USING MURDER

The Social Construction of Serial Homicide

SOCIAL PROBLEMS AND SOCIAL ISSUES

An Aldine de Gruyter Series of Texts and Monographs

SERIES EDITOR

Joel Best

Southern Illinois University at Carbondale

USING MURDER

The Social Construction of Serial Homicide

Philip Jenkins

ALDINE DE GRUYTER

New York

About the Author

Philip Jenkins is Professor of History and Religious Studies, Pennsylvania State University. His publications include *A History of Wales 1536–1900* (London, Longman, 1992) and *Intimate Enemies: Moral Panics in Contemporary Great Britain* (Aldine de Gruyter, 1992), as well as numerous articles in historical and criminological journals. His major interests involve the means by which social problems are constructed and presented in politics and the media. Dr. Jenkins is currently researching the problem of child sexual abuse by the clergy.

ALDINE DE GRUYTER
A division of Walter de Gruyter, Inc.
200 Saw Mill River Road
Hawthorne, New York 10532

This publication is printed on acid-free paper ⊗

Library of Congress Cataloging-in-Publication Data

Jenkins, Philip, 1952–
    Using murder : the social construction of serial homicide / Philip Jenkins.
        p.   cm. — (Social problems and social issues)
    Includes bibliographical references (p.   ) and index.
    ISBN 0-202-30499-X (cloth : acid-free paper). — ISBN
0-202-30525-2 (paper : acid-free paper)
    1. Serial murders—United States.   2. Serial murders—Europe.
3. Criminal psychology—United States.   4. Criminal psychology—
Europe.   I. Title.   II. Series.
HV6529.J46   1994
364.1'523—dc20   93-50051
                                                                      CIP

Manufactured in the United States of America

10   9   8   7   6   5   4   3   2   1

Contents

Acknowledgments

I would like to record my thanks to those researchers and scholars who have done so much to establish as a reputable discipline the academic study of extreme violence, and from whom I have learned so much. This group includes Steve Egger, Tom Fleming, James Fox, Eric Hickey, Ron Holmes, Jack Levin, Elliot Leyton, Robert Ressler, and Candace Skrapec. I suppose it is remarkable that such a potentially unsavory topic attracts such able investigators, who are moreover such balanced, decent, and generous individuals.

I would also note a debt of gratitude to other friends and colleagues who have assisted in the making of this book, especially Baruch Halpern, Kathryn Hume, Jennifer Jackson, and Melinda West. My wife, Elizabeth Jenkins, remains my best advisor. As ever, Joel Best has provided invaluable advice and commentary.

The errors in the book are all my own work.

Chapter 1

The Construction of Problems and Panics

COMPREHENDING MURDER

When police searched a Milwaukee apartment in July 1991, the discovery of extensive human remains indicated not only that the occupant Jeffrey Dahmer had killed repeatedly, but also that he had been involved in numerous bizarre activities such as cannibalism and necrophilia. Ultimately, Dahmer was associated with the deaths of some seventeen boys and young men, and the case created a national sensation. So much is beyond dispute, but the question then arises as to how such aberrant behavior is to be understood and contextualized. The vast majority of people are likely to agree that Dahmer's actions were unacceptable and wrong, but there is little consensus on whether the incident should be seen as a symptom of individual pathology or if it could plausibly be linked to broader social issues. And if the crimes are in fact a component of a wider social problem, exactly what sort of problem do they represent?

According to their ideological perspectives, different individuals emphasize varying elements of the story to produce radically different conclusions, together with the appropriate policy consequences. One observer might focus on the individual and developmental factors that shaped Dahmer's personality; another might emphasize the failings of police and official agencies; a third might stress the poverty or social breakdown in the areas from which the victims came. Based on these diverse approaches, a religious or moral enthusiast might blame the killings on declining moral standards, and perhaps the pernicious effects of promiscuous homosexuality. A gay rights activist might understand the incident as the consequence of the violence so often inflicted on homosexuals, as "murder by homophobia"; while others might emphasize the fact that a white man had systematically killed black men and boys, and draw parallels with other instances of racial violence and

1

persecution. If a comparable incident had occurred in a prescientific society, the crime might be understood as a manifestation of demonic evil or divine wrath. In every case, moreover, the incident would probably be employed as a powerful exemplar to support a particular moral or political lesson, each embroidering and reinforcing the narrative with appropriate cultural cross-references.

A single instance of multiple homicide can be cited in support of divergent rhetorical messages, and none is self-evidently correct or objectively true. Nor is the Dahmer case untypical in this regard. In the last decade or so, repeat homicide carried out over a period of weeks or months (*serial murder*) has come to be seen as one of the most pressing and widely discussed social problems; and the rich diversity of interpretations suggests the usefulness of the theme for various audiences. It has also proved valuable for the disparate claims-makers to assert that actions like Dahmer's are frequent or even commonplace, suggesting quite misleadingly that serial killers pose a substantial menace to public safety.

In recent years, there has been increasing scholarly concern with the construction of social problems. Topics such as child abuse and molestation, satanism, AIDS, and drug abuse have all provided the basis for influential case studies, which explore themes such as the creation and misuse of questionable statistics, and the exploitation of underlying public fears by both bureaucratic agencies and private "claims-makers" (Best 1989; Goode 1989, 1992, 1993). However, the popularity and diverse interpretations of serial murder make this one of the most promising fields of research into social problems in contemporary North America.

THE SERIAL MURDER BOOM

This type of crime has attracted enormous public attention. Serial killers are frequently discussed in the popular media, and interest reached a new height in the early 1990s, with incidents such as the trials of Jeffrey Dahmer, Aileen Wuornos, and Joel Rifkin, and the publicity surrounding the fictional works *The Silence of the Lambs, American Psycho,* and their countless imitators. This type of crime is now the subject of most of the numerous "true-crime" books published in the United States each year. Both in fiction and in true crime, there were considerably more publications in the three years from 1991 through 1993 than in the 1960s and 1970s combined. The serial killer novel is now a well-established subgenre in the mystery/thriller world. "The serial killer has become an American original, a romantic icon, like the cowboy" (Achenbach 1991).

There is clearly a huge public demand for such accounts, to say nothing of the frequency with which the topic is covered on television documentaries and talk shows. Multiple murder has also attracted significant attention from agencies of government and law enforcement. Partly in response to pressures emanating from the media and the culture at large, far more resources are devoted to tracking, identifying, and stopping the tiny number of serial killers than to preventing the great majority of routine homicide cases, in which victim and offender are related by marriage, kinship, or close acquaintance.

Both in popular and scholarly literature, the phenomenon of serial murder is generally approached through case studies of particular individuals. There are numerous book-length accounts of notorious killers such as Ted Bundy, Jeffrey Dahmer, John Wayne Gacy, or Henry Lee Lucas. More recently, a number of books have attempted to take a broader and more scholarly view of the phenomenon [Levin and Fox (1985) was the pioneering work but see now O'Reilly-Fleming and Egger (forthcoming) Segrave (1992), Wilson and Seaman (1992), Sears (1991), James (1991), Newton (1990, 1992), Hickey (1991), Egger (1990), Keppel (1989), Holmes and DeBurger (1988), Norris (1988), Cameron and Frazer (1987), Leyton (1986), Brown (1991a)]. The new scholarship has had the advantage of moving beyond the purely individualistic accounts to seek a social dimension in terms of causation and victimization; but the emphasis is still on attempting to understand the behavior itself, often with the laudable goal of improving the processes of detection and investigation. Very little has been written on the social reaction to the offense, the underlying factors that explain the construction of the "serial murder problem." It is this constructionist approach that differentiates this study from its predecessors.

There is still remarkably little of a systematic nature on some of the most interesting aspects of multiple homicide, in areas that can broadly be characterized as political, cultural, and rhetorical. Why are the cases portrayed in the way they are, and what significance is the observer meant to deduce from them? Some multiple-murder cases are far better known than others, and it will be argued that these incidents (like the Dahmer affair) have achieved the notoriety they have not because they are intrinsically more dangerous or threatening, but because they are more "useful" than others. Serial murder is commonly exploited by a wide variety of official agencies and interest groups, and the issue has been used as a multifaceted weapon in political debate. It has been employed by radical feminists, by advocates of black rights or by white supremacists, and by either defenders or critics of homosexual rights. It can be employed by moral traditionalists and fundamentalists, nativists, or antimodern reactionaries. In terms of policing, serial murder cases are as likely to be cited by law and order campaigners as by the harshest critics of the police. There is nothing in the behavior per se that lends itself to any particular ideological perspective, but it has proved very tempting to stigmatize various forms of conduct by portraying them as components of the larger serial murder problem.

The notorious cases thus tend to be those which offer the greatest potential for rhetorical development, using rhetoric in the broad sense of "the study of the process of public persuasion . . . the study of how symbols influence people" (Zarefsky 1986:5). A particular case might produce a wide array of such possible messages and themes, depending on the nature of the events and the different agendas of the various types of claims-makers involved. However, interpretations tend to follow certain general themes and directions, and these same themes occur in broad cross-cultural perspective. Our understanding of the weight and meaning attached to a particular case will therefore depend on a complex process of social construction and cultural work. Public recognition of serial murder is unlikely to diminish in the near future, and the problem will continue to provide a valuable resource for claims-makers. The social and rhetorical construction of multiple homicide is thus a continuing cultural process.

THE PROCESS OF SOCIAL CONSTRUCTION

Sociologists have long employed techniques of rhetorical analysis to address questions such as public perceptions of the amount and seriousness of criminal behavior, and the reasons for the appeal of crime as a topic in popular media. Terms like the *social construction of crime* have a lengthy scholarly pedigree, especially in the context of crime waves, wars on crime, drug wars, and similar events. In the 1970s, this sort of approach was often associated with radical or Marxist theorists, who wished to explain public concern over street crime in terms of manipulation by official agencies and other powerful social interests (see for example Hall et al. 1978; Quinney 1970, 1979).

It was also suggested that perceived crime waves reflect deeper social tensions, often arising from conflicts based on class, race, age, or gender (Cohen 1972; Cohen and Young 1973). British scholars often used the phrase *moral panics* to describe such artificially generated waves of concern over issues like mugging, drug abuse, and welfare cheating. The book *Policing the Crisis* (by Stuart Hall et al. 1978) is a classic of this genre, an attempt to use a short-lived panic over street robbery to reconstruct the concerns and tensions of Great Britain in the 1970s.

Radical approaches lost much of their influence during the 1980s, but there is now a vigorous social constructionist approach that seeks to determine the interest groups and moral entrepreneurs seeking to mold public attitudes through their depictions of crime and other social problems (Holstein and Miller 1993; Miller and Holstein 1993; Ben-Yehuda 1990; Best 1989; Spector and Kitsuse 1987; Schneider and Kitsuse 1984; Gusfield 1981). There is a growing literature on the complex role of the media in depicting crime and deviance, examining the role of the press and television both in reflecting public perceptions and in turn shaping those attitudes (Sparks 1992; Surette 1992; Leyton, O'Grady, and Overton 1992; Soothill and Walby 1991). While not denying that "new" problems may involve authentic changes in underlying social behaviors, the tendency is to interpret these phenomena chiefly as symbolic campaigns that reflect the interests of particular movements and pressure groups.

Among recent case studies, Best's important work (1990) examines the myths surrounding threats to children such as child abuse, child abduction, and Halloween sadism; while another collection of essays has addressed *The Satanism Scare* (Richardson, Best, and Bromley, 1991). In *Intimate Enemies* (1992a), the present author traced the origin of a connected series of panics that emerged in Great Britain during the 1980s, chiefly involving the threat of sexual violence directed toward children and (to a lesser extent) women.

In each case, the authors accept the basic premise that social phenomena may exist and be recognized for a lengthy period before they are synthesized into a new problem. The fundamental question for study concerns the ways in which various claims-makers undertake the work of construction, how they establish the significance and threat potential of "their" particular problem within the arena of public debate. Constructionist research focuses on three related themes: the interests particular groups have in promoting a problem; the resources available to them; and the ownership they eventually secure over the issue, or the degree to which their analysis is accepted as authoritative (Best 1990:11–13; Gusfield 1981).

These studies pay close attention to the rhetorical devices employed to project a particular view of the social reality of crime, and to the several stages involved in formulating and presenting a problem such as child abuse or serial murder. First, events must be identified and contextualized, or placed in a context that will be familiar to the assumed audience. This process will usually occur through the mass media:

> If the world is not to be represented as a jumble of random and chaotic events, then they must be identified (i.e., named, defined, related to other events known to the audience), and assigned to a social context (i.e., placed within a frame of meanings familiar to the audience). This

process—identification and contextualization—is one of the most important through which events are "made to mean" by the media. (Hall et al.
1978:54)

The importance attached to a particular event will vary according to
circumstances and timing, and the event can be placed in a number of
different contexts or frames. *Framings* are

> cultural combinations and constructions that put selected phenomena into
> comprehensible and consumable focus. Frames . . . are systems of selec-
> tion, presentation and accentuation: they are patterned mechanisms of
> cognition and interpretation that package social experience for produc-
> ers and purchasers of the frames. (Papke 1987: xvii; see also Goffman
> 1974)

Framing is achieved through a number of familiar rhetorical techniques. Best emphasizes the significance of domain statements, i.e.,
determining which phenomena do and do not fit within the domain of a
particular problem. For example, this means that the Dahmer case might
be seen as a part of the problem of racial conflict and injustice, or that the
Matamoros murders should be placed within the domain of the problem
of satanic or ritual murder. Linked to this concept is the process of
typification, which suggests that an issue is really one sort of problem
rather than another, and therefore requires a particular set of solutions.
This might mean that a serial murder case should be seen as a mental
health issue rather than a criminal justice problem, with all that implies
for official responses. Another claims-maker might see the same events
as representing religious or moral failings. A feminist could present the
same incident as an example of gender-based oppression.

Other devices are used to contextualize an event by placing it within
the framework of a previously established problem. In Best's terms,
issue x is significant because it can be portrayed as a part of known
problem y, and therefore requires the package of responses and reactions that have already been felt appropriate for problem y. This is the
process described by Hall et al. as "convergence":

> [C]onvergence occurs when two or more activities are linked in the pro-
> cess of signification so as to implicitly or explicitly draw parallels between
> them. Thus the image of "student hooliganism" links student protest to
> the separate problem of hooliganism—whose stereotypical characteristics
> are already part of socially available knowledge. . . . In both cases, the net
> effect is amplification, not in the real events being described but in their
> threat potential for society. (Hall et al. 1978:223)

Also significant here is the concept of stigmatizing one form of behavior by linking it ("mapping together") with another phenomenon that is perceived as far more dangerous. Few would question that serial murder represents an extreme form of dangerous and pathological predatory behavior: It is almost inconceivable to imagine even the most libertarian thinker claiming it as an acceptable or tolerable form of deviancy. It represents an "ultimate evil," and any behavior that can plausibly be linked to it will be regarded as a much greater menace than might otherwise be the case. In terms of the passage quoted above, the "threat potential" of the associated behavior is enormously amplified, whether that other behavior is satanism, sexual deviance, pedophilia, racial bias, and so on. Interpreting one individual as a pedophile killer serves to enhance the menace inherent in the word *pedophile*, and similarly for terms such as gay serial killer and satanic serial killer.

This process of escalation has been further described by Hall et al. as part of a "signification spiral," a "*self-amplifying sequence within the area of signification*: the activity or event with which the signification deals is *escalated*—made to seem more threatening—within the course of the signification itself" (p. 223, emphasis in original). The authors postulate the existence of "certain thresholds which mark out symbolically the limits of social tolerance" (p. 225). These proceed from the lowest level, of mere "permissiveness," to the higher thresholds of legality and ultimately of violence:

> [T]he higher an event can be placed in the hierarchy of thresholds, the greater is its threat to the social order, and the tougher and more automatic is the coercive response. . . . One kind of threat or challenge to society seems larger, more menacing, if it can be mapped together with other apparently similar phenomena—especially if by connecting one relatively harmless activity with a more threatening one, the scale of the danger implicit is made to appear more widespread and diffused . . . [A]s issues and groups are projected across the thresholds, it becomes easier to mount legitimate campaigns of control against them. (pp. 225–26)

Serial murder stands at the highest of these thresholds, and associating any kind of behavior with that phenomenon offers rich rewards in terms of claims-making. It is especially valuable in justifying "campaigns of control," or the expansion of legal sanction and bureaucratic power to combat or suppress a perceived social evil.

DEFINING THE PROBLEM

The ideological directions in which these rhetorical tactics are employed will depend on the broader political context. In the case of serial murder, the concept (if not the exact term) has existed for over a century, but only in the 1980s were there systematic descriptions and analyses of a multiple-murder problem, with appropriate solutions being described. The new attention paid to the issue from the mid-1970s probably did indeed reflect a genuine increase in the volume of serial murder activity (see Chapter 2). Between about 1976 and 1981, a group of highly publicized cases made a dramatic impact in the news media and in popular fiction: Ted Bundy was perhaps the most celebrated individual offender. By 1980–1981, there was a sharp increase in the number of novels and cinematic treatments of the topic, as well as in true-crime accounts in print and on television. This was a critical period in the social and cultural construction of the issue, but it remained unclear as yet what directions might be taken in emerging public responses.

Interpretations of the serial murder phenomenon naturally reflected prevailing social and political currents, which in the United States at that time tended to be strongly conservative. The election of Ronald Reagan to the presidency in 1980 marked the apogee of a New Right movement whose rhetoric and politics profoundly influenced social reactions to crime and violence. As the New Right approach will so often be discussed in this study, it is useful to summarize here the major beliefs and ideology of the movement.

THE RHETORIC OF DECADENCE

Fundamental to the conservative perspective was what might be termed the rhetoric of decadence. This was based on a highly pessimistic view of recent American history, which was seen as a time of critical decline and demoralization. For moral conservatives in 1980, the events of the previous fifteen years had had a catastrophic effect on the fiber of American society, and the tolerance of divorce, abortion, homosexuality, drugs, and sexual promiscuity had contributed to a pervasive moral breakdown that urgently needed to be reversed. Central to this vision was the perception that the radical social changes of the 1960s had represented not a valuable process of liberalization and experimentation, but a collapse of much that was desirable and necessary for an integrated society (Conover and Gray 1983). This was illustrated by rapidly growing problems of crime and violence, and in 1980–1981 recorded rates of violent crime reached unprecedented heights that would not again be achieved for another decade (Jenkins 1984; "Curse of Violent Crime," 1981). Contemporary anarchy was contrasted with the idealized family-oriented society so frequently depicted in the "Morning in America" advertising campaign, which was a centerpiece of Republican public relations during 1980. The solution to recent decay lay in the reaffirmation of traditional values and discipline, through law if necessary, and the renewed stigmatization and penalization of immoral behaviors.

From the mid-1970s, conservative and rightist political forces mobilized around a broad range of issues that generally concerned the perceived weakness of American society. There were several critical campaigns between 1977 and 1980: gay rights referenda in Florida and California, the negotiations over the Panama Canal treaty, the debate over the SALT II nuclear weapons treaty, the movement against the Equal Rights Amendment. New Right ideologue Richard Viguerie described 1978 in particular as "our critical year" (1981:65). Suggestions of international weakness appeared confirmed by events of 1979, especially the gasoline shortages, and the Iran hostage crisis, which lasted from November 1979 to January 1981. Perceptions of decay and ineptitude culminated in the failed hostage rescue mission of April 1980.

In foreign policy, the Right advocated a military buildup and a more confrontational attitude toward Communist and anti-Western forces. In domestic policy, traditional Republican emphases on fiscal conservatism were combined with a new politics of morality, which sought to appeal to conservative and fundamentalist Christians (Conway and Siegelman 1982). Conservatism found a solid base in the evangelical Christian groups that had grown so dramatically during the 1970s and that achieved visibility through networks of Christian publications and bookstores, and the work of television evangelists like Jerry Falwell and Pat Robertson. The Christian conservative movement found a structural base in the Moral Majority, which was founded in 1979, but it represented a wider social trend. Moral and military reconstruction would proceed hand in hand (Bennett 1990).

The growing public interest in serial murder following 1977 thus coincided exactly with a strong political trend toward a reevaluation of the etiology of social problems, a general tendency toward viewing wrongdoing and deviancy as issues of personal sin and evil rather than social or economic dysfunction. For conservatives of the Reagan era, the central issue in morality (as in economics) was a renewed emphasis on the responsibility of the individual, and a denial of the effectiveness or validity of solutions that emphasized the state or the social dimension. This theme gained special power from its frequent reiteration in the speeches of President Reagan himself. It has justly been remarked that "in modern American society the presidency is the primary source of symbols about public issues," and this was never more true than in the Reagan years (Zarefsky 1986:6–7).

In terms of crime and wrongdoing, the new policy was epitomized by a presidential speech in September 1981, in which Reagan argued:

> Many of the social thinkers of the 1950s and 1960s who discussed crime only in the context of disadvantaged childhoods and poverty-stricken neighborhoods were the same people who thought that massive government spending could wipe away our social ills. The underlying premise in both cases was a belief that there was nothing permanent or absolute about any man's nature—that he was a product of his material environment, and that by changing that environment—with government as the chief vehicle of change through educational, health, housing and other programs—we could permanently change man and usher in a great new era.
>
> The solution to the crime problem will not be found in the social worker's files, the psychiatrist's notes, or the bureaucrat's budget; it's a problem of the human heart, and it's there we must look for the answer. (quoted in Jenkins 1984:37–38)

Reagan stressed the value of "permanent truths," such as "right and wrong matters; individuals are responsible for their actions; retribution should be swift and sure for those who prey on the innocent" (p. 38).

This stress on moral responsibility, on good and evil, was crucial to the political rhetoric of the next few years, especially in the context of law enforcement. The obverse of the rhetoric of decadence was an emphasis on "manly" traditional values, epitomized by concepts such as standing up, standing tall, and fighting back, which were extolled as much in the war on crime as in the international arena (Slotkin 1992). This meant, for example, expanding the resources and legal powers available to police. There was also a much harsher and more punitive response to crime, replacing the social and therapeutic policies that had been advocated during the Great Society years and afterwards. Drug abuse was a particularly symbolic issue, and the new conservatism was aggressively expressed in the drug war declared in middecade, which sought to reassert the moral discipline that had been so widely questioned in recent years (Goode 1993; "Text of President's Speech" 1989; Reinarman and Levine 1989).

The practical consequences of these changes can be quantified by examining the nation's soaring prison population. The number of people incarcerated in state and federal institutions grew by 130 percent between 1980 and 1990, even though the actual rate of violent crime was essentially the same in 1990 as it had been at the time of Reagan's inauguration. In the same years, there was a widespread restoration of the death penalty, the ultimate form of purely retributive punishment. There were no executions in the United States between 1967 and 1976;

four between 1977 and 1981; but 82 between 1984 and 1987 (see Chapter 6 for the role of serial murder as an ideological weapon in promoting this change).

DANGEROUS OUTSIDERS

In the early 1980s, conservative political rhetoric was permeated by themes of external threat, national vulnerability, subversion, and internal decadence. These concerns focused on a number of "dangerous outsiders," most obviously the Soviet Union, which Reagan characterized as "the evil empire" in a 1983 speech to the National Association of Evangelicals. There were a number of other panics or waves of concern about these various external forces who appeared to represent grave threats to the American people. These included not only serial killers but also drug dealers and drug kingpins, terrorists both foreign and domestic, and of course the child molesters and pornographers believed to pose such a danger to American children.

In the political context of these years, all these apparently diverse groups served essentially similar social and rhetorical functions, by personifying the immorality and outright evil that had arisen in consequence of the moral and political decadence of recent administrations. These outsiders were readily portrayed as the product of the family breakdown and sexual hedonism of the previous fifteen years. It was common to personify these dangers by focusing on a particularly notorious or unpopular individual, like Muammar Qaddafi or Daniel Ortega in international affairs, John Wayne Gacy or Ted Bundy in domestic politics.

Dangerous outsiders were useful in justifying bureaucratic and legal changes to reverse the perceived decay. During the 1970s, the exposure of illegalities by intelligence and internal security agencies had led to the imposition of congressional restraints, and successive investigations had left a heritage of considerable suspicion of federal law enforcement. The incoming Reagan administration in 1981 had stated its intention to weaken such controls on federal agencies, but there remained stiff opposition. Over the next three years, there was a consistent and largely successful effort to reduce such hostility by citing the dangers from a variety of external enemies, including Communist espionage, international terrorism and the "narcoterrorism" of drug cartels (Woodward 1987). A 1981 armed robbery by leftist radicals in New York state provided the justification for a substantial expansion of internal security operations, and a revival of draconian legislation against political conspiracy and sedition. In the context of "normal" domestic crime, federal authority was reasserted by focusing on those apparently nonpolitical areas that could convincingly be depicted as posing a menace to ordinary citizens, themes such as child abuse and abduction, drug dealing, and serial murder.

THE RHETORIC OF PERSECUTION

Of course, not all the claims-makers active in shaping the serial murder problem were conservatives, still less adherents of the New Right, but interpretations derived from this perspective played a crucial role throughout the decade. The Reagan Justice Department formulated what became the dominant construction of the murder problem, promulgating statistics and evidence that were used by other theorists, including feminists and ethnic minority groups, who were among the bitterest critics of Reagan-era policies.

This conservative dominance must be placed in the context of the partisan divisions of the early 1980s. To employ a rather clichéd phrase, the Reagan conservatives enjoyed ideological hegemony through the early 1980s, and both economic and defense policies were legislated into effect with little effective resistance. This does not mean that left-wing or radical opponents were silenced, but their rhetoric and policies had to be adapted to the range of issues identified by the Right. For example, the concept of a drug menace was so firmly established that it could not simply be denied, and instead radicals had to propose alternative interpretations or solutions.

This process of adaptation can also be seen in the context of serial murder. During the late 1970s, claims-makers from the radical or feminist left had been among the pioneers in drawing attention to multiple homicide, specifically because the crime victimized women, blacks, or homosexuals, and it was common to suggest that serial murder was a manifestation of generalized injustice and persecution. This construction of the problem continued unabated through the Reagan era, and in fact it could be suggested that the level of persecution or victimization had been enhanced by conservative attitudes or policies. Radical and feminist groups thus tended to promulgate and even exaggerate the claims about serial murder made by the conservative or moralist right, and this was often achieved by drawing on the most inflated statistics derived from federal agencies. Knowingly or not, the critics of federal policies became tactical allies of the most conservative claims-makers.

THE STRUCTURE OF THE BOOK

This book includes three major sections. The first, comprising Chapters 2 through 4, describes the dramatic growth of concern over serial murder from the later 1970s onwards, and emphasizes the bureaucratic and political interests most active in promoting the issue as a social problem. The middle section, Chapters 5 and 6, explores some of the cultural meanings attached to the emerging problem, meanings that explain the enormous impact made by the bureaucratic claims-makers. The third section, Chapters 7 through 10, examines the main ideological and political perspectives that have been brought to bear on the serial murder issue in contemporary America.

From the late 1970s, many activists and groups attempted to interpret the accumulating evidence of increased serial murder activity in order to construct the problem in a manner advantageous to their particular interests or ideological stance. In most cases, this meant asserting that the problem was very large in terms of the number of individuals involved and the amount of social damage caused, and that the harm could be quantified in widely accepted statistics. It was also argued that the problem was rapidly growing, with the implied threat that the upward trend would continue unless urgent action were taken. Finally, each claims-maker normally suggested that the typical serial killer represented a particular type of individual, acting with a distinctive motivation, and would choose exemplars accordingly. For example, feminist theoreticians placed the greatest emphasis on the male sex-killer, to the exclusion of virtually any other type.

In order to assess such claims, it is important to discuss the evidentiary bases for these assertions, and to describe what can be known with some certainty about the reality of the serial homicide phenomenon. The limitations of evidence will be discussed in Chapter 2, "The Reality of Serial Murder," which will show that prior to the 1980s there were no estimates or even plausible guesses about the true scale of this behavior, though media sources and official documents now permit statements to be made with much greater confidence.

It will be suggested that serial murder has increased significantly in the United States in the last three decades, so to that extent the claims-makers are correct; but even today, this type of violence accounts for only about 1 percent of American homicides, and possibly less. And while there has been an increase, contemporary America is not facing an "unparalleled" threat, in that quite comparable behavior existed in the early twentieth century, both in Germany and the United States itself. Finally, this chapter will show that serial killers are considerably more diverse than is suggested by some recent claims. Women and racial minorities are quite well represented, while sex-killers do not hold quite the monopoly they appear to.

Chapter 3, "The Role of the Justice Department," describes how interpretation of the new problem was dominated from 1983 by law enforcement agencies, and specifically the federal Justice Department, which clearly achieved ownership of the issue. The "federal" view of serial murder asserted that serial murder was a vast menace, with some four to five thousand related fatalities each year, or up to a quarter of all American homicides. According to this view, the problem was novel, without historical precedent, and the threat potential was all the greater because killers were highly mobile, wandering freely between different states and jurisdictions.

This construction of the problem implied solutions, above all an emphasis on the federal role as the only way of combating the limitations of local agencies. The data on which this analysis was based were at best seriously misleading, but they remained little challenged for several years, and this helped the federal agencies achieve major rewards in terms of resources and prestige. This was an important political coup for the Reagan administration, as it reinforced its image as being "tough on crime" in the approach to the 1984 elections, while disseminating the conservative and individualistic view of the etiology of crime that they were anxious to promote. Moreover, the panic permitted the expansion of federal police powers, a trend that would have been strenuously opposed only a few years earlier.

The Justice Department interpretation of serial murder was at its height between 1983 and 1985, but a series of cases in the early 1990s gave renewed weight to these bureaucratic claims-makers. More specifically, the new emphasis on the phenomenon reinforced the technocratic belief in the work of the Justice Department's experts: the computer scientists who collated the data that permitted the recognition of serial crimes; the forensic technicians who examined physical evidence; and above all, the psychological profilers and behavioral analysts who provided invaluable information to local investigators.

Much of this success resulted from the fictional depictions offered in Thomas Harris's novels (and subsequent films) *Red Dragon* ([1981] 1990) and *Silence of the Lambs* ([1988] 1989), both of which inspired numerous imitators. Chapter 4, "Popular Culture," examines the development of images of the serial killer in popular culture, and attempts to explain this intense interest in terms of changing political concerns and social realities.

Constructionist studies often place major emphasis on the interpretation and dissemination of problems through the news media, but fictional and popular works also play a decisive role in determining cultural attitudes in an area like serial murder, and relevant works include novels, films, comics, true-crime books, and even trading cards. It is essential to pay due attention to these cultural artifacts, on the model suggested by Best's (1990) analysis of the "threatened children" theme in 1980s popular literature. There exists a complex feedback relationship between fact-based and fictitious accounts of the serial murder phenomenon. Fictional accounts often derive heavily from real-life cases, though with significant alterations; while in turn, the fiction has done at least as much to shape popular stereotypes of the serial killer as any avowedly factual book or news program. This is most apparent in the work of Thomas Harris, but Robert Bloch played a comparably influential role in earlier decades. There is also some evidence that actual serial killers may pattern themselves on fictional accounts.

In understanding the contributions of popular culture, much use will be made of the insights of the contemporary cultural studies movement, which originated in Great Britain with the work of scholars like Raymond Williams, Richard Hoggart, and Stuart Hall. This movement is fundamentally concerned with the multiple definitions and meanings of *culture*, and the complex relationship between elitist high culture and the broader meaning of the term, which includes and legitimizes "subcultures, popular culture, and ways of life: the construction of culture in this extended sense as the forcing ground for forms of symbolic opposition to culture in its more restricted dominant and aesthetic forms" (Grossberg, Nelson, and Treichler 1992:26). "Cultural studies" employs a variety of other disciplines and their methodologies: "it is now an alchemy that draws from many of the major bodies of theory of the last several decades, from Marxism and feminism to psychoanalysis, poststructuralism and post-modernism" (p. 2).

A cultural studies perspective analyzes texts or materials including popular artifacts that assuredly would not be viewed as suitable for critical discussion by more traditional literary scholars. The culture addressed might well include genre fiction such as detective stories, science fiction novels, or pulp romances, as well as men's magazines, popular music, and advertising: "[A]ll forms of cultural production need to be studied in relation to other cultural practices and to social and historical structures. Cultural studies is thus committed to the study of the entire range of a society's arts, beliefs, institutions and communicative practices" (p. 4). "Cultural studies has long been concerned with the everyday terrain of people, and with all the ways that cultural practices speak to, of and for their lives" (p. 11). Mass or popular culture is likely to offer a particularly valuable tool for the critical analysis of a society and its structures (Leps 1992; Papke 1987).

Also characteristic of most cultural studies work is the range of questions to be asked about a particular text or body of texts, and about the relationship between the text and its presumed audiences. It is generally assumed that culture very much mirrors the political and economic structures of hegemony and oppression, domination and displacement, that are believed to permeate the wider society. Texts are often discussed in the context of the patterns of domination and repression that they are felt to exemplify, whether this exploitation is based on class, gender, ethnicity, or sexual orientation. Essays in cultural studies are thus likely to focus on the oppressed and disinherited, and there is a fascination with issues of boundaries, marginality, and "otherness," all of which will be shown to be central to the serial murder literature.

The popular literature thus has important ideological implications, and much can be learned from the changing assumptions of such works and their associated stereotypes. Particularly important is the shift of interpretation away from the earlier psychiatric/therapeutic discourse in the direction of moralistic and even supernatural imagery, evinced most clearly in the "slasher films." From being a person whose sickness derived from family or social circumstances, the serial killer of the 1980s was increasingly seen as a ruthless incomprehensible monster undeserving of sympathy, and meriting only destruction at the hands of heroic "mind-hunters," like those portrayed by Thomas Harris. This world of monsters and mind-hunters dominated fictional depictions by the 1990s, and closely reflected changes in the analyses offered by law enforcement agencies.

However, the appeal of this imagery had roots far deeper than the opportunistic claims of the federal agencies, and Chapter 5, "Serial Murder as Modern Mythology," explores the presentation of popular culture depictions of serial murder. True-crime books in particular demonstrate strong sexual themes, and might be seen as appealing to a prurient interest, but the popular literature also addresses other equally powerful concerns of the presumed audience, above all in the manipulation and regulation of fear. Serial murder has come to provide an elaborate contemporary mythological system, in which the killers are believed to represent "the worst thing in the world," the ultimate other, denizens of a moral and spiritual realm with values wholly contrary to those of mainstream society. In recent years, popular stereotypes of these threatening outsiders have come to assimilate most of the characteristics that in earlier societies were attributed to a variety of chiefly imaginary external enemies, including vampires, werewolves, and cannibals. All represent the threat of a reversion to primitive savagery, manifested most blatantly in acts of cannibalism and mutilation.

Such social and psychological fears are very widespread, arguably universal, and the appeal to this imagery goes far toward explaining the success of the serial murder issue in popular culture, where offenders like Ted Bundy represent the nearest approach to pure demonic evil that can plausibly be described in an ostensibly secular world. Constructing an ultimate evil also offers great rhetorical opportunities to claims-makers wishing to suggest that a particular issue or phenomenon should really be mapped together with the serial murder problem. The evil is already established, its stereotypical qualities widely known, so that all that remains to be done is to demonstrate that its domain extends to include the issue in question, be it pornography, racism, homosexuality, child abuse, or rapid social change.

Chapter 6, "The Kind of Society We Have Now," examines the diverse social critiques manifest in both true life and fictional accounts of serial murder cases, politicized responses that might be presented in either conservative or radical guises. From a conservative stance, the central theme is that any given society has so departed from traditional norms as to produce individuals as bizarre and threatening as the celebrated serial killers. In the 1980s, the political dominance of conservatism ensured that this interpretation would be widely cited, and would specifically be used to attack the alleged immorality and individual self-gratification of the previous two decades. This rhetoric of decadence pervaded the ostensibly objective analyses of law enforcement officials who were so widely quoted in the media. Their apparent authority encouraged widespread acceptance of this view, which naturally favors conservative political solutions.

However, it was possible to interpret serial murder incidents in other ways, and some of the rival framings were remarkably radical in tone. It could be argued that the social flaws that permitted serial murder to continue were intimately connected with current social arrangements such as patriarchal dominance or racism, evils that were amplified by association with multiple homicide. Moreover, the inability of police to catch serial killers allowed these cases to be employed rhetorically against perceived biases within law enforcement. Such radical or critical perspectives have become powerful ideological buttresses for a number of political perspectives, especially feminism, for which the central reality of serial murder is that men (specifically) kill many girls and women for sexual motives. The crime is thus a part of a wider problem of "femicide," and is contextualized together with offenses such as rape, child molestation, and sexual harassment (discussed in Chapter 7, "Everyman Serial Murder as Femicide"). The monster or predator imagery discussed above is thus applied in a distinctively gendered fashion.

The feminist analysis stresses the role of offender and victim as representatives of the broader categories to which they appear to belong, and similar ideas have been employed from other ideological perspectives.

While feminists see the behavior in terms of men killing women, black activists have often seen the crime as one that characterizes *white* men, often assaulting minority individuals as an extreme symptom of generalized racial bias and harassment. This theme is discussed in Chapter 8, "The Racial Dimension." As serial murder is predominantly an intraracial crime, such an analysis may appear unpromising, but it has been cited in the context of two of the most notorious incidents of recent years, the Atlanta child murders of 1980–1981, and the Dahmer case of 1991.

Sexual orientation can provide a basis for the denunciation of a group, and the suggestion that this behavior somehow characterizes the broader social category from which the killer is drawn. Chapter 9, "A Homosexual Who Could Strike Again," describes the common tendency to discredit homosexuals by associating them with activities such as sexual murder and pedophilia. This is an example of what might be called the "politics of substitution," the stigmatization of a topic or issue as a surrogate to denounce some other theme that it is politically inexpedient to attack overtly. During the 1980s, the campaign against serial murder often won public support by focusing on crimes against children, but it will be suggested that the major concern was more specifically crimes by men against boys, notorious actions by killers like Dean Corll and John Wayne Gacy. The denunciation of serial murder had the surreptitious effect of drawing attention to the supposed pedophile inclinations of homosexuals, and the further association of both behaviors with extreme violence.

Serial murder can be used to stigmatize a social group or category, but it is also common to suggest that the crime might be the work of an organized movement. The exact group to be blamed will depend on the ideological outlook of the claims-making group or individual making the charge, and the political expectations and fears of the community in question. In recent years, serial murder cases have most frequently been employed to corroborate charges about the machinations of cults, usually of a satanic nature. Chapter 10, "Darker Than We Imagine: Cults and Conspiracies," traces the development of such charges to create what can only be described as an elaborate mythology of ritual murder in contemporary America. Here, common fears of atavism and primitive savagery focus specifically on the revival of supposed pagan rites, which are often associated with other ethnic groups. Though these ideas originated with secular sources in law enforcement and journalism, the claims were nurtured and promoted by religious and particularly fundamentalist Christian groups, for whom the cult theories served as an ideological justification during these years of expanding political influence.

Chapter 11, "Conclusion," will discuss the activities of various claims-makers in the creation and ongoing construction of the serial murder problem, and consider the implications for the broader study of social problems.

In a classic article from the 1940s, a social problem was defined as:

> a condition which is defined by a considerable number of persons as a deviation from some social norm which they cherish. Every social problem thus consists of an *objective condition* and a *subjective definition*. The objective condition is a verifiable situation which can be checked as to existence and magnitude (proportions) by impartial and trained observers. The subjective definition is the awareness of certain individuals that the condition is a threat to certain cherished values. (Fuller and Myers 1941:320)

Since the late 1970s, the offense of serial murder has clearly become a serious social problem, in that it is so widely if not universally viewed as a major social failing, a massive threat to social values. However, in this problem more than most, the gap between objective reality and subjective definition is enormous. This type of crime involves minuscule numbers of people, either as victims or perpetrators, and the likelihood of becoming a victim of this activity is extremely low.

In order to explain the vigor of public reaction, it is first necessary to appreciate the sizable disparity that separates perception and reality in approaching the statistics of the problem. The next chapter will suggest the methodological difficulties inherent in such an enterprise, but once these are resolved, it becomes apparent just how rare the offense of multiple murder really is.

Chapter 2

The Reality of Serial Murder

The phenomenon of serial murder can be found in many historical periods, and perhaps the most famous case of all—that of Jack the Ripper—occurred in London as long ago as 1888. At the end of the nineteenth century, Krafft-Ebing published a pioneering account of a group of serial sex-killers from several European nations (1978:53–80), and other such syntheses appeared in the 1920s (Douthwaite 1929). During the present century, there have been many celebrated cases of what were then known as mass murderers, such as Ed Gein and Albert Fish in the United States, and the Moors Murderers or the Yorkshire Ripper in Great Britain (Williams 1967; Harrison 1986). However, perceptions of this type of crime changed rapidly in the early 1980s, when American authorities drew attention to what appeared to be a rapid proliferation both of multiple-murder cases, and of the number of victims involved in each.

It was during the 1980s that the recently coined phrase *serial murder* was popularized by the media. The concept distinguishes between types of multiple homicide, depending on the time intervals that separate individual attacks: Murders committed in a brief period in one place are *mass murders*, while those carried out over a few days or a week are characterized as *spree-killings*. Serial murder implies that the killings are spread over months or years, with a cooling off period intervening.

It became common from about 1983 to talk of a distinctive serial murder *problem* that appeared to be quite novel in scale and severity. There now emerged an influential stereotype of the serial killer, who was seen as a white male in his thirties or forties, a sexually motivated murderer who preyed on either men or women depending on his sexual orientation. Jeffrey Dahmer, Ted Bundy, and John Wayne Gacy would all fit this image perfectly. The serial murder problem was therefore quite clearly defined: The phenomenon was vast, it was relatively new, and it tended above all to affect individuals of a particular age, gender, and ethnic background.

It is necessary to understand the objective reality of the behavior before addressing the ways in which the phenomenon has been socially and culturally constructed. In the literature on social problems, we are often reminded that it is difficult if not impossible to achieve a fully accurate perception of the scale of a given phenomenon. This is certainly correct, but it does not follow that no attempt should be made to understand the real substance of an issue. While admitting that our bases for interpretation contain much that may be subjective or otherwise flawed, it is still possible and indeed essential to use critically materials like media accounts and official statistics to assess the truth of claims presented.

Based on such analysis, it is clear that the shape of the problem outlined above is far from accurate, whether we consider the number and type of both offenders and victims, the historical development of the offense, its international context, or the accuracy of the stereotype of the normal multiple killer. In reality, serial homicide accounts for a very small proportion of American murders, and the claims frequently made in the 1980s exaggerated the scale of victimization by a factor of at least twenty. Moreover, such offenses are far from new, and the volume of activity in recent years is little different from conditions in the early part of the present century, while the phenomenon is by no means distinctively American. This chapter will show that the factual assertions commonly made about the serial murder problem are incorrect or misleading in virtually every particular.

THE STATISTICS OF THE DEBATE

In the early 1980s, it was common to hear very high figures for the extent of serial murder activity in the United States. One of the most egregious (and widely quoted) claims from this era suggested that the number of victims each year might approach four or five thousand, some 20 or 25 percent of the total of all homicide victims, compared to only 1 or 2 percent in earlier decades. This suggested a social crisis of considerable magnitude. However, the specific claim about the number of contemporary victims was soon challenged, and it is now generally accepted that the four or five thousand figure was largely spurious (see Chapter three). But popular and journalistic accounts still recite the statistic, and some even push it to further extremes, stating for instance that the number of serial *killers* presently active in the United States is four or five thousand (Van Hoffman 1990:7)!

The debate over such excessive claims highlighted the fact that little concrete was then known about the volume of serial murder activity either past or present, and much of the most basic research needed to be done. Even issues as fundamental as the definition of the offense remain contentious, and there are many other questions: Can an accurate database be compiled? Is it possible to measure the changing frequency of serial murder over time? Do apparent changes of frequency reflect actual changes of behavior, or are they an artifact resulting from developments in police perceptions, or reporting practices by the media? Today, some certainty is possible, but it is important to describe the problems encountered in reaching this point.

DEFINING THE PHENOMENON

If we wish to write a history of serial murder in the United States over the past century, the first step is to define the activity to be studied and quantified. The term *serial murder* should simply mean multiple acts of criminal homicide committed over a period of time, but in common usage it has come to have a more limited meaning, and the reasons for excluding some types of behavior are quite arbitrary. For example, most discussions of the act will not include homicides that have an apparently "rational" basis, such as crimes committed in the context of political terrorism, organized or professional criminality, or drug dealing. Accounts generally focus on homicides that lack a clear or comprehensible motive, acts of "irrational" murder such as rape-homicides or thrill-killings. In this study, a serial murder case will be defined as involving an offender associated with the killing of at least four victims, over a period greater than seventy-two hours. Excluded are cases where the offender acted primarily out of political motives or in quest of financial profit.

The serial murder phenomenon is composed of a number of individual cases with discrete offenders; but contrary to the impression that may be gained from fictional works, the nature and dimensions of such cases may be far from obvious, and interpretations will depend on processes of social and bureaucratic construction. In some cases, it is questionable if there are indeed authentic connections within what is widely reported as a "series" of murders, and there may be doubts about whether a particular series of deaths does in fact involve criminal activity. In Miami during 1989, police and medical examiners were at odds about whether a series of nineteen deaths of prostitutes was in fact murder, or merely the result of drug abuse (Schmalz 1989).

Even if foul play is established, the connections within an apparent series of murders can be quite tenuous. Between 1984 and 1987, it was commonly accepted that a "Southside slayer" was undertaking a series of murders in Los Angeles, and that one individual might have claimed up to seventeen victims (see Chapter 8). However, subsequent investigations suggest that as many as four or more different and unrelated killers might have been involved. Two of the victims should be attributed to one serial killer, Daniel Lee Siebert, while several others were associated with a killer named Louis Craine. At least one other killing was the work of a third offender, who was not believed to be a multiple murderer. What initially appeared to be a lengthy string of connected murders may thus turn out to be an artificial construct, and the question inevitably arises how many other apparent series should be placed in this uncertain category. The increased recognition of the serial murder phenomenon in the 1980s may have encouraged agencies to be oversensitive to possible linkages.

Also, the decision to label a case as serial murder is undertaken by bureaucratic agencies that certainly have their own political agendas, overt or otherwise. In one contentious case, it was alleged that over forty San Diego prostitutes had been killed by a single offender between 1985 and 1988, and that the crimes might be connected to forty or more other deaths in the Green River case in Seattle (1982–1984). This analysis was often accepted in the late 1980s, so that one hypothetical individual was presented as perhaps the worst serial killer in U.S. history, with almost ninety victims. In 1990, however, it became apparent that some of the early San Diego victims had been killed at a time when they were involved as witnesses in investigations into official corruption. At least some of the deaths might well have been the result of organized crime or even official malfeasance, rather than an irrational killer, and in one such case, several police officers were reported to be under investigation (Mydans 1990). During the late 1980s, it was generally stated that the San Diego murders and the Southside Slayings represented two of the worst murder series then in progress; but in retrospect, it must be asked what if anything can be said with certainty of either case. It remains to be seen how many currently unsolved series will prove to be equally dubious.

Also, the exact number of cases in a particular series is questionable. In fiction, murder series are quite well defined and there is no serious doubt that the police catch the correct perpetrator. There are no such guarantees in reality, and guilt is often difficult to ascribe. Alleged series often continue after the authorities have apprehended their leading suspect, and false accusations have been known. In one bizarre incident in 1981, Detroit prosecutors found themselves simultaneously pressing charges against two unconnected individuals for identical murders in the recent series of killings of prostitutes in that city. At least one of the parties must have been innocent, although both had confessed (Newton 1990:96–97).

A given offender is commonly said to be *associated* with a number of killings, but this word poses a large and perhaps insurmountable problem. Police agencies and prosecutors might attribute crimes to an individual in the hope of clearing the books of unsolved offenses. The killers themselves might wish either to maximize their criminal records or deny them altogether, and disturbed personalities often confess to large numbers of quite impossible crimes. Formal conviction is a valuable indicator, but it is rare for any serial killer to be formally charged and convicted in all the cases in which he or she is a strong suspect. We thus have to rely on much less certain evidentiary criteria to assess the real number of victims (compare Worthington 1993). In one well-known case, Ted Bundy was executed in 1989 for a murder committed in Florida, while the same state had tried and sentenced him for two other homicides. However, it has been suggested that Bundy was guilty of anywhere from 25 to 300 other murders across the United States. Estimates for the number of Henry Lee Lucas's victims range from about 5 to over 350 (see Chapter 3).

In the present study, an individual is listed as a serial killer if law enforcement and mainstream media sources consistently reported that the offender was believed to be implicated in four or more deaths. Clearly, this evidence is far from satisfactory, especially where it is based on confessions. It is also likely that media and police estimates are sometimes exaggerated or simply wrong, but such a reputational approach is perhaps the only means of proceeding in such a contentious area.

ASSESSING JUSTICE DEPARTMENT DATA

As the Justice Department and the FBI played so central a role in presenting the serial murder problem as a major social menace, it is instructive to examine their own internal lists of offenders, compiled at the Behavioral Sciences facility in Quantico, Virginia, and based largely on news clippings services (U.S. Justice Department 1992, 1993). It must be emphasized that these are purely working lists, not intended as comprehensive scholarly documents, but the implications are significant. Above all, they confirm what is implied from other sources about the extreme rarity of the offense, even in contemporary America.

By the end of 1992, the main list of serial murderers in the United States had grown to 447 names, of which some 82 were active between

1900 and 1970, and a further 365 from 1970 through 1992 (U.S. Justice Department 1993). This group of offenders was said to have killed 2,636 victims, to have attempted 367 killings, and to be implicated in 1,839 other deaths. Combining the known and suspected murders provides a total of 4,475 victims over the whole century, a very rough average of under 50 a year.

There are many problems with this document, which certainly omits names and incidents from the nineteenth and early twentieth centuries. However, most of the errors tend to lie in the direction of exaggerating the scale and importance of the problem. A number of cases listed are only credited with two or three victims, and would not fit the criteria for serial murder stated in this book. Other instances may not in fact be authentic series, such as the putative Atlanta Child Murders of 1979–1981, in which many unrelated deaths may have been combined to create an artificial murder series. [Dettlinger and Prugh (1983) offer a devastating critique of the Atlanta case: see Chapter 8.]

There is also clear duplication in the list, which becomes apparent if we consider the related list of spree-killers. Susan Atkins appears as guilty of seven murders committed in 1969, which are obviously the Tate and LaBianca killing carried out by the Manson "family," of which Atkins was a member. However, the same list also contains entries for Leslie Van Houten and Tex Watson, other family members, and they too are credited with seven victims. One incident is therefore listed three times, with the implication that the number of victims of spree-killing in 1969 was three times greater than it actually was.

The Manson murders are among the best known crime series of the century, and it is not difficult to discern an error here, but the same difficulty recurs in other cases, where an unsuspecting reader is more likely to be misled. In serial murder cases, for example, the "arsenic murder ring" active in Philadelphia in the mid-1930s is repeatedly mentioned, with each of four key participants (Herman and Paul Petrillo, Carmina Favato, and Morris Bolber) being "credited" with fifty victims, presumably the same fifty individuals in each instance (Young 1992; see also below). Similarly, both Leonard Lake and Charles Ng are separately credited with the twenty-five victims whom they jointly murdered. The eighteen individuals killed by the Chicago "cannibal murders ring" of 1981–1982 are listed under *each* of the four participants (Robin Gecht, Edward Spreitzer, Tom Kokoraleis, and Andrew Kokoraleis; see also Chapter 10). Removing the duplication from just these three cases would reduce the total of alleged serial murder victims for the century by about 225, or 5 percent of the whole; and there are assuredly other such instances.

There are also real problems with the area of suspected murders,

Table 2.1.   Serial Killers Allegedly Involved in Forty or More Murders, 1970–1992

Name	Killed	Suspected	Dates active
William Bonin	14	26	1979–1980
Thomas Creech	26	16	1965–1981
Robert Diaz	12	48	1981
Green River Killer	49		1982–1985
Donald Harvey	37	18	1970–1987
Genene Jones	1	40	1981–1982
Randy Kraft	16	29	1972–1983
Gerald Stano	41		1969–1983
Alan Stevens	1	42	1985–1989
Ottis Toole	3	100	1961–1981

crimes that have been attributed to an offender. This is illustrated if we consider the most serious cases in the list, the ten individuals who are said to have been involved in forty or more murders, listed in Table 2.1. Extensive courtroom testimony and journalistic investigation confirmed the very high estimates of victims attributed to four of these individuals: William Bonin, Donald Harvey, Randy Kraft, and Gerald Stano. On the other hand, without an arrest, it is very difficult to know if the Green River murders are in fact the connected series they currently appear to be, or if several separate killers were at work; while the claims of victims attributed to Robert Diaz, Thomas Creech, and Genene Jones seem quite unjustified. In the Jones instance, the forty victims may reflect the number of suspicious deaths that were reopened for further investigation after her apprehension, but of which little more was heard subsequently. Another Justice Department list in 1992 linked her to nine murders and attempts, a far more realistic estimate. The forty-two suspected attributed to Alan Stevens are in fact the dubious series of San Diego murders, discussed above, where there is significant controversy about the existence of any underlying pattern or linkage between the cases.

Especially dubious is the claim of over a hundred victims for Ottis Toole, who confessed to numerous crimes with which he had little connection. He had been associated with another killer, Henry Lee Lucas (see Chapter 3) and between them the pair had laid claim to a chain of several hundred victims in the 1970s and early 1980s. However, Lucas's claims have been culled ruthlessly, and the Justice Department list has brought the estimate of his activity from 160 victims to about 10. Presumably a similar divisor should be employed in Toole's case, and another Justice Department list prepared in 1992 omitted Toole's name altogether, perhaps reflecting serious doubts about any and all of his allegations (U.S. Justice Department 1992, 1993). The plausibility of suspected murders varies enormously from case to case, and the grounds for inclusion are often tenuous in the extreme.

But let us assume for the sake of argument that all the suspected victims are correctly attributed, and we ignore the (quite significant) padding of the list caused by duplication. Even so, the FBI data offer a portrait of the extent of serial murder activity that is radically different from what it and other agencies proposed in the early 1980s. It was implied at this time that many offenders might kill dozens or hundreds of victims in any given year, and several hundred over an entire "career" of murder. The FBI data provide no support for such a figure, suggesting rather that the average "kill" for a serial murderer over his or her lifetime would be about ten. Moreover, such murder series would generally be spread over four or five years or even more, so that the "average" serial killer would claim only two or three lives each year. Since 1970, there have been only three or four cases that can be said with any confidence to have involved forty or more victims.

Even if we grant that the rate of multiple homicide accelerated substantially over the century, the actual number of victims in the 1980s does not appear to be anything like as large as was often claimed. In 1992, the Justice Department compiled a list of known multiple-murder cases from 1977 through 1991 (U.S. Justice Department 1992), shown in Table 2.2. This suggests that 331 serial offenders had killed 1,964 victims, and were suspected in a further 1,285 killings, giving a total of 3,249 known or alleged victims. Even if every one of these cases is correctly attributed, that would mean that serial murder was accounting for about 200 victims a year, barely 1 percent of all American homicides.

However, problems of definition, duplication, and simple error mean that this figure is somewhat high, and an audit undertaken for a CNN documentary shown in 1993 reduced the kill substantially. This gave a figure of 191 killers active between 1977 and 1991, with the total known confirmed victims a mere 1,007 over fifteen years, or less than 70 a year.

Table 2.2.   Justice Department Data on Multiple Homicide
in the United States 1977–1991

Type of murderer	Killed	Attempted	Suspected
Mass (N = 157)	964	262	65
Spree (N = 112)	483	150	130
Serial (N = 331)	1,964	247	1,285

This is excessively cautious, as there is certainly some merit to the *suspected* category, and the estimate makes no allowance for cases yet to be discovered, but the implications are clear. In quantitative terms, serial murder represents an extreme fringe of the American homicide problem, and any estimate that suggests that it involves significantly over 1 percent of all murder victims should be greeted with great suspicion.

A HISTORY OF THE OFFENSE

If the reality of contemporary serial murder has been so radically misstated, what does this imply about the historical development of the phenomenon? This is a critical issue, as so much of the recent writing on serial homicide is predicated on the assumption that the behavior is historically new, and must therefore have arisen through novel social circumstances. It is a "nontraditional crime," "an alarming new phenomenon" (Wilson and Seaman 1992:1). This picture appears to be confirmed by FBI data in Table 2.3, which suggest that recorded serial murder cases have accelerated rapidly over time, with the mid-1960s as the crucial turning point in this trend. However, there are serious difficulties with this table, especially for the years before about 1950.

In order for this information to be reliable, we need to make two assumptions: First, that earlier cases are as likely as contemporary incidents to come to light and to be preserved in official records or media; and second, the search methods used for this project were equally reliable for the earlier periods as the later. Serious doubts can be expressed

Table 2.3. Justice Department Figures on the History of Serial Homicide in the United States

Period	Known serial murder cases
1795–1849	5
1850–1899	20
1900–1924	13
1925–1949	20
1950–1974	66
1975–1992	331
Total	455

Source: U.S. Justice Department (1992).

on both counts, so that the apparently large increase can in part be explained as an artifact of the processes of recording and searching. For the 1970s and 1980s, the researchers who compiled these statistics had access to computerized search facilities, which permitted a wide trawl of local newspapers and national wire services, so that the total of cases is inflated by numerous small-scale local incidents. For earlier years, the study relies on much chancier data, including book-length case studies of well-known offenders, and less systematic newspaper searches undertaken by earlier scholars. The data for the earlier and later periods simply cannot be fairly compared. In fact, it is remarkable that the findings for the nineteenth century produce as many cases as they do; and it is astonishing to find authors asserting that the serial murder phenomenon simply did not exist before about 1870 (Wilson and Seaman 1992:3).

Especially troubling is the nature of cases listed for the different eras. In the 1980s, we have numerous instances of cases involving "only" two or three victims, in addition to the legendary incidents with twenty or thirty killings. For the years between 1890 and 1940, by contrast, the vast majority of the cases listed are instances of "extreme" serial killing, with very large numbers of victims. This either means that early killers were all vastly more successful than their modern counterparts, or else the searches are failing to locate the (hypothetically) numerous petty cases of that era. The latter explanation is far more probable. Moreover, the known earlier cases are overwhelmingly drawn from major cities, especially in the Northeast and Midwest, from New York and Chicago, Cleveland, and Cincinnati. It is again possible to argue that urban conditions were more likely to produce violent behavior, but issues of recording and searching must also play a role in explaining this imbalance.

CHANGING MEDIA PATTERNS

This does not mean that the apparent increase is entirely false, but the historical pattern must be reconstructed more systematically. It is necessary both to compile an accurate listing of known serial murder cases over time, and to consider possible objections that apparent changes might result more from developments in trends of reporting or recording crime than from actual changes in the behavior itself.

In order to compile a database to supplement the Justice Department lists, cases can be located in several major sources. The first involves well-indexed and authoritative newspapers like the *New York Times, Los Angeles Times,* and *Chicago Tribune.* This material must be supplemented from a variety of secondary sources on serial murder, which have been fully listed elsewhere (see Jenkins 1988a, 1988b, 1989; major sources include Wilson and Seaman 1983; Wilson and Pitman 1984; Gaute and Odell 1979). Eric Hickey's important study *Serial Murderers and Their Victims* lists some 202 cases from 1795 to 1987; while Michael Newton has published valuable "encyclopedias" of serial murder, *Hunting Humans* (1990) and *Serial Slaughter* (1992; see also Newton 1988).

Taken together, this evidence provides prima facie confirmation of a rise in the volume of serial murder activity from the 1960s onwards, although not as dramatic as Justice Department data would suggest. However, the validity of this finding ultimately depends on the evidence of newspapers and other mass media, and the crucial issue then arises whether the nature of reporting is fairly constant over time. If a study of media sources in the 1920s or 1950s produces far fewer cases than we find in the 1990s, can we safely assume that this indicates a change in the frequency of the offense, or might this simply reflect changes in the workings of the mass media?

There is some evidence that metropolitan papers like the *New York Times* or *Los Angeles Times* did expand their coverage of regional news from the 1950s onwards (Jenkins 1992b). Also, local newspapers were increasingly likely to form part of large chains or corporate groupings, and those chains themselves grew from statewide or regional concerns to national status. One consequence of this was that stories of any sensational value were less likely to be confined to a purely local market, and were instead disseminated throughout the chain. Stories thus reached a national audience, and were picked up (or at least referred to) by other major journals like the *New York Times*. As the trend toward chain ownership was most marked in the late 1960s, it is at least possible that the increased reporting of serial murder might in part reflect a growing nationalization of news. Furthermore, journalistic practices in the 1980s were marked by a growing trend toward sensationalism, and the growth of what has been described as a tabloid approach to news gathering, so that we would expect an acceleration in the spiral of crime reporting.

On the other hand, these trends would not in themselves be a sufficient explanation for any perceived changes. Throughout the century, a major serial murder case has usually been viewed as a story of great journalistic interest, and the *New York Times* between about 1900 and 1940 reported extensively and enthusiastically on serial murder cases as far afield as Colorado, Iowa, Alaska and South Dakota. There is no reason to believe that media practices or public taste changed suddenly during midcentury. Moreover, cases that today might seem comparatively minor or commonplace would then have received enormous attention in terms of column inches in the newspapers, or in numbers of published books and magazine articles. The suggestion is that had more cases occurred in earlier years, they would have been reported at length. If a case like that of Ted Bundy had occurred in, say, the early 1920s or mid-1950s, it is impossible to believe that its sensationalistic potential would have been overlooked.

It might also be suggested that cases were as likely to be reported in midcentury, but that police agencies interpreted crimes differently before announcing their conclusions to the media. We might hypothesize that a police agency arresting a suspect in the late 1930s might be slow to investigate his or her involvement in a series of crimes over many years in a number of states; while their modern counterparts would be more familiar with patterns of serial homicide, and would thus tend to speculate with greater freedom. Modern agencies also have superior record-keeping techniques, and more experience of interagency cooperation, enhancing the likelihood that a suspect could be linked to a large number of earlier offenses. It was only in midcentury that the duty of investigating suspicious deaths passed from elected coroners to professional medical examiners.

This view is superficially attractive, but the contrast with earlier eras is too sharply drawn. Between 1900 and 1940, American police agencies often demonstrated their familiarity with the concept of serial murder and pursued investigations accordingly, so that such offenders were frequently detected and apprehended. As a matter of course, investigators traced the earlier movements of suspects, and attempted to link them with crimes in other jurisdictions or even other nations. There is no evidence that police agencies in midcentury were any less aware of these issues and problems, especially in the aftermath of widely publicized affairs like the Cleveland Torso Murders of the 1930s. Moreover, the attention focused on the stereotypical "sex maniac" in the 1950s ensured that police and media were constantly aware of the possibility that a sexually motivated attack might well be one of a lengthy series.

It is therefore likely that the accounts of cases we can compile from media and secondary accounts are representative of broader trends, even if they are not, of course, comprehensive. Based on this evidence, a number of statements can be made about the changing frequency of serial murder in the United States, and they offer only qualified support to the claims made during the 1980s.

THE FREQUENCY OF SERIAL HOMICIDE 1900–1990

Serial murder of the type observed in the 1980s was by no means a new phenomenon. There were numerous cases of multiple killers during the nineteenth century, and there are published accounts of perhaps hundreds of incidents other than the legendary Jack the Ripper affair (see, for example, McClaren 1993; R. Harris 1989; Altick 1973; Adelman 1970; Lindsay 1958). In the United States, the best-known case involved H. H. Holmes ("Herman Mudgett"), who killed perhaps thirty people in the 1890s, and especially victimized women visiting the Chicago World's Fair of 1893.

During the present century, celebrated cases have included Melvin D. Rees, who raped and killed a Maryland woman in 1957, and massacred a family of four in Virginia in 1959. He was also believed to have carried out four other sex-slayings near the University of Maryland. Equally modern in character was the case of Jake Bird, a drifter who killed two women in Washington state in 1947. When arrested, he confessed to over forty homicides in the previous decade, with confirmed offenses recorded in Illinois, Kentucky, Nebraska, South Dakota, Ohio, Florida, and Wisconsin. The reconstruction of his travels and crimes bears obvious resemblances to the investigation of more recent itinerant killers, like Henry Lee Lucas or Gerald Stano. In the 1950s, Stephen Nash of California resembled other homosexual serial killers of later years.

Broadly, the American experience with serial murder can be divided into three periods: a time of quite intense activity before about 1940; a time of relative tranquility in the mid century; and finally a "murder wave" that began in roughly the mid-1960s and continues unabated today.

1900–1940: A "Murder Wave"?

Between about 1900 and 1940, there was an absolute minimum of a hundred serial murder cases, and the total may be far greater. Moreover, there were at least twenty-four extreme serial killers, individuals who each killed ten or more victims (Jenkins 1989:380). In other words, such a case of extreme serial homicide could be expected to break in the news media at least every twenty months. By way of comparison, the number of such extreme cases in the 1970s and 1980s was about sixty, but the overall population at this point was far greater.

Serial murder was less common in America in this era than in the last two decades, but not much less. The offense was common, and the United States produced most of the types of multiple homicide with which we are familiar today. To illustrate this, we might consider two periods of peculiarly intense concern with multiple homicide, both of which bear many resemblances to recent years: respectively, the years between 1911 and 1915, and between 1935 and 1941.

1911–1915. FBI data record just thirteen serial murder cases for the whole period from 1900 to 1924. However, unsystematic use of just one major source, the *New York Times*, allows us to locate seventeen cases for just the five-year period 1911–1915, a rate of reporting quite comparable to modern conditions. Rippers and axe-murderers frequently made national news in these years. "Jack the Ripper" was credited with a still unsolved series of over twenty killings of black women in Atlanta between 1910 and 1912 (*New York Times*, May 12, 1912), and the press used the same name for a repeat child-killer active in New York in 1915 (*New York Times*, March 20–30, May 4–18, 1915). In 1912, there was a murder series in Aurora, Colorado (*New York Times, August 12, 1912*). In 1913, Cincinnati reported a new suspect in the notorious Ripper case that had been such a major story over the previous decade (*New York Times*, December 19, 1913).

In 1915, the arrest of alleged axe-murderer Loving Mitchell led to revived investigations of a series of attacks on families in five Midwestern states, which had claimed perhaps thirty victims; while Henry Lee Moore massacred over twenty victims in separate axe attacks on rural families before his arrest in 1912. One of Moore's attacks, the slaughter of a family of eight in Vilisca, Iowa, remained in the news sporadically through 1917 (*New York Times*, June 11–12, 1912, September 2, November 25, 1917). In its day, the Vilisca massacre made a national impact quite comparable to the Gainesville murders of 1990.

Such extreme homicide cases were remarkably abundant in these years. Syd Jones confessed to thirteen homicides before his execution in 1915 (*New York Times* March 22, June 26, 1915); and the same year, the demolition of a house in Grand Forks, North Dakota, proved that the previous owner had been a "maniac" who had left six bodies on the property (*New York Times*, June 27, 1915). In Aberdeen, Washington, Billy Gohl was convicted of two murders of itinerant seamen in 1912, but he was suspected in up to forty other killings (Newton 1990). There were also celebrated cases involving women offenders, like multiple poisoners Louise Vermilyea, Mrs. Lindorf, and Ellen Etheridge (*New York Times*, April 7, June 21, 1912; Newton 1990).

Public reactions to these crimes were very similar to what might be expected today. The press treated these incidents as major stories, and in New York City the child murder scare of 1915 was probably the most intensely covered metropolitan story of that year. Public concern is suggested by impassioned editorials, as well as reports of mobs attacking suspicious strangers. The police also behaved in a strikingly modern fashion, and law enforcement agencies in this era were thoroughly familiar with the possible linkages between crimes. This is suggested by the 1912 arrest of Frank Hickey for a series of killings of boys in New

York and Massachusetts. Police duly reconstructed his previous patterns of residence and employment and attempted to connect him with other unsolved murders in those areas (*New York Times*, December 6, December 17–26, 1912). The Villisca massacre of 1912 was auspicious in being one of the first multiple homicide cases where federal law enforcement became involved to track interstate linkages.

The authorities were also quite familiar with types of crime that we tend to regard as distinctively modern including ritual killings and medical murders. Nearly fifty victims were killed by a still unidentified axe-murderer in Louisiana and Texas in 1911–1912, crimes that may have been connected with an obscure black religious sect (*New York Times*, March 3, 1912). In the medical arena, there was a lengthy series of child murders in a Brooklyn hospital in 1911 (*New York Times*, February 23–March 1, 1912), while Frederick Mors killed between eight and twenty elderly patients in New York City in 1914 (Nash 1980). Nursing home proprietor Amy Archer-Gilligan killed anywhere between twenty and a hundred patients in her charge between 1907 and 1914.

1935–1941. A similar impression of apparently modern conditions emerges if we consider the cases that came to light in the years between 1935 and 1941, a period about which a recent book argues (on the basis of the Justice Department statistics) that "multiple murders were quite rare in America. And those which were recorded were so isolated and bizarre as to appear to have nothing to do with the reality of American life" (Jeffers 1992, 24–25). This view appears quite incorrect.

The period began with the 1935 arrest of Alonzo Robinson for a series of sex murders in the Midwest, the crimes involving cannibalism, mutilation, and decapitation. The same year, Californian Earl "Bud" Kimball confessed to a series of twenty-five murders in the Sierra Nevada (*New York Times*, August 23, 1935). Also in 1935, multiple rapist Gerald Thompson was on trial in Chicago for the murder that was the culmination of his long series of sex crimes, while Albert Fish was on trial for the last of fifteen child murders committed over the previous quarter of a century (see below, and Chapter 8). The year 1937 brought the case of Anna Hahn, a Cincinnati woman who poisoned at least five elderly men in her care.

It was about 1934 that there began the most spectacular murder series of the era, the Cleveland Torso Killings, in which an individual killed and mutilated up to seventeen victims in poor areas of the city (Nickel 1989). The crimes may also have been connected to other killings in western Pennsylvania, all of which remain unsolved. Just as this case was at its height in terms of media excitement in the summer of 1938, the fourteen or so murders of Joe Ball were being discovered in southern

Texas (*New York Times*, September 27, 1938). In 1941, Jarvis Catoe was arrested for a series of at least nine rape murders in Washington, D.C., and New York City, and he was also questioned in connection with the New Jersey "lovers' lane" murders, which had begun in 1938. However, these crimes were later connected with Clarence Hill, who confessed in 1944 [compare Chapman (1982) for a similar case about this time].

In 1939 and 1940, the media focused on the organized crime death squad known as Murder, Incorporated, based in New York City but operating across the nation. These were also the years of the sensational "poison for profit" ring discovered in Philadelphia, an insurance fraud operation that may well have claimed fifty lives (Young 1992). This case was all the more intriguing because of its apparent ritualistic associations, and the media freely speculated on the occult interests and activities of the various participants, who included Jewish Qabalists and *Hexerei* folk-magicians, as well as Italian folk-healers and witches (McDonnell 1939a, 1939b, 1939c). The police also explored the possibility of ritual and voodoo elements in the Cleveland torso slayings (Nickel 1989:154; compare Chapter 10).

This short period therefore produced at least ten cases that earned national notoriety, and as with their counterparts in the 1970s and 1980s, American serial killers like Albert Fish and the Cleveland Torso Killer became internationally famous (Nickel 1989; compare Douthwaite 1929). It is very likely that a detailed search of local newspapers and police records from the early part of the century would produce dozens more cases that have since been forgotten, especially instances involving far fewer victims than the legendary incidents. However, it is also striking how many cases with numerous victims have slipped from the public record since their celebrity in the 1930s, and are not mentioned in most recent lists of serial killings. This includes such then-famous murderers as Bud Kimball and "Texas Jim" Bakerien (*Literary Digest*, January 2, 1937, p. 34).

By 1940, the American public was thoroughly accustomed to stories of serial murder in the news media, which also carried stories about overseas cases, especially from Germany. The incidents often included grotesque acts of mutilation, torture and sexual perversion, and there was even a minor undercurrent of ritualistic murder. There were also many films and fictional depictions, so that the mass murderer or maniac sex-killer was a familiar popular stereotype by the late 1930s (see Chapter 4).

This is illustrated by Joseph Kesselring's 1938 play *Arsenic and Old Lace*, which imagines the encounter between two separate "teams" of serial killers. This black comedy was filmed by Frank Capra in 1941, and it became a popular classic following its release in 1944. The villain, Jonathan Brewster, thus became one of the best known fictional stereotypes of a multiple killer, and in every way his imaginary career bears close resemblances to those of authentic modern cases. He has claimed twelve lives, and has roamed freely: "Then the first one in London, two in Johannesburg, one in Sydney, one in Melbourne, two in San Francisco, one in Phoenix, Arizona . . . the filling station. Three in Chicago and one in South Bend." He has also been involved in extreme actions of torture and mutilation, as in "the Melbourne method—two hours!" which his partner regards with such horror. However, this brutal killer has claimed no more victims than his aunts, who poison elderly men as a form of mercy killing ("a very bad habit"). In real life, such multiple poisoners (who were often women) were indeed the killers most likely to have claimed the largest number of victims.

In summary, both periods (1911–1915, 1935–1941) bear many resemblances to conditions in the contemporary United States, and a similar picture could be given for any period of comparable length in the first four decades of the century.

1940–1965: The "Sex Crime Problem"

In contrast, the rate of activity certainly declined in midcentury. Between 1940 and 1969, there were only about fifty serial murder cases recorded in the United States, and the real number might be smaller (Jenkins 1992b). Between 1970 and 1990, there was an absolute minimum of three hundred. In terms of extreme cases, with ten or more victims, there were seven between 1940 and 1965, compared with over sixty between 1971 and 1990. A serial murder case was recorded on average every 10 months or so between 1940 and 1964; and one extreme case every 43 months. Between 1971 and 1990, a serial case could be expected to emerge in the media every 24 days, and an extreme case every 120 days. By this coarse measure, serial murder cases overall were eight times more likely in the later period than in midcentury; and extreme cases were reported over ten times as frequently.

The decline of serial homicide is a phenomenon that merits explanation. A number of reasons have been suggested for this change, including the growing demographic stability following the end of the age of mass immigration, a change that reduced the number of potential victims who could disappear with little trace. There were also the somewhat draconian civil commitment laws, which may have removed from public circulation many individuals who might otherwise have become multiple killers, or their victims; but the discussion remains speculative (Jenkins 1992b).

The reality of the decline in the volume of activity is confirmed by an examination of the contemporary literature on violent crime. The dominant intellectual trend of this period within criminology was psychiatric and psychoanalytic, and there was much interest in the life histories of strange or bizarre offenders who might illustrate unusual aspects of the human mind. Collections of case studies were published by reputable scholars who devoted great attention to psychopathy (Abrahamsen 1944, 1960, 1973; Karpman 1947–1948, 1954; Bromberg 1948; Wertham 1947, 1949, 1966; Neustatter 1957). We would therefore expect scholarly attention to be paid to real-life serial killers if they were available.

There were indeed numerous accounts of serial homicide and lust-murder, while the important distinction between mass and series murder was beginning to enter the literature (MacDonald 1961:175, 1968, 1976; Banay 1956; Galvin and MacDonald 1959; MacDonald 1961:175). However, very few of these subjects were drawn from the United States. The classic case studies were mainly German murderers of the 1920s and 1930s like Fritz Haarman, Karl Denke, and Peter Kürten, each of whom claimed ten or twenty victims in circumstances of extreme brutality and sexual perversion (Wertham 1949:259; MacDonald 1961). A similar emphasis on European cases is also found in the sensationalistic literature, which recounted gruesome homicide cases in prurient terms.

Modern accounts of multiple homicide would probably draw all their examples from American cases, but domestic examples did not then exist in anything like comparable numbers. In a sentence that today seems quite remarkable, Bromberg could write in 1948, "The paucity of lust-murderers in modern criminologic experience makes an analysis of the basic psychopathology difficult." There were "few actual cases" to compare with "Jack the Ripper or other legendary sex-fiends" (p. 87); and the author felt he had to return to 1913 to find an American parallel.

This is not to suggest that no American cases attracted interest, but the same small group of incidents was described repeatedly. Albert Fish occupied a central place in the literature for many years after his execution in 1936, due to the detailed analysis of the case published by Fredric Wertham (1949). In fact, he represented the prototypical multiple killer in his day as definitively as Ted Bundy did in later years. As late as 1952, the film The Sniper had to return to Fish to find an exemplar of an American sex-killer (see below, and also Chapter 4). Not until the later 1950s would there again be American cases that would have such a cultural impact, with the notoriety accorded to Ed Gein, Charlie Starkweather, and (later) Albert DeSalvo (Schechter 1991; Allen 1976; Frank 1967; Reinhardt 1960, 1962; DeFord 1965).

There was a sense that the multiple killer was a phenomenon that had definitely been relegated to the American past, a point illustrated by Ray Bradbury's classic 1957 novel Dandelion Wine. This elegiac work provides a romantic portrait of rural America during the summer of 1928, in which all the old familiar features were being replaced by the modern world. Among the traditions passing away is the notion of the multiple killer, exemplified by a serial strangler called "the lonely one." The theme of lost innocence is suggested by the failure of the killer to claim a female victim, and in fact it is the woman who takes his life. This is seen as yet another turning point, like the replacement of the buggy by the automobile, and it is implied that the community is the poorer for losing the sense of thrill and romance that the killer had provided. Significantly, this serial murder story is located in the 1920s, rather than in a contemporary setting when serial killers appeared so much less appropriate or plausible. The ripper seemed to be a remnant of the gaslight era.

Multiple homicide (mass murder) continued to be recognized as a phenomenon during midcentury, but the issue was subsumed into the broader problem of sex crimes or sex psychopaths, which included a spectrum of behavior that included child molestation and rape as well as nuisance offenses like voyeurism and exhibitionism (Halleck 1965). Perceptions of a problem spread rapidly from the late 1930s, and Kittrie (1971) suggests that it was the Fish case above all that caused the public identification of the sex offender with the child killer (compare Schechter 1990; see Chapter ten below).

Sex crimes were often discussed in the periodical literature, and the *Literary Digest* (April 10, 1937) used recent FBI data to argue that the nation was facing a crisis from sex offenders. In 1937, New York City was said to be in a state of panic after the sexual murders of four children by "murderous-minded perverts" (*New York Times*, August 14, 1937). The stereotype was decisively reinforced by the 1946 case of William Heirens, a Chicago multiple killer whose confessions offered a textbook instance of Freudian inner conflict. At one murder scene he had left a note reading, "For Heaven's sake catch me before I kill more. I cannot control myself" (Freeman 1955; Kennedy, Hoffman, and Haines, 1947). From the late 1930s onwards, most states passed draconian and ill-defined "sex psychopath" laws to stem the alleged tide of sexual violence, and these often remained in place until the late 1960s (Sutherland 1950). The issue of sex fiends reached a new height in the early 1950s, and in 1955 Paul Tappan suggested that in popular mythology "tens of thousands of homicidal sex fiends stalk the land" (quoted in Cohen 1980:669).

Contemporary images are well reflected in the 1952 film *The Sniper*. This adopted a crusading tone, suggesting that multiple murder was an extreme type of sexual offense, which required sympathetic proactive action, with an emphasis on treatment, therapy, and rehabilitation. This is epitomized by the didactic prologue, which asserted, "High among police problems is that of the sex criminal, responsible last year alone for offenses which victimized 31,175 women. Adequate and understanding laws do not exist. Law enforcement is helpless. Here in terms of one case is the story of a man whose enemy was womankind." The very limited scale of serial murder activity in these decades goes far toward explaining why the issue was seen as a subset of a larger problem, rather than a menace in its own right.

1965–1994

It is in this context that we should see the acceleration in multiple homicide activity from the 1960s, the murder wave claimed by most authors. The phenomenon did exist, but it was a return to earlier historical patterns rather than a wholly new phenomenon; and it only seems new and dramatic when considered against the immediately preceding period. In fact, it should perhaps be the tranquility of midcentury that deserves explanation, rather than the apparent violence of recent years. The low violence rates of the earlier period also encouraged observers of the 1960s to see the conditions of their own day as unprecedented, which they were not. An account of the Boston Strangler case of 1963 notes that "Not since Jack the Ripper murdered and dismembered women in the gaslit streets of London three quarters of a century before had anything comparable been experienced" (Frank 1967:29), a comment that would have astonished Americans of the Progressive era or the 1930s.

In the mid-1950s, the United States enjoyed very low rates of serial homicide, while a quarter of a century later, the country would be in the midst of an apparent murder wave; and the transition between the two stages can be dated to the mid-1960s. The increase of extreme and seemingly irrational homicide was frequently remarked on during these years, and many writers focused on a short period during 1966. In July, Richard Speck killed eight nurses in a Chicago hostel, and in August, Charles Whitman killed sixteen people during a shooting spree in Texas (Breo and Martin 1993; Altman and Ziporyn 1967). Only slightly less celebrated were two murder sprees later in the year in Arizona and Utah.

Over the next three years, such acts were widely discussed in the context of a general "violence problem," which was also manifested in political assassinations, urban riots, and soaring crime rates (U.S. Government 1969–1970). However, specific interest in multiple acts of irrational murder was stimulated by the Manson family murders of 1969, as well as a sharp rise in the number of ripper crimes or lust murders of the sort that had been dismissed as so rare in the 1940s. The late 1960s were the years of notorious offenders like John Norman Collins (Keyes [1976] 1977), Jerry Brudos (Rule 1983a), Antone Costa (Damore [1981] 1990), George Putt (Meyer 1974), "Zodiac" (Graysmith 1987), and others (Hilberry 1987; Moser and Cohen 1967). These crimes marked the beginning of an authentic upward trend that continues into the present decade.

Serial murder has become far more frequent since the late 1960s, and offenders tend to kill larger numbers of victims (Jenkins 1992b). Holmes and DeBurger write of a "surge" in "multicide" dating from about 1960 (1988:16). Norris comments, "Since 1960 not only have the number of individual serial killers increased but so have the number of victims per killer, and the level of savagery of the individual crimes themselves" (1988:19). Leyton (1986) suggests that reported acts of multiple homicide in the United States were ten or twelve times more frequent after the 1960s than before. On a related topic, Fox has remarked that 1966 marked "the onset of the age of mass murder" ("Experts Say . . . " 1988). We may agree with all these remarks, without accepting the implied corollary that there is something unique or unprecedented about contemporary American conditions.

AMERICAN UNIQUENESS?

The distinctiveness of American conditions has been a frequent theme in writings on serial murder over the last decade, and one researcher indicates that 74 percent of all twentieth-century serial killers derived from the United States (Newton 1990). If true, this suggests that there is a peculiarly American vulnerability to this sort of crime, but this conclusion would be difficult to justify. For example, it has been suggested that serial killers account for perhaps 1 or 2 percent of homicide victims in the United States, which is not significantly greater than the proportion in Great Britain over the last half-century (Jenkins 1988b). The difference between the two societies is not that Americans necessarily have a greater proclivity for random irrational homicide, but that U.S. murder rates are simply far higher overall than those of any comparable developed society.

It might also be suggested that the high frequency of recorded multiple-homicide activity in the United States reflects a greater awareness of the offense than in other countries, and a greater willingness by law enforcement agencies to recognize linkages between murders. Legal factors may play a role here. Most English-speaking countries outside the United States base their laws on British precedent, in which a case remains *sub judice* until its final resolution. Courts place severe restrictions on coverage, and they enforce these limitations with the harsh penalties of the contempt laws, which include imprisonment. In Canada, for example, much still remains obscure about the Clifford Olson case decided in 1982, though a recent writer has speculated that Olson may have been involved in forty murders rather than the eleven previously known (Worthington 1993). During the sensational Paul Bernardo/Teale rape-murder case of 1992–1994, American journalists encountered severe legal difficulties trying to treat Canadian courts with the same freedom that prevails in their home country. In contrast, Jeffrey Dahmer was already the subject of several books before the completion of his trial.

Moreover, libel laws are much harsher in British-influenced nations, so that it is very risky to suggest that a given individual was convicted of two killings, "but is suspected of eight more" (Jenkins 1991, 1992a). When William Lester Suff was arrested in 1992, a typical newspaper headline reported "California Worker Charged with Two of Nineteen Deaths," implying that he was a strong suspect in the remaining crimes in Riverside County, and that further charges were simply a matter of time. Such speculations are the source of most of the high estimates of serial murder activity in U.S. cases, but they would not be possible in Britain, Canada, or Australia, in which reference could only be made with safety to cases proven in court. The Suff headline would certainly be actionable in these countries. Convicted killers have used such legal protections to ensure that no charges are published other than those actually established in court (Worthington 1993).

In this environment, it is not surprising that British or Canadian killers are usually credited with only two or three murders, while their U.S. counterparts are linked to thirty or forty (Andrew Rule 1988). Furthermore, the lack of detailed media accounts means that it is much harder for researchers to list serial killers by searching databases. Finally, Britain and British Commonwealth police forces tend to be much less amenable to publicizing information to press and public, especially about ongoing investigations. It might even be that if such factors are taken into account, British Commonwealth nations could actually have a *higher* incidence of serial murder than the United States.

THE GERMAN EXPERIENCE

American uniqueness may thus be exaggerated. In addition, contemporary American rates are not that unusual when compared with some

Table 2.4. Major German Serial Murder Cases 1910–1950

Name	Dates active	Number of victims
Grossman, Georg Karl	1914–1921	50?
Denke, Karl	1921–1924	30
Haarmann, Fritz	1918–1924	50?
Kürten, Peter	1899–1929	12+
Ludke, Bruno	1928–1943	80?
Seefeld, Adolf	1933–1936	12
Pleil, Rudolf	1946–1950	9–25?

Source: Wilson and Pitman (1984), Newton (1990), Nash (1990).

past societies with high rates of serial homicide, most notably Germany in the early twentieth century (Jenkins forthcoming). Between 1910 and 1940, there were several cases of extreme serial homicide, often characterized by gross deviations such as necrophilia and cannibalism, and in which dozens of victims perished. Table 2.4 indicates the best-known cases.

These cases have all been frequently described, but a brief recapitulation might be useful in emphasizing some common themes in the cases (Douthwaite 1929). The Grossman case involved a child molester who had often come to police attention. The chaos of the war years allowed him to kill unmolested, and he is alleged to have sold the flesh of some of his female victims as meat for human consumption. Similar stories like these frequently surrounded the killers of these years, such as Fritz Haarmann of Hannover (see Chapter 9). Typical of this era was the case of Karl Denke, a cannibal who preyed on vagrants and transients in his Silesian town. At the end of the decade, the terrifying image of the serial killer was reestablished by the case of Peter Kürten. Kürten had been killing sporadically since his childhood, in the 1890s, but it was in Düsseldorf in the Weimar years that he earned his greatest notoriety as a multiple rapist, "vampire" killer, poisoner, and arsonist. His trial in 1931 created an international sensation.

It is not known whether the major cases were accompanied by a plethora of lesser known series where fewer than ten victims died. This seems probable, but the local German newspapers of that era remain to be examined by a researcher with the appropriate linguistic and scholarly competence. A memoir of Weimar Berlin records, "Hardly a month passed without some terrible murder becoming known. In many cases, ordinary criminal instincts were combined with sexual perversion, typical of the day" (quoted in Wilson and Seaman 1992:314). Such cases did much to disseminate awareness of multiple homicide in Germany, where the topic even provided a subject for Expressionist painters. The serial murder theme entered popular culture through such cinematic works as *The Cabinet of Dr. Caligari* (1919) and Fritz Lang's *M* (1931), which draws on the incidents of Haarmann and Kürten (see Chapter 4). There was also lively academic and professional work, and scholars like Karl Berg undertook the pioneering taxonomic work that has survived in such concepts as *Lustmörder*, which is so often mistranslated as lust-killer. This work became significant for American attitudes toward crime and violence as so many German psychiatric and medical experts fled to the United States during the 1930s. The German experience confirms that in historical terms, there is little that is truly novel about the phenomenon of multiple murder in the contemporary United States.

EXAMINING THE STEREOTYPE

Quantitative and comparative evidence also allows us to challenge the stereotype of the serial killer as a lone white male, an image that is questionable on various grounds. For example, in the literature as in fictional depictions, the stereotype of the serial killer is usually the lone ripper or mad slasher. In reality, there are a great many cases where murders are perpetrated not by an isolated individual, but by two or more offenders working in close concert: what has been characterized as "group serial homicide." Group activity may account for 10 or 20 percent of all serial murder cases (Jenkins 1990). This is significant for the understanding of the offense, because it challenges the idea that the crime results solely from individual pathology rather than cultural environment.

Serial killers do not always act alone, nor do they invariably act from obvious sexual motives. There are certainly cases where a male killer rapes his female victim, clearly enjoying great sexual satisfaction from the commission of violent and perverted activities; and it can be argued that sexual motivations underlie other cases where the sadistic element is not quite so explicit. However, numerous cases lack the apparent sexual motive, and this is especially true of the prolific "medical murderers" like Donald Harvey or Genene Jones, nurses or doctors who kill their patients. Such cases include some of the largest number of victims found in accounts of multiple homicide (Mandelsberg 1992; Furneaux 1957). It can be argued that such crimes arise from an urge to express power over others, which might be ultimately sexual in nature, but the linkage should not be accepted uncritically.

It is also questionable whether "the serial murderer almost without exception is a male" (Osterburg and Ward 1992:596). In 1991–1992, the trial of Florida murderer Aileen Wuornos led to media claims that this was America's first female serial killer, but this assertion is quite impermissible (see Chapter 7). There have been several attempts to list and quantify known serial murder cases, and such endeavors always tend to produce a surprisingly high proportion of female killers. In his study of American serial murder from the 1790s to the 1980s, Eric Hickey (1991) suggests that women comprise at least 15 percent of the whole. The Justice Department databases name thirty-six female serial killers over the present century, some 7 percent of the total.

Moreover, such lists will always be counting *known* cases, and will thus exaggerate the significance of crimes that are easily recognized as serial homicide. In particular, they will always include a disproportionate number of ripper-type acts, while understating crimes of less obvious violence, involving asphyxiation or poisoning. Before the age of modern forensic medicine, it was quite possible for poisoners to claim dozens or hundreds of victims undetected, and this type of killer was far more likely to be drawn from the women who prepared food and supervised drugs and medicines (see Chapter 7). Women serial killers are thus likely to be seriously underrepresented in any list of offenders. A similar point can be made about killers from ethnic minority groups, who form so small a component of public perceptions of the serial murder "menace." Though minority offenders are rarely represented in either true-crime or fictional depictions of serial killers, they undoubtedly exist (see Chapter 8).

Finally, serial killers do not generally "roam." This was an issue of moment in the 1980s when it was alleged that the typical killer wandered freely across the country, killing in ten or twenty states; and it was also said that such extreme mobility was a recent development. This assertion was made chiefly in order to justify increased federal involvement in the problem, but it is questionable. Certainly, there always have been a number of killers who have wandered widely across state and jurisdictional boundaries. In a sixteen-month period in 1926–1927, Earle Nelson killed about twenty victims in at least eight states, before his final apprehension in Winnipeg, Canada, while the 1947 case of Jake Bird has already been mentioned (Jenkins 1989, 1992b). In the 1920s, Carl Panzram confessed to murders as far afield as Africa; and he may have served as one source for the fictional Jonathan Brewster (Gaddis and Long 1970). However, such offenders were and are a small minority, and the majority of killers tend to operate within one city or even one neighborhood, often preying on a particular victim population, much in the way that the original Jack the Ripper carried out his attacks in a small area of East London in the 1880s. In this matter, as in so much else, recent accounts of serial murder have tended to exaggerate the distinctiveness of contemporary American conditions.

A CONTEXT

Public fascination with serial murder seems difficult to justify solely in terms of the objective damage caused by the activity. It is often hard to estimate precisely the objective content of a social dysfunction that is constructed as a major problem, but the offense of homicide can be operationalized and measured with a fair degree of confidence. We have unusually reliable statistics, which demonstrate that in terms of the number of victims, homicides of all sorts represent a small proportion of all deaths in the United States; and mass and serial murders constitute a tiny element of this category (Daly and Wilson 1988; Block 1987; Riedel and Zahn 1985; Newman 1979).

In a typical year in the early 1990s, about 23,000 individuals became victims of homicide in the United States, representing a murder rate by far the highest in the industrialized world. However, these killings accounted for only about 1 percent of all U.S. deaths, and the numbers appear relatively small in comparison with deaths from smoking-related conditions (perhaps 350,000). Heart disease, cancer, and strokes together accounted for about two-thirds of all deaths. Murder figures were also smaller than the number of fatalities resulting from motor vehicle accidents (about 45,000) or suicide (about 31,000). Through the 1980s, the annual number of deaths resulting from accidents ran at an annual average of about 100,000.

Moreover, only a small proportion of murders result from mass and serial killings. Among perpetrators of homicide, almost 60 percent are relatively close to their victims in the sense of being spouses, family, or acquaintances. About 40 percent of homicides result from conflicts, such as lovers' triangle situations, brawls under the influence of alcohol, or quarrels over money. The typical American homicide occurs between intimates, acquaintances, or neighbors, and it has an understandable (if apparently trivial) cause, in stark contrast to the irrational lust-murders believed to typify serial killers. Indeed, mass, spree, and serial murders combined represent at most 2 percent of all American homicides.

Of course, simple death statistics cannot convey the full extent of the social harm inflicted by violent death, with all its complex effects on families, friends, and communities, but the figures do give a sense of proportion. In any given year, serial murder will account for perhaps one out of every ten thousand deaths that occur in the United States, a mere 0.01 percent—99.99 percent of Americans will die from causes other than irrational multiple homicide.

The question then arises why such a relatively minor issue attracts so much interest, so much fear, and is presented as such an over-whelmingly threatening social problem. To answer this, it is necessary to understand the wide range of symbolic meanings that have been attached to the phenomenon, and how these meanings have been manipulated for the purposes of a number of interest groups and bureaucratic structures. The ensuing process is a model of the developing construction of a social problem.

Chapter 3

The Role of the Justice Department

In the previous chapter, it was suggested that serial murder activity in the United States genuinely did increase from the mid-1960s onwards. This phenomenon offered the potential for the construction of a murder problem substantially different from earlier perceptions. Throughout American history, there have been notorious cases of serial murder that attracted widespread public attention, reflected in fictional portrayals, true-crime studies, and serious academic works. However, these individuals were never contextualized as part of a distinct murder problem, and were often instead seen as components of the larger issue of sex crimes or sex psychopaths (see Chapter 2; for the earlier "homicide problem," see Brearley 1932, Hoffman 1925). In contrast, from the late 1970s the image of a multiple-murder problem began to be discussed, with the suggestion that such behavior reflected a systematic crisis in American society. This chapter will describe how the proliferating number of multiple-murder cases came to be constructed as part of a broader phenomenon, and how the newly identified problem was constructed and typified.

From the mid-1980s, both the rate of growth and the actual scale of the multiple-murder problem became a hotly contested issue, and it was widely claimed that serial murders annually represented a fifth or a quarter of all homicides in the United States. Few would now support such an extravagant claim, but the origins of this statistic are of great interest for what they suggest about the legislative and bureaucratic politics of a social problem. The very high statistics for serial murder activity resulted from the competing claims of various bureaucratic agencies, together with the activism of pressure groups seeking to enforce and expand the rights of victims, especially children. Together, the two types of claims-maker succeeded in creating and promulgating a powerful picture of an enormous social threat, in which Americans were portrayed as being at the mercy of dozens or hundreds of monstrous

49

random killers, each of whom might be responsible for hundreds of deaths and kidnappings.

DISCOVERING SERIAL MURDER, 1973–1982

Serial murder cases proliferated from about 1966 onwards, and during the early 1970s, there were several cases of extreme serial murder, all of which attracted national and international attention. Between 1971 and 1974, there were notorious incidents involving the murders by Juan Corona, Herbert Mullin, and Edmund Kemper, all in California; and the ring associated with Dean Corll in Texas. The cases of Corona and Corll in particular drew attention because of the very high number of victims involved—about thirty in each instance—and both instances were claimed as marking a radical departure from earlier patterns of multiple homicide. From 1974 onwards, the genre of true-crime studies concerning such cases began to proliferate, reaching an unprecedented volume by 1980–1981 (Damio 1974; Gelb 1975; Gardener 1976; see table 3.1).

Media coverage intensified significantly from 1977 onwards, with the reporting of several cases that attracted intense public interest and that would shape perceptions of the emerging problem. Numerous instances of multiple homicide were reported in these years, but six in particular attracted the most attention. In three instances, the notoriety can be partially explained because they occurred in major metropolitan areas readily convenient for the media. Respectively, these were the Son of Sam killings in New York City, the John Wayne Gacy murders in Chicago, and the Hillside Stranglings in Los Angeles. There were also the Atlanta Child Murders, which became notorious because of the nature of the victims, the racial conflict implicit in the investigation, and the protracted inability of the police to solve the crimes; and there were the murders associated with Ted Bundy in several states. Meanwhile, the California Freeway Killings allegedly claimed the lives of over forty young men between 1976 and 1980, though subsequent prosecutions would show that the crimes were actually the work of at least two unrelated serial killers.

All these cases continued to be viewed as newsworthy over months or years, and all attracted attention years after the conclusion of the trials. There was thus a lengthy period when all these incidents more or less simultaneously enjoyed great prominence in the media, with the most intense coverage concentrated in 1980 and 1981 (see Table 3.2). In New York, the Son of Sam killings continued from July 1976 through August 1977, with the trial of David Berkowitz lasting several months after-

Table 3.1. True Crime Books Dealing with Serial Murder 1971–1981

Subject	Author	Title
Charles Manson	Sanders ([1971] 1972)	*The Family*
Albert Fish	Heimer (1971)	*The Cannibal*
Dean Corll	Olsen (1974)	*The Man with the Candy*
Dean Corll	Gurwell (1974)	*Mass Murder in Houston*
Charles Manson	Bugliosi and Gentry (1974)	*Helter Skelter*
Charlie Starkweather and Caril Fugate	Beaver, Ripley, and Trese (1974)	*Caril*
Juan Corona	Kidder (1974)	*The Road to Yuba City*
Herbert Mullin	West (1974)	*Sacrifice Unto Me*
George Putt	Meyer (1974)	*The Memphis Murders*
Ed Kemper	Cheney (1976)	*The Coed Killer*
Charles Starkweather	Allen (1976)	*Starkweather*
Kemper/Mullin	Lunde (1976)	*Murder and Madness*
John Norman Collins	Keyes ([1976] 1977)	*The Michigan Murders*
John Norman Collins	Wilcox (1977)	*The Mysterious Deaths at Ann Arbor*
(Several cases)	Godwin (1978)	*Murder USA*
Paul Knowles	Fawkes (1978)	*Killing Time*
Dean Corll	Linedecker (1980)	*The Man Who Killed Boys*
Herbert Mullin	Lunde and Morgan (1980)	*The Die Song*
Ted Bundy	Winn and Merrill (1980)	*Ted Bundy: The Killer Next Door*
Ted Bundy	Rule (1980)	*The Stranger Beside Me*
Ted Bundy	Larsen (1980)	*Bundy: Deliberate Stranger*
Zebra murders	Howard (1980)	*Zebra*
Ted Bundy	Kendall (1981)	*The Phantom Prince*
Antone Costa	Damore ([1981] 1990)	*In His Garden*
Ed Gein	Gollmar (1981)	*Edward Gein*
Kenneth Bianchi	Schwartz ([1981] 1982)	*The Hillside Strangler*
Peter Sutcliffe	Cross (1981)	*The Yorkshire Ripper*
David Berkowitz	Klausner (1981)	*Son of Sam*

[a]This list does not include books on the original Jack the Ripper case.

wards (Terry 1987; Abrahamsen 1983, 1985). The Hillside Strangler affair was at its height in the last months of 1977, but Kenneth Bianchi was not arrested for over a year afterwards; and the trial of his coconspirator Angelo Buono followed in mid-1981. The Atlanta Child Murders were first identified as a crime series in the summer of 1980, but Wayne Williams was not arrested in this case until May 1981, and not convicted until early 1982. The several arrests in the Freeway Killings began in

Table 3.2.   Major Serial Murder Stories, 1977–1981

Jan. 1976–Mar. 1977	Child murders case in Oakland County, MI
July 1976–Aug. 1977	Son of Sam killings in New York City
April–June 1977	Son of Sam letters published in New York media
June 1977	Ted Bundy's first prison escape
Aug. 1977	Arrest of David Berkowitz
Oct.–Dec.	Hillside Stranglings in Los Angeles
Dec. 1977	Ted Bundy's second escape from prison
Sep. 1977–April 1978	Stocking Strangler cases in Columbus, GA
Jan. 1978	Ted Bundy kills women in Florida sorority house; Richard Trenton Chase carries out "vampire" killings in Sacramento, CA
Feb. 1978	Ted Bundy arrested after final killing in Florida
Oct.–Nov. 1978	Ten killed in Los Angeles Skid Row Stabbings, later attributed to Bobby Joe Maxwell
Dec. 1978	Discovery of many bodies in John Wayne Gacy's house
Jan. 1979	Arrest of Bobby Joe Maxwell
June 1979	Kenneth Bianchi indicted in Washington State
June–Nov. 1979	Southern California murder series by Lawrence Bittaker and Roy Norris
July	Ted Bundy convicted in Florida
October	Angelo Buono arrested
May 1979–June 1980	Twenty one victims recorded in Californian Freeway Killings
Dec. 1979–Jan. 1980	Murder spree in Pennsylvania by Michael Travaglia and John Lesko
Dec. 1979–May 1980	Prostitute Murders by Richard Cottingham in and around New York City
Jan.–Feb. 1980	New York police investigate confessions to over twenty murders by Joseph Fischer (claims remain questionable)
Jan.–Dec. 1980	Eighteen women killed in apparent murder series in Detroit
Feb.–March 1980	Trial of John Wayne Gacy
April 1980	Arrest of Gerald Stano in Florida leads to his confessions in over forty murders
April–Nov. 1980	Sunday Morning Slashings in Ann Arbor, MI, later attributed to Coral E. Watts
June 1980	William Bonin arrested in Freeway Killings
June–Aug. 1980	Sunset Strip Murders in Los Angeles, later attributed to Douglas Clark
July–Aug. 1980	Other arrests in Freeway Killings case
Nov. 1980	Arrest of Gerald Gallego in murder series in California and Nevada
March 1980–May 1981	Missing and Murdered Children case in Atlanta
January 1981	Suicide of Freeway Killings suspect Vernon Butts; Arrest of Peter Sutcliffe in English Yorkshire Ripper case

(*continued*)

Table 3.2.   (Continued)

March 1981	Execution in Indiana of serial killer Steven Judy; End of preliminary hearings in Buono prosecution; Arrest of I-5 Killer Randall Woodfield
May	Questioning of Wayne Williams in Atlanta case; Arrest of David Carpenter resolves Trailside Slayings in northern California
June	Conviction of Randall Woodfield; Arrest of Wayne Williams
Nov. 1981–Jan. 1982	Trial of William Bonin
Nov. 1981–Nov. 1983	Trial of Angelo Buono
Dec. 1981–Feb. 1982	Trial of Wayne Williams

mid-1980, but the final convictions did not occur until the end of the decade. The Gacy murders were discovered at the end of 1978, with his trial attracting the vigorous interest of the media into early 1980. The number of Gacy's known victims (thirty-three) represented a new record in American history, exceeding the previous figure associated with Dean Corll in 1973.

In each case, discussion and comment was kept alive for several years afterwards by true-crime books and television documentaries [On the Hillside case, see for example Schwartz and Boyd (1981), Schwartz ([1981] 1982), O'Brien (1987); see also PBS's 1984 "Frontline" programs on "The Mind of a Murderer." On Gacy, see Cahill (1986) and Sullivan and Maiken (1983)]. There were also television movies such as *The Atlanta Child Murders* (1985) and *The Case of the Hillside Stranglers* (1989). The Son of Sam case was even commemorated in rock music, and may have provided the basis for the 1977 Talking Heads song, "Psycho Killer." It also earned the distinction of being parodied in the syndicated comic strip "Doonesbury" during 1977, when it was used to attack the sensational tone of New York tabloid journalism (the would-be killer adopts "Son of Arnold and Mary Lieberman" as his "nom de tabloid").

Ted Bundy

The best known incident was that of Ted Bundy, who was the most notorious serial killer since Albert Fish, if not since Jack the Ripper. This is a good illustration of how a criminal comes to be perceived as newsworthy, and retains this degree of public interest long after his detection and apprehension. The affair first came to light in 1974 with a series of unsolved murders in Washington State and Utah. These crimes were widely reported, and were discussed in sensationalistic papers as far afield as Great Britain. Further murders in Utah and Colorado followed over the next two years, and Bundy was arrested in January 1977. Regional news media focused attention on this as a major crime series, and there were television interviews that were frequently repeated over the next decade.

The affair reached national notoriety with Bundy's 1977 escape from custody in Colorado, at which point the killer joined the FBI's "ten most wanted" list. There is also some evidence that he achieved the status of a folk-antihero, and became the subject of jokes and popular legends. Following his escape, restaurants were reported as selling "Bundy-burgers," which were found on examination to contain no meat (for the emerging folklore of Ted Bundy, see Caputi 1987:5). Bundy was already a figure of national notoriety when he carried out his final series of murders in Florida in early 1978, and this status was consolidated by the widespread televising of his trial in that state, culminating in his conviction and sentencing in July 1979.

The trial, together with the 1977 prison interviews, left an impression of a handsome and articulate individual with a lively sense of humor, a figure who many observers found striking and even likable. The judge at the Florida trial congratulated Bundy on his legal acumen, and remarked that he felt "no animosity" toward the offender. At the same time, the number of murders with which Bundy was linked was believed to have few parallels in American history, and all of the victims were female, including the child of twelve killed in his last known attack. These aspects contributed to making Bundy a highly effective popular villain, who could epitomize evil without being a simple mindless brute. He was rather a complex individual who could provide the basis for elaborate speculation on the nature of evil and mental illness, and his articulate and apparently intelligent conversations were widely viewed. In 1983, a further series of interviews offered what appeared to be a lengthy autobiographical statement of a career of serial murder, albeit told in the third person (Michaud and Aynesworth 1983, 1989).

The Bundy case was the subject of several book-length true-crime treatments, which suggests that publishers were responding to considerable public interest. Four such studies appeared between 1980 and 1983, and one became the subject of a network television movie, *The Deliberate Stranger* (1986). In addition, one of Bundy's biographers was Ann Rule, who had known him personally in Washington state, and who became one of the most widely quoted authorities on serial murder (Rule 1983a, 1983b, 1984, 1993).

The case also had a lengthy "afterlife," ensuring that the images and issues associated with Bundy continued to influence thinking long after his sentencing to the electric chair in 1979. He was not ultimately executed until 1989, and in the interim there were several occasions when execution appeared imminent. Each incident gave the news media an opportunity to revisit the case and to recapitulate the gruesome circumstances. One abortive execution date encouraged the NBC news show "1986" to air a segment consisting largely of the earlier interviews. The tapes also appeared on several general documentaries on the topic of serial murder, including the 1984 HBO program "Murder: No Apparent Motive." Bundy's actual execution was the occasion of intense news coverage and the appearance of yet another book on the case.

Even death could not prevent Bundy from achieving a high degree of postmortem celebrity. Religious groups did much to perpetuate his memory, in consequence of his final interviews with James Dobson, in which he blamed his wrongdoing on the malign influence of pornography. The affair was thus cited as conclusive evidence of the nefarious influence of obscene literature, and one survivor of a Bundy attack traveled widely to lecture on the evils of pornography. Continued fascination with the figure of Bundy is also suggested by Michael Perry's fictional crime thriller *The Stranger Returns* (1992), which imagines that Bundy survived his execution, and was continuing his career of violence. Through such means, Ted Bundy has lived on as a figure in popular culture for almost two decades.

Defining the Serial Murder Problem

Between 1977 and 1982, multiple homicide had come to be a well-known phenomenon in the mass media, and public interest was reflected in the popularity of books and especially films dealing with the topic (see Chapter 4). Multiple murder was the theme of more American films in 1980 and 1981 than in the previous two decades combined. However, there were as yet no systematic attempts to discuss the scale of the phenomenon or to offer general explanations. Interpretations of the new problem soon emerged, largely defined by the interests and preoccupations of federal law enforcement agencies.

New views of serial murder derived chiefly from the Behavioral Sciences Unit (BSU) of the Justice Department, with its headquarters at Quantico, Virginia, within the FBI National Academy. This unit had been established in the early 1970s, and rapidly developed an interest in "profiling" violent offenders (Ault and Reese 1980; Hazelwood and Douglas 1980; Hazelwood and Burgess 1987; Hazelwood and Warren 1989). It was this group that popularized the terms *serial crimes* and *serial murder*, though there is some question about the actual origin of the phrases. Robert Ressler (Ressler and Schachtman 1992:29) asserts he coined the phrase to describe the activities of offenders such as Son of Sam about 1976–1977, while it only gained popularity following the discovery of the Gacy murders; but there are earlier occurrences (see, for example, Lunde 1976).

From 1978, the group pioneered the use of lengthy interviews with incarcerated felons, including mass and serial killers, in order to assist the process of profiling criminals still at large (Ressler and Schachtman 1992:36). This operation was formalized as a Criminal Personality Research Project. In 1982 and 1983, Ressler and John Douglas coordinated an investigation funded by the National Institute of Justice to undertake detailed interviews with thirty-six incarcerated multiple killers, the results of which provided the basis for wide-ranging taxonomies of serial offenders (Ressler, Burgess, and Douglas 1988). The group hoped that such schemes would be of great value to investigators in using the analysis of crime scenes to reconstruct the likely characteristics of the offender concerned (National Center for the Analysis of Violent Crime, NCAVC 1986). In 1981–1982, the BSU achieved its most visible public success to date when it assisted in both the arrest and prosecution of Wayne Williams.

From about 1980, the BSU experts were increasingly concerned about "linkage blindness," the failure to note connections between serial crimes committed in various jurisdictions, and the observed tendency of killers like Ted Bundy to operate in several states or jurisdictions over a short period of time (Egger 1984, 1985; Brooks, Devine, Green, Hart, and Moore 1987). In 1981, the new attorney general William French Smith sponsored a Task Force on Violent Crime to explore means of improving interagency cooperation. The following year, there was a formal proposal to create a National Center for the Analysis of Violent Crime (NCAVC), under the auspices of the BSU (Jeffers 1992; Ressler et al. 1988:99–120, 196–204). In the Summer of 1983, this scheme was developed by a conference held at Sam Houston State University in Texas.

The creation of a new databank called the Violent Criminal Apprehension Program (VICAP) was also proposed to collate information about unsolved crimes from different jurisdictions (Brooks et al. 1987). For example, we might imagine that six murders had been committed in different states, each involving similar victim characteristics or crime scene patterns, for example, that each victim was a red-haired woman whose body had been discovered near an interstate exit. There was at that time no official mechanism to share such information, so that each team of investigators operated in ignorance of what its counterparts might discover, and no agency suspected that it might be dealing with a crime series. The VICAP scheme would ask or require local police departments to submit information on unsolved crimes, responding to quite detailed questions about every aspect of the offense: The form eventually developed had 189 separate questions spread over 15 pages (Osterburg and Ward 1992:803–20). Data would be collected and analyzed at the NCAVC, which would provide leads to local investigators and lay the foundation for information-sharing that would lead to the arrest of roaming violent offenders.

The proposals for both VICAP and the NCAVC might have proved difficult, since they required the infusion of significant resources, while the immediate political context deserves notice. It has already been noted that the incoming Reagan administration had to battle against a heritage of grave suspicion that the FBI would abuse its powers as it had during the Hoover years, and there were acrimonious debates in Congress. In 1982 and 1983, controversy resulted in the failure of a proposal to expand FBI databanks to include records of individuals suspected of serious criminal activity. The inclusion of the names of "people not wanted for a specific crime but who were suspected of being drug traffickers, terrorists and associates of wanted persons" was proposed (Burnham 1984).

Opposition could also be expected from state and local law enforcement agencies, which often resented federal intrusions into their jurisdictions. Contrary to widespread public impressions, the FBI has no jurisdiction in serial murder cases as such, and can only act if an offender crosses a state line or commits a related felony such as kidnapping. Expanding the federal role in homicide investigation was thus a major innovation, and was likely to be contentious. However, the portrayal of the serial murder threat in the 1980s was sufficiently plausible to win broad support both for the new NCAVC, and the expanded computer facilities required for VICAP.

The Threat to Children

The serial murder threat was particularly convincing because it seemed to be especially directed against children, an association formulated in the years between 1980 and 1983. The late 1970s and early 1980s witnessed dramatically intensified concern about dangers to children in the United States, with powerful claims about the supposed extent of dangers like child pornography, sexual abuse, and kidnapping (Best 1990). Controversial claims about missing children placed the numbers at tens of thousands annually, with the suggestion that most were sexually abused and many murdered. Claims about threatened children were widely reported in the media, and they formed part of numerous congressional investigations. While the genuine concern of the political activists should not be underestimated, it is also true that expressing concern for protecting children is usually a sure and risk-free way of garnering public support.

The suggestion that serial murder formed part of the domain of the larger problem of threats to children was encouraged by a number of incidents involving the victimization of children or teenagers, including the cases of John Wayne Gacy and Dean Corll. Also crucial were the Atlanta Child Murders, and the Reagan Justice Department created an unprecedented federal task force to investigate these crimes (see Chapter 8). Shortly after an arrest was made in the Atlanta case, the kidnapping and murder of a child named Adam Walsh occurred, an incident that earned national notoriety following a TV movie in the fall of 1983. Adam's father John Walsh became a national spokesman for both victims' and children's causes. The Walsh case attracted the attention of Senator Paula Hawkins of Florida, who cited the affair in her ongoing campaign against child abuse and molestation. Together, the Gacy, Atlanta Child Murders, and Walsh cases served to contextualize serial murder as part of the perceived problem of child disappearances and abductions. (It will also be suggested in Chapter 9 that the specific focus on young *male* victims may have reflected an antihomosexual agenda.)

Concern about missing and abused children led to federal action (see Appendix to this chapter). In late 1981, the House Committee on Civil and Constitutional Rights held hearings on a proposed Missing Children's Act, which provided the opportunity for interest groups to present a picture of a vast social menace. (There is an extensive discussion of the hearings and investigations of the early 1980s in Best 1990:27–40.) However, the most active committee on this area was the Juvenile Justice Subcommittee (chaired by Arlen Specter) of the Judiciary Committee of the U.S. Senate, which between 1982 and 1984 held hearings on a string of related menaces: child pornography, child molestation, and the effects of pornography upon both women and children (U.S. Senate 1982, 1983, 1984, 1985). In April 1982, the committee held the first in a series of hearings on "missing and exploited children," which gave the opportunity for the systematic presentation of a serial murder problem.

At the 1982 hearings, witnesses included Paula Hawkins and John Walsh (U.S. Senate 1982). It was Walsh in particular who stated the issue of missing children as in large measure a problem of repeat killers. He described several serial murder cases, including the Atlanta killings, but also the cases of Bundy, Gacy, Corll, and the California Freeway Killer. Walsh emphasized that such activity was widespread, and that much of the harm resulted from linkage blindness, the failure of justice agencies to coordinate information and intelligence. This made it possible for children and young people to disappear without a trace, until finally they might be located in a mass grave.

Concern about missing children soon found legislative expression. In 1982, the federal Missing Children's Act gave the role of information clearing-house to the FBI's National Crime Information Center; and a National Center for Missing and Exploited Children was operational by 1984. The linkage with the serial murder issue was made explicit by a Justice Department spokesman who stated, "They're coming at two different ends of a problem. While VICAP is aimed at tracking down the offender, this [National Center] will help parents and law enforcement get children back" (Lindsey 1984b).

However, the Specter committee had by no means exhausted its agenda. In February 1983, the committee held hearings on child kidnappings, and over the following months attention turned to the issue of serial homicide. In April, there was correspondence on the matter between Specter and FBI director William Webster, in which the director presented extremely high statistics for the estimated scale of serial murder activity. This new interest was reflected in committee hearings that July "on patterns of murders committed by one person in large numbers with no apparent rhyme, reason or motivation": a term that in effect became a synonym for serial murder (U.S. Senate 1984).

Among the witnesses were familiar faces such as John Walsh and Paula Hawkins, but two new individuals were also influential. These were Roger Depue, of the BSU, an expert on serial crimes and multiple homicide, and Ann Rule, the true-crime author who had written best-selling studies of serial murderers Ted Bundy, Jerry Brudos, and others. Depue, Rule, and Hawkins presented a frightening picture of the nature and scale of serial homicide, recounting numerous cases including the familiar images of Bundy, Stano, Speck, Bianchi, Carlton Gary, and others.

In keeping with the juvenile theme of the Specter committee, witnesses tended to emphasize cases in which children had been targeted, such as the unsolved Michigan child murders of the 1970s; and they also focused on the theme of murderers escaping capture or detection for their crimes. It was repeatedly suggested that killers were very likely to get away with it, and that offenders might commit numerous crimes before arrest. Ann Rule was the main exponent of the view that killers were likely to roam far afield, killing in several states, which naturally reinforced the need for some federal or interjurisdictional information network, such as the proposed NCAVC and VICAP (U.S. Senate 1984).

The Statistics of Serial Murder

The various witnesses agreed about the severity of the serial murder problem, and the inadequacy of existing resources to cope with it. They were also in broad agreement that the menace could be quantified, and they made much use of statistics throughout the hearings. These met little challenge at the time, but in retrospect they seem remarkably high. For example, the number of victims linked to Ted Bundy was placed at anywhere between 24 and 300, while Ann Rule suggested that Harvey Carignan might have been involved in as many as 180 attacks (compare Rule 1983b).

These specific allegations seem modest compared with the statistical claim that emerged and that was one of the most powerful elements in the construction of the new problem: that serial murders represented about a fifth of all American homicides. It was estimated that there had been some 3,600 "random and senseless murders" in 1981. Over the following months, the committee's figures were widely reported and somewhat exaggerated, and this was the origin of the suggestion that serial killers claimed some four to five thousand victims each year.

This figure seems counterintuitive, to say the least; current FBI estimates of the problem suggest that the annual number of victims is closer to two hundred than four thousand. The 1983 figures were certainly not produced at random, and they initially appeared to have some statistical authority, but a closer consideration of the evidence suggests grave problems of interpretation. The creation of the murder estimates is a striking illustration of the way in which statistics are generated and largely accepted, although they might be wildly misleading.

Briefly, the problem lies in the definition of serial murder, and its relationship to the phenomenon described in 1983 as random and senseless murder. In order to understand this, it is necessary to describe the whole process by which felonies are recorded and quantified. When a serious crime is committed, a police agency files a Uniform Crime Report (UCR) with the Justice Department, and in the case of murder, a Supplementary Homicide Report (SHR) is also submitted. Both UCR and SHR data are extensively used by criminologists as an invaluable means of seeking information on patterns of violent crime. The SHR is a rich source, providing information on the identity of both offender and victim together with data on factors such as the age, sex, and race of both parties. It also notes the circumstances of the crime, listed under headings such as Lovers' Triangle, Brawl under the Influence of Alcohol, Gangland Killing, Argument over Money, and so on.

For the purposes of the 1983 hearings, the critical part of the data was found in the SHRs, in the number of homicides that could not be classified under one of the supplied headings. Between 1976 and 1985, for example, about 17 percent of all homicide circumstances are listed as *unknown*. In the same period, 29 percent of murders indicate an unknown relationship between offender and victim; and an additional 16 percent suggest that the offender was a stranger to the victim. During 1983, the law enforcement experts studying serial murder presumed that most of these *unknown* and even *stranger* categories were the work of serial killers like Bundy or Gacy; and this was the source of the four or five thousand victims idea.

If this was correct, it permitted an estimate of the changing frequency of serial murder over time. In 1966, for example, only 6 percent of American murders involved unknown circumstances or motive; by 1982, the figure was 18 percent, and the proportion steadily grew during the decade. This appeared to substantiate claims about an explosion of multiple homicide:

> In an increasingly large number of stranger homicides, the killer seems driven to murder not by some "rational" reason but by a serious psychological disorder. The FBI estimates that as many as 25 percent of killings may now fall into this category. . . . [O]verwhelmingly, the victims of bizarre murder are women and children; the killers are almost invariably men. (Porter 1983:2)

However, this interpretation of the data is quite unwarranted. In effect, it suggests that an *unknown* homicide circumstance equates to *no apparent motive*, which in turn means that the murder is *motiveless*, or "with no apparent rhyme, reason or motivation." This is unpardonable. All that can be legitimately understood from the fact of an *unknown* circumstance is that, at the time of completing the form, the police agency in question either did not know the exact context of the crime, or did not trouble to fill in the forms correctly.

When a murder is detected, the police file the requisite paperwork, with the deadline being within five days of the end of the month in which the incident occurred. At this early stage, the police might well know neither the offender nor the circumstances, and thus enter an *unknown* response in the appropriate categories. Weeks or months later, the situation might well change, and the correct procedure would be for the police department to submit a new report to amend the first. Here, though, there is enormous room for cutting corners. The Justice Department has already been notified of the death, and whether a further form is submitted will depend on many factors. A conscientious officer in a professionally oriented department with an efficient recording system probably would notify the reporting center that the murder was no longer unsolved or lacking known circumstance, especially in an area where murder was a rare crime. Other officers in other departments might well feel that they have more important things to do than to submit a revised version of a form they have already completed, which would in fact represent a third recension on a single case.

The chance of follow-up information being supplied will therefore depend on a number of factors: the frequency of murder in the community; the importance accorded to record-keeping by a particular chief or supervisor; the organizational structure of the department; and the over-all professional standards of the unit. The vast majority of departments are likely to record the fact of a murder being committed, but only some will provide the result of any subsequent investigation. Since the UCRs were instituted in 1930, repeated audits and investigations have suggested the extremely low priority that police agencies attach to accurate reporting, and the chances of error grow significantly with the quite elaborate SHRs. (For the UCR, see, for example, Mackenzie, Baunach, and Roberg 1990; Gove, Hughes, and Geerken 1985; Skogan 1975.) This pattern may bode ill for the chance of agencies complying effectively with the still more complex VICAP forms.

Murders depicted in the SHR as having a known suspect and motive are likely to be those where there is a very clear-cut situation, with the offender immediately identified and probably apprehended at the scene. If there is any delay or confusion, for whatever reason, the case is likely to fall into the statistical limbo of motiveless crimes. If a suspect is not found within the same month that the actual killing is discovered, then the case is likely to be entered as *no suspect*, and to remain so despite later events. It is even probable that the later in the month the crime occurs, the more likely it is to be described as lacking known motivation or offender. Put another way, the remarkable fact about the SHR data is that so many murders *do* produce immediately known motive and suspects. Even when no suspect is ever found, it does not necessarily mean that a serial killer is to blame. Both Chicago and Miami have long records of organized crime–related killings, which often remain unsolved in the sense of lacking known offenders.

Confirmation that the SHR's *unknown* categories do not correspond to serial murders is provided by the regional variations in reporting. Every study of regional differences in serial murder suggests that the rate of activity is relatively low in northeastern cities such as New York and Washington, D.C., but particularly high in California cities such as Los Angeles, where in the 1980s the police felt the need to create a specialized serial murder investigations unit. However, the SHR data would appear to imply an exactly contrary result. Between 1976 and 1985, the proportion of murders described as *unknown offender* stood at 17 percent nationwide, but local figures ranged from zero percent in Los Angeles to 4 percent in Chicago, 32 percent in Washington, D.C., and 50 percent in New York City. It would be ludicrous to suggest that murders "without rhyme or reason" accounted for half of all homicides in New York City, while such crimes were entirely absent from Los Angeles. The conclusion must be that the vast contrast between the Los Angeles and New York figures reflects local police reporting practices.

Furthermore, the emphasis on murders with *no known motive* probably conceals the fact that many serial killings are in fact listed in the SHR reports, but under another category. When a body is found with evidence of sexual assault, the crime is usually categorized as the result of *instrumental felony—rape*, and this would account for many cases where the unidentified victims of serial killers are discovered. Presumably, this is how the Los Angeles police categorized the crimes of the Hillside Strangler, the Night Stalker, the Sunset Slayer, the Southside Slayer, and the other notorious murderers of these years.

The use of the SHR's *unknown* categories was statistically impermissible; but the resulting figures were virtually unchallenged at the time, and profoundly influenced public perceptions. They were especially attractive because they were so memorable and convenient, and the figure of four thousand victims entered the media in much the same way as fifty thousand missing children, or the same number of human sacrifice victims alleged later in the decade. Also critical was the thorough confusion of the different categories of murder, and the identification of *stranger* and *motiveless* murders as serial homicides. This is well illustrated by the fictional treatment in Derek Van Arman's bestselling *Just Killing Time*, where he states, "In order for a homicide to become a VICAT [*sic*] investigation, the crime either had to classify as serial or be an atrocity committed by a total stranger, what was referred to as motiveless homicide" ([1992] 1993:33).

THE PANIC, 1983–1985

The Specter committee set the tone for reporting on serial murder issues over the following months, and prepared the media for the dramatic upsurge of concern that occurred in the fall of that year. In October 1983, the Justice Department held a news conference on the danger of the growing danger of serial murder. Justice Department experts Roger Depue and Robert Heck confirmed once more that the number of victims annually might reach several thousand, but they also enunciated another statistic that would enjoy wide notoriety when they stated that there might be thirty-five such killers active in the United States at any given time ("Thirty-Five Murderers" 1983). VICAP provided the only effective response to such an appalling menace. (Heck incidentally was research project director for the Office of Juvenile Justice and Delinquency Prevention, indicating once more the link between the serial murder issue and the broader theme of threats against children.)

Thirty-five killers, four thousand victims: Both figures were freely quoted and generally accepted, although the juxtaposition of the two presented definite problems. In order to produce four thousand victims, each of the putative killers would have to kill at least a hundred people annually, and there was no case on record where an offender was known to have killed at anything like so high a rate. The only parallels to such activity were to be found in some of the largely speculative figures cited in the Specter committee for individuals like Ted Bundy, but these assumed that each killer claimed a huge "dark figure" of victims. In reality, very few recorded killers have ever claimed more than ten or so victims in a given year, and most were associated with far fewer deaths (see Chapter 2). It was therefore likely that one of the popular figures was wrong: Either there were more than thirty-five killers at any one time, or there were far fewer than four thousand victims.

Ironically, we know in retrospect from their own figures that the Justice Department officials were actually underestimating the number of killers active at any given time. In any given year in the early 1980s, there were at least fifty individuals who had already killed multiply, and who would kill again. For 1981, we can now trace fifty-eight such cases then active, and there were at least fifty-six in 1982. However, it was years before such information became available. In the short term, the claims-makers faced an apparent contradiction.

The Lucas Case

Fortuitously for the incipient panic, reporting of the Justice Department news conference coincided almost exactly with the national attention paid to a news story from Texas, where convicted killer Henry Lee Lucas was claiming that he had been responsible for several hundred killings in the previous five years (Cox 1991; Norris 1991). According to his original story, Lucas had traveled the country with a number of friends, including murderer Ottis Toole, and had killed perhaps 360 people in over twenty states. This case seemed to reinforce the images presented in the Specter committee hearings, both of vast numbers of victims and of the roaming killer who wandered freely between jurisdictions. If there were thirty-five such individuals active at one time, then the serial murder problem represented an appalling social crisis, and there really might be four or five thousand victims. Toole also reaffirmed the linkage between serial murder and child victimization, by claiming to have been the killer of Adam Walsh, though his confession soon proved to be false (Joyce 1983).

Much remains controversial about the Lucas confessions, and it rapidly became apparent that many of his claims could not be substantiated. By 1985, it was suggested that his confessions were almost entirely spurious, and that his number of victims was in reality closer to the thirteen or so for which he was actually convicted than to 360 (though some credible authorities accept figures far larger than 13 (Cox 1991). It appeared that law enforcement agencies had been much too quick to accept his confessions, and that some had been anxious to clear unsolved killings in their jurisdictions without due investigation. However, at the time, Lucas seemed to epitomize the worst fears of the serial killer as an itinerant monster from whom no one was safe.

The impact of the story was all the greater because of what appeared to be the killer's lucid and extremely frank discussions of the most grisly crimes, which he recounted in interviews with police and press. During 1984 and 1985, interviews were shown on ABC's "20/20" and "Good Morning America," on CBS' "Nightwatch," and they also aired in the 1985 television documentary *Acts of Violence*. The reports inspired two feature films, *Confessions of a Serial Killer* (1987) and *Henry: Portrait of a Serial Killer* (1986, released in 1990), while there were also a number of true-crime books and detective magazine accounts (Norris 1992a; Cox 1991). In February 1985, a major interview with Lucas appeared in the pages of *Penthouse*.

In 1984 and 1985, concern about serial murder became intense, and the problem was clearly defined according to the model proposed by the BSU authorities (U.S. Congress 1986). Such images were enhanced by other events in 1984, especially the manhunt for a killer named Christopher Wilder. Wilder began his violent career in Florida, but in April he began a nationwide rampage in which he killed at least nine women in eight states in the West and Midwest. Wilder spent months on the FBI's ten most wanted list, prior to committing suicide in New Hampshire. This case regularly made headline news on the television networks, and ABC's "Nightline" used it as a vehicle for a program on the serial murder phenomenon. The story confirmed the Lucas image of the killer as a sexual predator roaming from state to state in pursuit of victims, who snatched innocent prey almost at random; and the *New York Times* reported current efforts at "Stopping Them Before They Kill Again and Again and Again" (Lindsey 1984b).

At exactly the time of the Wilder case, the Congress once more pro-

vided a platform for those warning of a national serial murder menace
(U.S. Congress 1984). In February and March of 1984, the Specter committee held hearings on the Missing Children's Assistance Act, a measure that was to be discussed further that April by the House committee
on Human Resources. Major witnesses included John Walsh, who was
introduced in reverential tones by the powerful Democrat Senator Paul
Simon of Illinois. Walsh claimed, "We found that the number of random
unsolved murders of women and children in this country rose from 600
in 1966 to 4,500 in 1981." At this point, he was apparently inflating the
July 1983 estimate of 3,600 victims, and further claimed that this corresponded only to the number of women and children victimized, a statement whose warrant is unclear. However, this was consistent with his
belief in the high rate of child victimization. Every hour, he stated, 205
children were reported missing in this country, a figure corresponding
to 1.8 million cases per annum, and many of these would be found
murdered.

The Media Response

Once these ideas were established, they were rapidly disseminated by
the media, who virtually never questioned the evidential bases for the
assertions. The new problem was presented on the network television
news programs, in journals as various as *Time* and *Newsweek*, *Life* and
OMNI, *Psychology Today*, and men's magazines like *Hustler*, *Penthouse*,
and *Playboy* (Darrach and Norris 1984; Kagan 1984; Porter 1983;
Abrahamsen 1983).

A characteristic statement of the problem was presented in a major
front-page story published in the *New York Times* in January 1984, on the
"rise in killers who roam U.S. for victims" (Lindsey 1984a). This emphasized that serial murder in contemporary America was a new phenomenon that had exploded since the late 1960s and that was distinctively
American in nature. The American murder wave was both qualitatively
and quantitatively different from anything recorded in previous history,
with vastly more victims, and much greater occurrence of savage torture
and mutilation. In short, serial murder had become an *epidemic*, a word
attributed to the Justice Department's Robert O. Heck. The term implied
widespread social pathology, rapid and uncontrollable growth, and
ubiquitous threat, as well as the need for urgent countermeasures.

According to the article, Justice Department officials "assert that history offers nothing to compare with the spate of such murders that has
occurred in the United States since the beginning of the 1970s." Heck
was quoted for the view "that as many as four thousand Americans a

year, at least half of them under the age of eighteen, are murdered in this way. He said he believes that at least 35 such killers are now roaming the country." Many of their victims were to be found among the thousands of bodies that turned up each year unidentified and unexplained. In August, the *Times* followed this with another lengthy story about the psychology of "mass killers," which quoted experts who believed that the serial killer represented an altogether "new personality type." This again confirmed that the scale of serial activity was quite unparalleled in American history, while claiming that of Lucas's 360 claimed victims, "more than 142 have reportedly been verified by police" (Berger 1984).

Newsweek presented a similar account in "The Random Killers" (Starr et al. 1984), a story that occupied four full pages and that employed the term *epidemic* in its subtitle. It similarly argued, "Law enforcement experts say as many as two-thirds of the estimated 5000 unsolved homicides in the nation each year may be committed by serial murderers." *Life* suggested that "hundreds" of serial killers might be at large (Darrach and Norris 1984; compare Holmes and DeBurger 1985).

Characteristic of the coverage at this time was the television documentary *Murder: No Apparent Motive*, made in 1984 for the HBO series "America Under Cover," though it was often repeated over the next decade on other cable channels. This begins with a photograph of one of Bundy's victims from the Florida sorority house, with the narrator stating, "Four thousand a year—dead. Killed by total strangers. It's an epidemic of murder in America—murder with no motive." The program then turns to a California police officer who remarks, "We have people that commit murders like you might go out and mow the lawn. That's about as much thought as they give. A term that's been used is *recreational murder*. Nothing else to do—they go out and kill." At that point, the screen fades to red.

Neither *stranger* homicide nor *recreational* murder is necessarily synonymous with serial murder, though all these terms are here presented as essentially identical, and the program that followed was based on reconstructions of celebrated serial cases Edmund Kemper, Ted Bundy, and Henry Lee Lucas, all of whom were interviewed. It was further suggested that these individuals were representative of a large social threat, defined in the now familiar terms of the Justice Department's experts. One of the authorities most frequently consulted was Robert Ressler, who remarks, "Serial killing—I think it's at epidemic proportions. The type of crime we're seeing today did not really occur with any known frequency prior to the fifties. An individual taking ten, twelve, fifteen, twenty-five, thirty-five lives is a relatively new phenomenon in the crime picture of the U.S."

In fact, the only time in which one of the BSU group was criticized involved their allegedly excessive *caution* in the face of the "epidemic." After Robert Heck is quoted as suggesting that "thirty-five is a minimum figure" for the number of serial killers currently at large, the narrator suggested "That's the official estimate from the Justice Department. But we've talked to the top crime investigators, and most thought that that estimate was way too low." The figure of thirty-five killers was "the tip of the iceberg," and the real number might be "dozens upon dozens upon dozens," "far more than thirty-five." *Newsweek* also argued that the FBI figure was conservative, in the view of local police agencies. Against this menace, both *Newsweek* and the television documentary presented the work of the BSU and VICAP as the most hopeful tool, the only way to prevent lengthy crime careers like those of Bundy and Lucas.

By the end of 1984, the serial murder problem had been formulated and projected with enormous vigor and success, and the claims-makers succeeded in achieving many of their policy goals. A number of federal agencies were indeed created to provide the investigative assistance and intelligence collation sought by the claims-makers. The formation of the NCAVC was regarded as sufficiently important to be announced by President Reagan personally, in a June, 1984 address to the National Sheriffs Association meeting in Hartford, Connecticut. Over the next year, the new unit was divided into a research operation, the Behavioral Sciences Services Unit, and an Investigative Support Unit, which housed VICAP (U.S. Congress 1986).

VICAP became operational in 1985, and began collecting information about "homicides or attempts . . . [that are] apparently random, motive- less or sexually oriented, or are known or suspected to be part of a series." The effects of the scheme are still difficult to judge, as agency compliance remains voluntary, and barely a fifth of all unsolved cases were being reported to the system by the early 1990s. In 1993, Washing- ton State investigator Robert Keppel suggested that VICAP had yet to establish a connection in *any* murder series, while Ann Rule pronounced herself "disappointed" (in CNN documentary, *Murder by Number*, 1993) However, several states established similar schemes tied in to VICAP, such as New York's HALT or Washington's HITS program, and these did require the participation of all relevant agencies (Keppel and Weis 1993). It was hoped that a more comprehensive national approach would be possible from about 1995.

THE HISTORY OF A NUMBER, 1985–1990

After 1985, the flood of serial murder stories abated somewhat, and over the following years, the very high claims about the numbers of offenders and victims were increasingly challenged. Interestingly, it was the FBI itself that first broke ranks, and at the 1984 press conference announcing the creation of the NCAVC, Roger Depue stated that "at least 10 percent of the 5,400 unsolved murders in the United States each year are the work of systematic, intelligent, transient killers" ("FBI Launches Frontal Attack" 1984). This did not of itself mean that these were the only crimes involving serial murder, but the number of victims implied was closer to 540 rather than to 4,000.

Later works scaled down claims far below the four thousand level, and in 1988, the *Criminal Justice Research Bulletin* published an article (Jenkins 1988a) suggesting that the actual scale of the problem had been greatly exaggerated, and that the annual number of victims might be closer to four or five hundred. Ironically, this article was controversial at the time for its revisionist views, though in retrospect even these figures appear excessive. In May 1989, CBS's news program "West 57th" introduced a story about the New Bedford serial murders with the words, "The FBI estimates that last year alone, 31 serial killers committed 313 serial murders." The estimated number of killers has remained roughly constant from the 1983 estimate, but the victim total has plummeted.

The most sweeping challenge to the earlier figures was presented in the 1993 CNN documentary *Murder by Number* (see Chapter 2), which radically reduced the estimated scale of multiple-homicide activity. Its figures (closer to one hundred victims annually) were praised by several academic and law enforcement experts, but Ann Rule made no apology for her earlier statements: "There's always been the choice for me, do you frighten people and maybe save their lives, or do you cover it over and we all put our heads in the sand; then the moment comes when you need to be prepared and you aren't. I have always chosen to err on the side that may save lives." While far from a retraction of her earlier statements, this does imply that she acknowledged an element of error or exaggeration, albeit with the best of motives.

However, the "epidemic" statistics survived in many quarters. In 1988, Stephen Michaud argued that the FBI's proposed laboratory for genetic testing would be "of special importance in tracking down serial killers and repeat sex offenders, who are thought to account for the bulk of sex crimes" (Michaud 1988). Though the linkage is not explicitly drawn, the suggestion is that serial killers are associated with very many sex crimes.

Also in 1988, Joel Norris wrote that about five thousand Americans each year,

fully 25 percent of all murder victims—were struck down by murderers who did not know them and killed them for the sheer "high" of the experience. The FBI calls this class of homicides serial murders and their

perpetrators recreational or lust killers. . . . [T]he FBI has estimated that
there are at least five hundred serial killers currently at large and unidentified in this country. (Norris 1988:15, 19)

In 1990, Clifford Linedecker suggested that about 30 percent of the
twenty-one thousand homicides in the United States remained unsolved, and "a disproportionate number" of these were believed to be
the work of serial killers: "A staggering number of these elusive criminals are serial killers" (Linedecker 1990a:ix). The importance of these
statements is that both Norris and Linedecker are among the best-selling
true crime authors, and their opinions thus carried far greater weight
than any more academic analysis. Such ambitious figures were especially prevalent among interest groups who wished to support a particular rhetorical position. Major claims-makers in this area included
advocates of children's rights, religious groups, and feminist writers (see
Chapters 7 and 10).

The Myth of the Mind-Hunter

After 1985, the panic over serial murder died away somewhat, due in
large part to the various activists having achieved their legislative agendas. However, the figure (and name) of the serial killer had decisively
entered the culture, and the second half of the decade witnessed a rapid
growth in both scholarly and true-crime publications on the topic.
Between 1985 and 1992, there appeared at least fourteen scholarly or
professional books on the general phenomenon, apart from the many
true-crime contributions (Segrave 1992; Wilson and Seaman 1992; Sears
1991; Newton 1990, 1992; Hickey 1991; James 1991; Egger 1990; Keppel
1989; Holmes and DeBurger 1988; Norris 1988; Cameron and Frazer
1987; Leyton 1986; Levin and Fox 1985; see also Holmes and Holmes
1993; Blair 1993; Athens 1992; Yarvis 1992; Chappell 1989; Toch and Adams 1989).

A serial murder problem had now been established on the lines advocated by the Justice Department; but during the late 1980s, the same
agency enjoyed continued success in redefining the issue along lines
that provided the maximum benefit and prestige for the FBI and its
investigators. Specifically, this meant presenting the FBI's behavioral
scientists (the "mind-hunters") as uniquely qualified to deal with the
serial murder menace, and this interpretation became very influential.
The mind-hunter image of the BSU was initially presented in a series of
highly laudatory media accounts, which reinforced the prestige of the
unit as the world's leading experts on serial violence.

One of the first such articles appeared in 1983 in the pages of *Psychology Today*, and like its many successors was largely based on interviews

with the leading BSU agents Robert Ressler, John Douglas, and Roy Hazelwood. Typically, such a report would describe true life cases in which uncannily accurate profiles led to the apprehension of unknown killers (Porter 1983). Among specific achievements, the most frequently cited was the use of FBI profiles to assist prosecutors in the trial of Wayne Williams. This was the format followed in a 1986 article in the highly visible setting of the *New York Times Magazine*, by journalist Stephen Michaud, who had earlier published his interviews with Ted Bundy. The article depicted the achievements of the NCAVC profilers ("The FBI's New Psyche Squad") in straightforward though admiring terms, while the article helped to popularize the FBI jargon then becoming popular, such as the distinction between *organized* and *disorganized* offenders, and the term *Unsub* for *unknown subject*.

Admiring articles were followed by book-length studies, including Paul Jeffers's *Who Killed Precious? How FBI Special Agents Combine High Technology and Psychology to Identify Violent Criminals* (1992). The book's blurb suggested, questionably, that "until now, [serial killers have] been almost impossible to catch," but that now the criminals had met their match in the BSU, "the only thing that stands between us and the country's most deranged psychopaths" (compare Clark and Morley 1993). FBI agents like Ressler and Douglas consulted extensively on this and other works, while Ressler himself became a visible public spokesman for the new techniques after his retirement from the bureau (Ressler and Schachtman 1992).

The public triumph of mind-hunting was neither assured nor inevitable. In fact, the adulatory works of the 1980s rarely made mention of the number of cases in which the FBI contribution had been negligible or actively counterproductive, and there were incidents that contributed little positive to the reputation of the BSU. For example, Roy Hazelwood is cited in a study of the Charlie Hatcher case as producing a profile that is justly described as "uncannily accurate" (Ganey 1989:22); but the same author also notes that an earlier profile "drawn up by Hazelwood in a Georgia case turned out to be the most inaccurate in the agency's history" (p. 22). In the Green River case, similarly, John Douglas had been involved in offering profiling assistance from the earliest stages of the investigation in 1982–1983, but the case still remained unsolved a decade later (Smith and Guillen 1990). The profiling endeavors of the BSU have been severely criticized within the FBI, and agent Paul Lindsay has denounced the claims made in Ressler's autobiography. Lindsay, an experienced homicide investigator, has also asked, "I mean, how many serial killer cases has the FBI solved—*if any*?" (Rosenbaum 1993a:124, emphasis in original; for Lindsay's critique of the Bureau, see also his 1992 novel *Witness to the Truth*).

However, it was not a serial murder case that caused the sharpest and most public criticism of the FBI's behavioral scientists. The incident that led to a public relations disaster for the unit followed the explosion of a gun turret aboard the U.S. battleship *Iowa* in April 1989, killing forty-seven sailors. The navy swiftly decided that the deaths were "equivocal," nonaccidental, and sought culprits. Attention focused on a small group of individuals, most of whom had perished in the disaster, and BSU profilers Roy Hazelwood and Richard Ault were requested to analyze information about this group. They soon concluded that the most likely suspect was Clayton Hartwig, who (they claimed) had sabotaged the gun turret in order to arrange a spectacular suicide (Jeffers 1992:177–229). The crime was thus one of mass homicide, and Hartwig was profiled shortly afterward in a true-crime study of extreme mass killers.

This account was publicized in September 1989, but it met widespread incredulity, in part because the navy appeared so anxious to avoid any interpretation that involved admitting blame for the service, or for its contractors. There was a skeptical "60 Minutes" report, and in December an angry congressional hearing summoned Hazelwood and Ault for a hostile public interrogation, in which they were especially criticized for accepting the navy's initial assumption that foul play had been involved. The ensuing report (March 1990) remarked,

> The FBI psychological analysis procedures are of doubtful professionalism. The false air of certainty generated by the FBI analysis was probably the single major factor inducing the Navy to single out Clayton Hartwig as the likely guilty party. The FBI should consider revamping its entire equivocal death analysis system. (Jeffers 1992:217)

This marked the nadir in the prestige of mind-hunting, while the FBI's expertise in forensic science was simultaneously under assault from independent scientists critical of the agency's treatment of DNA evidence (Neufeld and Colman 1990). The bureau was attacked for its apparent claims to infallibility in interpreting this data, and it was alleged that critics had been threatened with legal action and harassment (Kolata 1991). A public scandal followed in 1990 and 1991, tarnishing the unit with perhaps the most prestigious tradition in the whole FBI. Nineteen-ninety was in many ways a bleak year for the bureau, but the mass media soon allowed the Quantico investigators to recoup their reputation.

The Image of Jack Crawford

By far the most influential account of the BSU group came from the fictional work of Thomas Harris, author of *Red Dragon* ([1981] 1990) and

The Silence of the Lambs ([1988] 1989; see Chapter 4). Harris's writing were a critical contribution to the renewed upsurge of concern about serial murder in the early 1990s, and also ensured that the problem was defined according to the views of the Justice Department. It was *Red Dragon* above all that established the idea of the detective as mind-hunter, employing scientific crime-fighting skills well beyond the normal level of police procedures, and the book helped to popularize the methods of profiling and other investigative techniques characteristic of the BSU.

In fact, the detectives depicted as interviewing convicted killers are based heavily on real-life agents who had provided information for the book, so inevitably the FBI personnel are depicted as the heroic counterpoint to the villainous killers. The figure of FBI agent Jack Crawford was loosely synthesized from the real-life characters of Ressler, Douglas, and Hazelwood. (The British version of Robert Ressler's autobiography stressed that of all this agent's lifelong investigative accomplishments, the one deserving note was that he had served as adviser to Thomas Harris on *Silence of the Lambs*.) The BSU was portrayed as an elite team of superdetectives called in to assist local agencies facing the threat of savage roaming killers, while there was at least the impression that the unit had a special jurisdiction over serial murder cases wherever they occurred (see Chapter 5). This was an appealing and influential picture. Intentionally or not, Thomas Harris provided the FBI's violent-crime experts with invaluable publicity and unprecedented visibility, both crucial in the aftermath of the *Iowa* disaster. As Ressler has written in his remarkably candid autobiography, "The media have come around to lionizing behavioral science people as supersleuths who put all other police to shame and solve cases where others have failed" (Ressler and Schachtman 1992:241).

This is suggested by a report broadcast in November 1991 by CBS's "60 Minutes" on the Justice Department's Investigative Support Unit, the "psycho squad" headed by John Douglas. The preamble stated, "It would be comforting to think that the movie *Silence of the Lambs* was pure fiction. It wasn't. It was based on real crimes and a real FBI unit which is known affectionately as the Psycho Squad." The report suggested that this group and the subjects it investigated were in fact the true life equivalents of Harris's fictional creations. Harris's detective Crawford is presented (questionably) as a straightforward depiction of the real-life agent Douglas. An interview with killer Gary Heidnik is introduced with the words, "This is not a scene from *Silence of the Lambs* but it could have been." Such interviews are juxtaposed with clips from the film in which the fictional Hannibal Lecter is interrogated. The overall impression is both that Heidnik represents one of the monsters of fiction, while the Justice Department investigators really were the superdetectives suggested by the film. Agent Douglas even remarked that his aspirations for the unit would be that agents could intervene in a crime and depart suddenly, reminiscent of the Lone Ranger.

The CBS interviewer's questions and remarks were uncritical to the point of being quite reverential. For instance, the accuracy of the unit's profiles and analyses is said to be so uncanny that these are believed to result from mystical means: "The police say that you hold seances, and that you're weird, that you're sorcerers, and that you're the ouija board men . . . witch-doctors." Ironically, many of the occult terms often applied to the profilers were by no means intended to be flattering, and some of the harshest criticisms levied against Ressler and Douglas dismiss their work as "voodoo" (Rosenbaum 1993a). However, the news report leaves the disingenuous impression that such words reflect breathless admiration.

It would be difficult to conceive of a more favorable depiction, of brilliant and heroic mind-hunters combating the most savage enemies of society, yet never losing the fundamental humanity that causes them to sympathize deeply with the individuals who are the victims of these atrocities. Moreover, this was a report from "60 Minutes," the program that shortly before had led the assault on the *Iowa* verdict.

THE NEW PANIC, 1990–1992

The factual accuracy of *Silence of the Lambs* has been much criticized by law enforcement officers, including Ressler, Hazelwood, and other Quantico investigators themselves (see, for example, Ressler and Schachtman 1992:241). More hostile critics have denounced the "slavish P.R. the Bureau reaped from *Silence of the Lambs*," and Paul Lindsay has noted how the bureau's reputation was "vastly puffed up by the hype" from the film. He further describes the film itself as "far fetched, a fabrication . . . *totally* fiction" (Rosenbaum 1993a:122–24, emphasis in original).

But such criticisms were rarely heard in the media, and the Justice Department's specialists earned still more prestige during the renewed concern with serial murder in the early 1990s. Though not as intense or as exaggerated as the panic of 1983–1985, the events of 1990–1992 did substantially reshape perceptions of serial murder, and a concatenation of incidents made serial murder almost as keen a focus of media attention as it had been in the mid-1980s. In addition, there was even more debate about the role of the serial killer as a figure in art and literature (see Chapters 4 and 7). Media reporting constantly reinforced the idea that there was an overwhelming menace to society, and the only hope for combating it lay in Quantico, exactly the linkage that the Justice Department had been trying to establish for a decade. The delineation of the new panic demonstrated the federal agency's complete ownership of the murder problem.

Signs of renewed concern emerged in August 1990 with the reporting of a series of five gruesome mutilation murders on the University of Florida campus in Gainesville (Reynolds 1991). Though technically spree crimes, these attacks were universally construed as serial murders, and so the topic was brought back to the headlines. Within days, ABC's "20/20" estimated that eighty news reporters were covering the case. The impact of these crimes was all the greater because of the "innocent" nature of the victims. These were, after all, students, not people engaged in prostitution or homosexual activities, a distinction that often leads to an undervaluing of victims in other cases. The attacks seemed all the more threatening because they occurred in the apparent safety of the victims' homes; and the location inevitably recalled Ted Bundy's final spree on another Florida campus (Kunen 1990). In Gainesville, "You've got Jack the Ripper loose at the state's flagship university"; and it was soon recognized that the initial suspect was not in fact involved in the crimes, so that the real killer remained at large (report on ABC's "20/20," January 4, 1991). News coverage of Gainesville placed the incident in the context of a number of current and unsolved cases around the country: in New Bedford and San Diego, Philadelphia and New York, Norfolk, Virginia, and Washington D.C., reinforcing the concept of a generalized problem ("Cities Nationwide" 1990).

Over the next three months, serial murder remained in the news because of the dispute over Bret Easton Ellis's book *American Psycho* (see Chapter 7). In February 1991, the release of the film version of the *Silence of the Lambs* provided a central point of reference in the renewed concern with serial homicide, and the popular enthusiasm it generated lasted for several months. Just as that interest was beginning to fade, a number of true-life murder cases occurred that reawakened public fears.

In July 1991, the gruesome and cannibalistic elements of the Jeffrey Dahmer case ensured that this would become one of the best known of all serial murder incidents nationwide. In the *New York Times*, for example, there was a major half- or full-page feature on the case for each of the next ten days, and there were interviews and discussions on all the major talk shows and news programs (Achenbach 1991; Suplee 1991; Gammage 1991; Johnson 1991). According to several *Milwaukee Journal* reports, an estimated 450 journalists sought to cover the ensuing trial. The vast impact of the affair was also suggested by the wide popularity of jokes and tales based on the case, and the cannibalistic theme helped to reinforce the connection with the fictional Hannibal (see Chapter 5).

August 1991 found other serial murder cases in the headlines. For example, it was suggested that there had been a string of almost twenty related murders in Riverside County, California, the victims being mainly female prostitutes. (The following January, William Lester Suff was charged in two of these crimes.) The same August, there was also an abortive revival of the Lucas stereotype, when a drifter named Donald Leroy Evans was widely reported for his claim that he had killed up to sixty people in twenty states, and that he was "actually the worst serial killer in the nation's history" ("Troubled Past for Drifter" 1991; Schneider 1991). However, police were very anxious to avoid a repetition of "a Henry Lee Lucas kind of thing," and were very cautious about accepting these boasts. The allegations indeed proved difficult to substantiate, and little more was heard of the case, but the denial of the charges received far less publicity than the initial claim. Also during 1991, Aileen Wuornos was arrested for a number of murders in Florida and was promptly billed as "America's first female serial killer" (see Chapter 7). Interest in the phenomenon was maintained into 1992 by the televised trials of both Dahmer and Wuornos on the television cable channel Court TV.

In the spring of 1992, there was also widespread concern about a proposal to issue sets of trading cards depicting serial killers, an idea originally reported in a sensational story on the television program "Entertainment Tonight" in January. The concept appeared especially frightening because of the supposed appeal of such objects to children, and on the television talk show "Larry King Live," it was incorrectly stated that these cards were being sold through Toys 'R Us. By April, there were movements to ban sale of the cards in seven states and Canada, and the Maryland legislature proposed a sweeping measure prohibiting simple possession (Jones and Collier 1993).

These events gave the news media a new tag for the examination of serial murder on a level unparalleled since 1985, and stories were now likely to be adapted to fit the concerns and emphases of Harris's work, and thus the federal model of the problem (see Chapter 4). Virtually every feature on the subject included at least one interview on the subject of profiling and crime scene analysis, usually with one of the Quantico investigators; and reporting of the Gainesville murders disseminated awareness of terms like *blitz* attacks and *disorganized* offenders. On several occasions in these years, the present author was approached for interviews by journalists who assumed that anyone with a professional and academic interest in serial murder must automatically be an authority on profiling, which was seen as the chief or only methodology for studying the offense.

Over the next two years, the fictional Hannibal Lecter and his real-life counterparts featured prominently in news and magazine stories on all television networks, as well as in numerous magazines ("Secrets" 1992; Dubner 1992; Goodman, 1991). *People Weekly* used *Silence of the Lambs* as a vehicle to discuss the factors that gave rise to real-life serial murder. In *Village Voice*, director Jonathan Demme was quoted as an authority on the topic of authentic serial murder, and discussed the contributions made by child abuse to the causation of the offense (Taubin 1991). Such articles were especially likely to appear in periodicals chiefly aimed at younger women, perhaps suggesting the greater fear that this audience would be likely to have in the face of sexually motivated attacks (see, for example, the coverage in magazines like *Vanity Fair*, *Mirabella*, *Red Book*, *Mademoiselle*, *Cosmopolitan*, *Chatelaine*, or *Glamour*—Sikes 1992; Casey 1992; MacNamara 1991; Harrison 1991; Mailer 1991; Masters 1991b; Edmiston 1991; Rosenbaum, 1991, 1993a; Rule 1989).

Television often returned to the theme. Between 1991 and 1993, ABC's main news program "20/20" included segments on the Gainesville murders (January 1991), Leonard Lake and Charles Ng (April 1991), Andrei Chikatilo (October 1992), and Texas serial murderer Kenneth McDuff (October 1992). In May 1991, CBS's "48 Hours" presented a one-hour special entitled "Serial Killer," which included a case study of the then unsolved Riverside murders, as well as harrowing interviews that first brought the case of child killer Westley Alan Dodd to national attention. In April 1993 the show addressed another full program to the case of Kenneth McDuff. The same network's "60 Minutes" offered a report on the FBI's "Psycho Squad" (November 1991; see above), and in 1992 reported the case of Ray and Faye Copeland. NBC's news program "Dateline" presented two major reports on Aileen Wuornos (August and November 1992; see Chapter 7).

Meanwhile, PBS's "Frontline" series presented two full documentaries during 1992: "Monsters among Us" ostensibly concerned sex offenders and their treatment, but in reality focused on multiple-child killer Westley Alan Dodd. "Nova"'s "The Mind of a Serial Killer" was mainly concerned with the Arthur Shawcross case. The program focused on the achievements of the ISU, and intercut real-life footage of John Douglas's real-life office with scenes depicting Jack Crawford's desk from *Silence of the Lambs*. In 1993, another "Nova" examined the use of DNA testing to catch a serial sex-killer. In January 1993, CNN presented the five-part series, "Murder by Number," which included interviews with Dodd and other serial killers as well as psychologists and criminological experts. Moreover, this listing of news reports is far from comprehensive, and it does not include programs on related topics such as satanism or child abuse, which might well include accounts of serial killers.

The apparent surge of reported cases led to revived suggestions of a murder epidemic. In May 1991, CBS's "48 Hours" began by noting that "More than twenty-one thousand Americans are murdered each year." There were many motives for such crimes, "but the most horrifying deaths come at the hands of serial murderers, people who actually enjoy making other people suffer and die." Although it could not be quantified, the problem was thus immeasurably grave. It was "a crime against humanity, a race against time." The following April, Robert Ressler was quoted in *Mirabella:* "We're seeing an upward spiraling trend where one week you have Jeffrey Dahmer, the next week Donald Evans It just never stops. America is going to turn into *A Clockwork Orange*. The sexual psychopath will become the norm" (Sikes 1992).

FROM CLAIM TO OWNERSHIP

From the late 1970s, the dimensions and nature of the serial murder problem have been clearly delineated. It involves a war by representatives of normal society against semihuman criminal monsters, a conflict of heroes and villains, in which the only hope of achieving victory lies in entrusting adequate resources to those agencies with the expertise and commitment to undertake combat on our behalf. It is a problem of law enforcement rather than social policy or mental health, and it must be undertaken at a national and interjurisdictional level. Moreover, the battle must be won using the most sophisticated psychological and forensic techniques. In this view, the serial murder problem is perhaps the purest example of a "war on crime" ideology, defined in such a way as to attract maximum resources and prestige for law enforcement agencies, particularly those of the federal government.

The official view of serial murder is beyond doubt that propounded by the Justice Department. Its thorough ownership of the emerging problem owes much to the agency's skillful courting of the mass media, as discussed in Chapter 11. On the other hand, media manipulation is not in itself a sufficient explanation for the success of this particular interpretation of the phenomenon. It is very difficult to imagine any agency so successfully manipulating television and newspapers unless it is assumed that there was a preexisting public demand for portrayals of both menacing serial killers and heroic mind-hunters. The nature of these underlying public attitudes can best be studied from popular culture, in which serial murder has so long played a prominent role.

Appendix: Creating the "Serial Murder Problem": A Chronology 1981–1985

1981

- Attorney General's Task Force on Violent Crime explores means of improving interagency cooperation.
- May–June: Culmination of the Atlanta Child Murders case leads to the arrest of Wayne Williams.
- July: Adam Walsh disappears. His father John Walsh campaigns for children's rights and sets up the Adam Center in Fort Lauderdale, Florida. Etan Patz abduction confirms fears of predatory strangers.
- November: Hearings on the Missing Children's Act before the House Committee on Civil and Constitutional Rights.

1982

- April: Hearings on missing and exploited children before the Specter committee.
- November: Proposal to create a National Center for the Analysis of Violent Crime, NCAVC.
- December: Hearings on child pornography before the Specter committee.
- Federal Missing Children's Act gives the role of information clearing house to the FBI's National Crime Information Center.

1983

- February: Hearings on child kidnapping before the Specter committee.
- April: Correspondence between Specter and FBI director Webster.
- July: Hearings before the Specter committee "on patterns of murders committed by one person in large numbers with no apparent rhyme, reason, or motivation."
- Summer: Conference at Sam Houston State University proposes the establishment of NCAVC under the auspices of the BSU.
- Fall: Television movie *Adam* focuses concern on missing children.
- October: Justice Department news conference involving Roger Depue and Robert Heck popularizes idea of thirty-five active serial killers.

- October: Publicity given to the serial murder case associated with Henry Lee Lucas and Ottis Toole.

1984

- National Center for Missing and Exploited Children operational.
- February: Conviction of Alaska serial killer Robert Hansen.
- February–March: Hearings on the Missing Children's Assistance Act before the Specter committee.
- March: Kenneth Wooden's reports on "20/20" focus on child murders and disappearances. Wooden's book *Child Lures* is distributed to hundreds of thousands of homes.
- April: National concern about serial killers follows the Christopher Wilder case.
- April 9: Hearings before the House Committee on Human Resources on the Missing Children's Assistance Act.
- June: Ronald Reagan announces the establishment of NCAVC.

1985

- April: growing criticism of most of the Lucas serial murder allegations.
- May: VICAP computer system operational.
- May: Attorney General Meese supports the creation of a national center for education and research in the area of child abuse.
- August: Richard Ramirez arrested in Night Stalker case.

Chapter 4

Popular Culture:
Images of the Serial Killer

The impact of the alleged murder epidemic of the 1980s can only be explained if the supposed threat aroused fears and images already present in the public consciousness, and there is abundant evidence that serial killers and similar figures have long played a significant role in popular culture. The idea of using a serial killer as a fictional villain is by no means a recent innovation, but the volume of such depictions has expanded enormously over the last two decades. Publishers and filmmakers clearly believe that there is a vast market for stories on this theme, and the continuing success of these works suggests that their perceptions are quite correct. The scale of this interest is unprecedented, and so perhaps is the complexity of the images presented.

This chapter will trace the development of these cultural images, and especially the steady shift away from the portrayal of multiple killers as creatures of individual psychopathology ("psychos"), and toward more moralistic and even supernatural interpretations of ever more terrifying and dehumanized monsters. This transition occurred in both cinema and the novel, and it profoundly influenced media coverage of the topic. The growing tendency to view serial killers as exemplifying supernatural evil reflected trends in contemporary debate and investigation, which will be discussed in Chapter 10 below.

It is difficult to know whether the bureaucratic law enforcement attitudes toward serial murder preceded or followed changes in popular culture, and whether the specific image of the "monster" developed in the media before it was popularized by police agencies. It has been noted that in coverage of serial murder, the boundaries between fiction and real life were often blurred to the point of nonexistence. However, both true-crime and fictional depictions rendered great service to the Justice Department by promoting its orthodoxy in the interpretation of the offense.

EARLY TREATMENTS OF THE THEME

An interest in true crime can be traced at least to pamphlets of the seventeenth and eighteenth centuries, and the journalist Henry Mayhew has described a whole subculture of this type in the England of the 1860s. There were "death hunters" and "running patterers" who shouted in the streets the details of notorious crimes or murders. Itinerant "caravan shows" depicted the crimes as puppet shows and tableaux (Dietz, Harry, and Hazelwood 1986). In 1827, Thomas De Quincey discussed the "culture of murder" in *On Murder, Considered as One of the Fine Arts*, a response to a recent London case of serial homicide (Critchley and James 1971; James and Critchley 1987).

Specialized "true-detective" magazines date back to the *National Police Gazette* (1845), the linear ancestor of modern periodicals like *True Detective* and *Official Detective*. Some twenty such titles were published during the 1980s. These provided sensationalistic "instant reaction" accounts of major crimes, the tone of which is suggested by titles such as "Did alligators eat the pretty Texas waitresses?" or "Texas homosexual torture-murder horrors!" (Dietz et al. 1986). There were also numerous book-length studies of homicide cases, especially in the 1920s (from a very large literature, see Pearson 1924, 1928, 1936; Hoffman 1925; Smith 1927; Douthwaite 1929). The 1940s produced a popular "Regional Murder Series," books focusing on the bizarre crimes of a particular area: *Chicago Murders, Cleveland Murders*, and so on (Collins 1944; Wright 1945; Casey 1946; Bayer 1947; Hamer 1948; compare Derleth 1968). In 1947, Robert Bloch's novel *The Scarf* depicted a sensationalistic Hollywood journalist whose remarks suggest the popularity of bizarre violence as a media theme. Encouraging a colleague to write on the Cleveland Torso Murders, he urges: "People like to read about it. Look at the way those true detective magazines sell. Sex crimes. Blood. Everybody wants to know. . . . Ever hear about the ritual murders we had out here? The devil worshippers? They cut up a kid" (Bloch 1947:207–8).

The multiple killer has played a role in fiction for over a century, and there are many classic predecessors for the contemporary novel of suspense or horror fiction centered on this type of activity (Black 1991; Davis 1957). Among the most distinguished are classic novels like James Hogg's *Confessions of a Justified Sinner* (1824), or Stevenson's *Dr Jekyll and Mr Hyde* (1886), both of which describe repeat killers with multiple personalities. The genre received a fillip from the publicity accorded to the Jack the Ripper case, and Jack featured widely in European fiction from the 1890s through the 1930s (Rumbelow 1988:236–45). There was a collection of stories on the topic in Swedish from as early as 1892, and a few years later, Jack appeared in *Pandora's Box* (1904) and other plays by the

German writer Frank Wedekind. Wedekind's work provided the basis for the opera *Lulu* by Alban Berg (first performed in 1937), and thus the serial killer became a presence in high culture no less than true crime. Multiple homicide of the ripper type provided a theme for European authors like Friedrich Dürrenmatt (1959) and Georges Simenon (1979).

There were also many popular works about Jack the Ripper, and in the Anglo-American world the most influential early work was Mrs. Belloc Lowndes's story *The Lodger* (1913), which enjoyed enormous success on the stage. However, there had been pamphlet and music hall treatments of the crime within months of the actual events (Rumbelow 1988:236–41).

Films about serial murder can be traced back to the early days of the cinema, especially in Germany, where Jack the Ripper featured as a contemporary demon-figure in such Expressionist classics as *Waxworks* (1924) and *Pandora's Box* (1929; McCarty 1986; Green and Swan 1993:6–7, 33–34, 140–42, 197–98). The influence of contemporary German cases of multiple killers Fritz Haarmann and Peter Kürten was apparent in the film *M* (1931; see Chapter 2). It is likely that the German experience did much to influence Alfred Hitchcock's choice of the ripper theme in his version of *The Lodger* (1926); and partly through this example, the image reestablished itself in Anglo-American popular culture.

The Lodger was remade in 1932 and 1944, and there were other treatments of the multiple killer in following years. These included *Night Must Fall* (1937), *Stranger on the Third Floor* (1940), *The Brighton Strangler* (1945), *M* (remade in 1951), *The Sniper* (1952), and *While the City Sleeps* (1956). There was also the humorous treatment in *Arsenic and Old Lace* (1944; see Chapter 2). This featured Peter Lorre, who had established a reputation portraying a multiple killer in both *M* and *Stranger on the Third Floor* (Lorre had also drawn material from observations of a true-life repeat killer in a 1936 Los Angeles trial: Wolf and Mader 1986:299).

Hollywood's enthusiastic interest may reflect public awareness of the numerous such real-life cases reported up to the late 1930s (see Chapter 2). Multiple killers were frequent villains in films in the period during and after the second world war, and they were also a mainstay of pulp fiction. Serial killers occur in the work of fantasy and suspense authors like Robert Bloch, Ray Bradbury, and Ellery Queen, as well as in horror comics, in series like EC Comics' *Tales from the Crypt* (Branigan 1986; Barker 1984; Daniels 1974).

Robert Bloch himself has remarked on the postwar revival of the psychopath as a villain in fiction, and how "[p]sychopathology defied the deductive method. [T]he psychotics emerged to confound all the bright young men and little old ladies playing detectives" ([1943] 1977:8–9). Throughout his long career, Bloch would mine the history of American serial murder for fictional themes ([1946] 1977). His *American Gothic* recounts the story of H. H. Holmes, while the author tried unsuccessfully to persuade Hitchcock to make a film based on the Cleveland Torso Murders (Bloch 1993). His own novel *The Scarf* (1947) was widely influential in its device of telling the story through the autobiographical voice of the multiple strangler (see Chapter 10 for some of Bloch's other contributions). The book was regarded as a sufficiently important contribution to merit a laudatory review from Fredric Wertham in a professional psychiatric journal (Bloch 1993:197–200).

PSYCHO AND AFTERWARDS: 1960–1978

During the 1950s, Bloch developed in several short stories the idea of the killer as psychotic or multiple personality. The Ed Gein case provided the basis for an ambitious treatment of the theme, and Bloch's novel *Psycho* was the source of Hitchcock's 1960 film of the same name. The commercial and critical success of *Psycho* indicated the immense potential of the issue, and a boom began in films depicting multiple murder (Rebello 1991; Rothman 1982). Most were based on real-life cases, although with considerable fictional license being taken (see Capote 1965). The career of Ed Gein provided the basis for *Psycho* and *Deranged*, while later pictures followed the careers of Albert De Salvo (*The Strangler*, 1964; and *The Boston Strangler*, 1968) and Charlie Starkweather (*Badlands*, 1973). *Dirty Harry* (1971) freely synthesized the stories of Gary Krist and Zodiac.

Hitchcock's *Frenzy* (1972) marked a return to ideas he had pioneered in *The Lodger*, and thus ultimately derived from the Jack the Ripper story, though in modern-day guise. There were in addition numerous other treatments of the original Jack the Ripper case, which continued steadily from the 1950s through the 1980s (see, for example, *A Study in Terror*, 1966; *Hands of the Ripper*, 1971; *The Ruling Class*, 1972; *Murder by Decree*, 1979; *Time After Time*, 1980; or U.S. television movies like *Jack the Ripper* and *Jack's Back*, both 1988). Authentic incidents of mass murder inspired *In Cold Blood* (1967) and *Targets* (1968).

It is possible that the resurgence of interest in multiple homicide was fueled by the steadily increasing reports of actual cases, but there were also changes within the cinema industry, above all the rise of new and more relaxed standards of censorship. From about 1970, films in first Britain and then the United States depicted nudity and extreme violence of a type that would have been inconceivable even five years previously, and there was much controversy about films such as *Straw Dogs*, *A*

Table 4.1. Films About Multiple Homicide, 1967–1979

1967 *In Cold Blood* *Night of the Generals*	1974 *Deranged* *Texas Chainsaw Massacre*
1968 *The Boston Strangler* *Targets* *No Way to Treat a Lady*	1975 *Stranger in the House ("Black Christmas")* 1976 *Helter Skelter*
1970 *Ten Rillington Place*	1977 *The Town That Dreaded Sundown*
1971 *Dirty Harry* *Hands of the Ripper*	1978 *Toolbox Murders* *Halloween*
1972 *Frenzy* *Last House on the Left*	1979 *When a Stranger Calls* *Murder by Decree*
1973 *Silent Night, Bloody Night* *Badlands*	

Clockwork Orange, and *Soldier Blue* (all released 1970–1971). The new environment radically changed treatments of serial murder. In earlier years, it had been common to affect a social crusading tone to guard against charges that this unsavory subject matter was being exploited for prurient reasons, but such claims were no longer necessary. *Frenzy* graphically portrayed rape and multiple murder, and this pioneered a proliferating series of films that were widely criticized for gratuitously exploiting the violence and sexual content of the murders. It was these which formed the basis for the emerging "slasher movie" genre of the early 1980s (see Table 4.1).

In 1972, *Last House on the Left* drew to some extent on the Manson murders. The film was of particular significance because it established the reputation of filmmakers later important in the horror genre: Its producer, Sean Cunningham, went on to direct *Friday the Thirteenth,* while director Wes Craven was the maker of *Nightmare on Elm Street* and *The Hills Have Eyes.* Also influential was *Texas Chainsaw Massacre* (1974), which was inspired by the Gein case. This latter was a low-budget work that enjoyed great international popularity. It was *Texas Chainsaw Massacre* that introduced the idea of the killer as a deranged monster wielding bizarre weapons and thoroughly depersonalized by his use of a mask. *Stranger in the House* (1975) provided other influential themes: a college sorority setting that allowed the killer to stalk attractive young women, and the timing of the murders around a major holiday, in this case Christmas.

THE SLASHER FILM: 1978–1990

These themes coalesced in 1978 in John Carpenter's much-imitated *Halloween*, which tells the story of the fictional killer Michael Myers. Michael first appears as a child, when he kills his sister. After many years in a hospital for the criminally insane, he escapes and (masked) begins a spree in which he murders several teenagers now living in his former neighborhood. Finally, he is outwitted and defeated by the heroine, but on each occasion when he is apparently killed, it transpires that he survives to kill again (the resurrection is a device derived from Brian De Palma's 1976 film, *Carrie*). Michael Myers appears in the film as a thoroughly inhuman monster, voiceless and literally faceless, whose only function is to serve as a relentless killing machine. The film was not directly based on any specific case, but the concept of the multiple murders of young women over a single night may have owed something to Ted Bundy's rampage in a Florida sorority house earlier that year.

The influence of *Halloween* was soon seen in a wave of derivative films, which came to be known as *slasher* (or "slice and dice") movies. These were at their height in 1980 and 1981, at exactly the time when media attention was so focused on real-life cases of multiple sexual homicide, above all the cases of Bundy, Gacy, and the Atlanta Child Murders (see Table 4.2; compare Table 3.2).

Table 4.2. Some American Films About Multiple Murder 1980–1981

1980	1981
Cruising	*The Burning*
Don't Go in the House	*Friday the Thirteenth, Part 2*
Dressed to Kill	*Graduation Day*
First Deadly Sin	*Halloween II*
Friday the Thirteenth	*Happy Birthday to Me*
Maniac	*He Knows You're Alone*
Motel Hell	*Hell Night*
Prom Night	*My Bloody Valentine*
Terror Train	*New Year's Evil*
	Nightmare

Source: McCarty (1986).

With few exceptions, slasher movies closely followed a rigid formula. First, as in *Halloween*, the victims were almost invariably teenagers or young people. Generally, the story explained how a traumatic incident many years previously had caused an individual to become an irrational killer who wore a mask or distinctive costume in order to commit his crimes. Years later, a group of teenagers arrive at a place or setting where the killer is active. Introductory scenes depict the young people amusing themselves, and these scenes often provide the opportunity to depict the gratuitous sexual activity, and the female nudity or seminudity that was almost obligatory for the genre. College campus or high school settings were often used in this context.

Over the period of a night or more, the killer then tracks down the victims one by one, killing them in various gruesome ways that usually involve the use of cutting tools or weapons (Clover 1992). Often, the stalking of the victim is indicated from the killer's point of view, perhaps through the mask he wears. Finally, there may be one or more survivors (the "last girl") who discover the bloody remains of the victims and perhaps confront the murderer, though virtually every film contains a resurrection ending, where the apparent death of the offender proves to be an illusion, and he or she returns to kill again.

Some of the slasher movies enjoyed enormous success, and several were followed by one or more sequels, most notably in the case of *Friday the Thirteenth* (see Table 4.3).

The character of such films can be understood as a response to both commercial and technological factors, which permitted and even demanded the display of so much graphic violence. Slasher films were a subset of the wider genre of "gore" or extreme horror associated with cult directors like George Romero. This model flourished in the 1980s because of the advances in special effects, which permitted the simula-

Table 4.3. Slasher Film Series[a]

Film series	Episodes	Time frame
Friday the Thirteenth	9	1980–1993
Nightmare on Elm Street	6	1984–1991
Halloween	5	1978–1989
Silent Night, Deadly Night	5	1984–1991
Prom Night	4	1980–1990
Texas Chainsaw Massacre	3	1974–1990
Sleepaway Camp	3	1984–1989

[a]In addition, three sequels to the original 1960 *Psycho* were released between 1983 and 1990.

tion of the effects of grotesque violence, and which altered the level of audience expectations about such portrayals. Serial murder films often came from the same studios, directors, and special effects experts who were simultaneously involved with stories of purely supernatural horror, including, for example, the *Night of the Living Dead/Return of the Dead* films (five contributions to the series between 1978 and 1990) and the *Evil Dead* series (three between 1983 and 1992). Changing commercial standards and censorship criteria also go far toward explaining the strongly sexual character of the violence in these films (see Chapter 5).

THE THRILLER NOVEL

Cinematic treatments alone ensured that serial murder would enjoy a prominent role in popular culture during the 1980s. However, the boom in slasher movies at the end of the 1970s coincided with a revival of interest in horror themes in the popular novel (Best 1990:113–23). The horror genre was resuscitated by the work of author like Stephen King and Peter Straub, who employed both secular and supernatural themes, and who often made use of extreme and violent images. The success of such writing encouraged many imitators in search of new themes, especially as traditional villains like vampires and werewolves had become so hackneyed, implausible, and even humorous. Moreover, the new generation of writers was addressing an audience accustomed to the graphic violence of the gore films, which was far beyond what had been normal for traditional horror (Skal 1993). It is not therefore surprising that several authors were attracted by the serial murder stories then occupying such a prominent role in the media, and King himself used a campus serial killer as the basis for his 1978 novella *Strawberry Spring*.

There were several important novels from this era. In 1979, Shane Stevens's best-selling *By Reason of Insanity* ([1979] 1990) used the case of Richard Speck as a model for the killer's planned rampage in a women's hostel, while the fictional villain himself was obsessed by his supposed relationship with 1950s rapist Caryl Chessman. In 1981, Stuart Woods's *Chiefs* ([1981] 1987) portrayed a multiple killer attacking boys and young men, and burying their remains in a secret cemetery, a concept that owed much to the cases of both Corll and Gacy. Also in 1981, Lawrence Sanders's *Third Deadly Sin* ([1981] 1982) explored the theme of the female serial killer. The same year, Thomas Harris's *Red Dragon* ([1981] 1990) was influenced by several true-life incidents that he studied with the advice and assistance of the FBI's Behavioral Sciences Unit.

Red Dragon was by far the most influential book of its kind from this period, but all these works contributed to shaping an emerging genre. Serial murder books generally differ from mainstream murder mysteries in that the interest of the study does not lie in the quest to identify the killer. In fact, this information is usually provided at a very early stage, and the book focuses on the career of the criminal and the means used to catch him or her. The book often tells the story at least in part from the point of view of the killer, a key element of *Red Dragon*, *By Reason of Insanity*, and *The Face That Must Die*, by the British horror author Ramsey Campbell ([1979] 1985).

The ideas presented in *Red Dragon* enjoyed a resurgence in 1988 with the publication of Harris's *The Silence of the Lambs* ([1988] 1989), which is to some extent a sequel. This book was an enormous best-seller, and among other distinctions it became a main choice of the Book of the Month Club (Stasio 1989; Richter 1989). Harris draws on real life cases in both books, especially in the portrayal of Hannibal Lecter, "Hannibal the Cannibal," who is presented as an evil sadistic genius rather than a confused inadequate like *Psycho*'s Norman Bates. This shift of perceptions reflects the influence of real offenders, chiefly Ted Bundy, but also the intelligent and articulate Edmund Kemper, who had provided Robert Ressler with some of his most valuable interviews. The Buffalo Bill killer of *Silence of the Lambs* is based on a synthesis of Ed Gein and Gary Heidnik, but the killer also employs tactics pioneered by Bundy to entrap his victims.

The influence of Harris's work was vastly enhanced by the release of film versions. *Red Dragon* attracted a little attention under the title of *Manhunter* in 1986, but the film version of *The Silence of the Lambs* (1991) was an international sensation, with Anthony Hopkins offering a terrifying portrayal of Hannibal. This success attracted imitators, and there was soon a wave of both fact and fiction books with covers boasting their serial murder theme. Some novels claimed to be in the tradition of *The Silence of the Lambs*, or to have villains in the tradition of Hannibal Lecter, while a number came close to imitating the butterfly motif of Harris's best-seller. Robert L. Duncan's *The Serpent's Mark* ([1989] 1990) depicted a behavioral scientist nicknamed "the Monster Catcher," while Joe Monninger's *Razor's Song* ([1991] 1993) asserted that its villain could be compared to both Hannibal Lecter and Ted Bundy.

The overlap between fact and fiction is especially blatant (and problematic) in the true-crime literature, where case studies of serial killers frequently refer to Harris's work as if it were the definitive account of the true-life phenomenon. The fictional Hannibal became a villain as well known as any authentic offender, and was even cited in journalistic accounts as if he were a real figure. The cover of a 1992 paperback studying Randy Kraft describes the book as "the true story of a real-life

Hannibal Lecter" (MacDougal 1992). Child killer Charlie Hatcher was "the real-life embodiment of Hannibal Lecter" (Ganey 1989).

Harris's work also established a precedent in using a Quantico setting, and focusing on the mind-hunting endeavors of the FBI's behavioral scientists. Van Arman's *Just Killing Time* was typical in including a scene at Quantico, in which the head of the agency VICAT [*sic*] is lecturing about the vast scale of the serial murder problem:

> In 1985, there were 14,516 murders in America classified as without mo-
> tive. . . . [F]rom this group of killers, only sixteen suspects have been
> captured. . . . [T]hat number does not include an additional five thousand
> bodies that simply turn up each year in the category of unidentified. . . . If
> you are a middle or upper middle class family of four, the chances are 37
> percent that you will meet a serial killer in your lifetime. . . . [L]ess than
> one percent of all motiveless homicides were ever solved. (Van Arman
> [1992] 1993:20–21, 34)

David Lindsey's *Mercy* ([1990] 1991) was one of many novels to popularize the characteristic BSU terminology and worldview, while there
was even a series of thriller novels under the generic VICAP title. Literary critics scoffed at the invasion of the crime genre by the behavioral
science fad: "There were three separate books this year in which the
killer set fires, tortured animals and wet his bed as a child, just because
the FBI profile said it" (quoted in Stasio 1989).

THE NEW BOOM 1991–1994

The film of *The Silence of the Lambs* further stimulated popular fascination with this topic. In the *New York Times*, "a fiction editor at a major
publishing house" was quoted as saying that 1989 appeared to be "the
year of the serial killer" (Stasio 1989). The theme attracted the interest of
some of the best-selling contemporary authors, such as P. D. James,
Robert B. Parker, Jonathan Kellerman, and Ed McBain. Over the next
three years there was an upsurge of novels on serial killers, works such
as David Lindsey's *Mercy* ([1990] 1991), James Neal Harvey's *By Reason of
Insanity* ([1989] 1990), and Herbert Lieberman's *Shadow Dancers* ([1989]
1990; see Appendix to this chapter). The most commercially successful
books from these years included Ridley Pearson's *Undercurrents* ([1988]
1989), Peter Straub's *Koko* ([1988] 1989), and John Sandford's *Rules of Prey*
([1989] 1990), all of which were followed by multiple sequels (there were
five *Prey* books by 1993). In different forms, the serial murder theme
came to occupy a prominent role in several related genres, in mystery

and detective novels no less than in horror and suspense. The theme also appeared in "serious" literary works, in novels by Peter Ackroyd, Paul West, Philip Kerr, and Carol DeChellis Hill.

Publishers now took the opportunity to reprint earlier volumes on serial murder, some of which had been out of print for years. Other volumes had originally appeared from very minor or local presses, but they now achieved major circulation. This provided the opportunity to republish books like Mark Clark's *Ripper* ([1987] 1989), Michael Slade's *Ghoul* ([1987] 1989), and even Shane Stevens's classic *By Reason of Insanity* ([1979] 1990). The fictional interest in serial murder was clearly evident in further publications through the early 1990s, and the topic spread into other genres, even including science fiction. In "young adult" writing, authors like Chris Pike developed the ideas and teenage settings of the slasher movies. The serial murder boom was also evident in the cinema, where the theme appeared in films like *Candy Man*, *Split Second*, *Jennifer Eight*, and *Basic Instinct* (Broeske 1992; James 1991; Love 1991; Sharrett 1991).

The new stereotype achieved a quirky culmination in the television series "Twin Peaks" (1989–1991), which features a FBI agent of awesome forensic and investigative powers summoned to investigate a serial murder in a small rural community. Perhaps parodying the excessive media claims for the mind-hunters, the fictional agent Cooper receives his most significant clues in dreams and visions.

TRUE CRIME

The issue was covered as extensively in the news media and other "factual" sources as in fiction. The spate of news reports during the panic of the early 1990s has already been noted (see Chapter 3), On television, serial murder stories became a staple of semidocumentary shows about police and crime investigation, which often used sensationalized dramatic reconstructions of crimes and other incidents in the career of the offender; and multiple murder was the theme of many talk shows hosted by celebrities like Geraldo Rivera or Phil Donahue. These programs often tried to involve the viewing audience to the point of encouraging the fantasies that the public itself was helping to solve the crimes.

On December 7, 1988, there was a two-hour prime-time television special entitled *Manhunt Live!*, which reported on current serial murder investigations with particular emphasis on the Green River case. Viewers were urged to call a special telephone hot line with possible leads, a pioneering idea that became the basis of the popular "America's Most Wanted" series, hosted by John Walsh. A book on the same case included an appeal for information to the Green River telephone hot line, offering a publisher's reward of fifty thousand dollars for evidence leading to the killer's conviction (Smith and Guillen 1990). Recently, a number of books have been sold with accompanying audiocassettes, so that readers can place themselves in the imaginary position of investigators interrogating Arthur Shawcross or Henry Lee Lucas (Norris 1991, 1992a). Court TV allows viewers to "attend" serial murder trials, and the channel has sought to broadcast every available case, including quite obscure events like the Alejandro Henriquez trial in New York City.

The interest in factual true-crime accounts was especially apparent in published accounts of real-life cases, and there is now a True Crime Book Club. Of course, multiple homicide is by no means the only theme of true-crime books, and in recent years, other topics that have enjoyed considerable attention include organized crime, tales of family murders among the rich and famous, and sensational crimes of passion like the Amy Fisher case of the early 1990s. However, serial murder stories usually account for between a third and a half of the output of such books.

Moreover, the volume of multiple-murder accounts has expanded significantly in recent years. In 1974, the Corll and Kemper cases led to a then unusual spate of at least seven books in a single year, and major cases like that of Gacy and Bundy were also widely discussed in the early 1980s. The genre thrived during the following decade (from a large literature, see, for example, Markman and Bosco 1989; Wambaugh 1989; Bakos 1989; Biondi and Hecox 1988; Molloy 1988; Moore and Reed 1988; Emmons 1987; Hilberry 1987; Keyes 1986; Brian 1986; Harrison 1986). In 1990, *Publisher's Weekly* remarked on the growing spate of serial murder books, and the pace at which books appeared accelerated to unprecedented heights in the aftermath of *The Silence of the Lambs* (Jeffers 1992:231). There is some evidence that the true-crime flood was beginning to abate by the end of 1993, but the theme remained in vogue in the thriller novels (see Appendix to this chapter).

In the four-year period from the start of 1990 to the end of 1993, over forty book-length studies of individual cases appeared, in addition to general accounts of the serial murder phenomenon, and at least twenty collections of briefer studies, often drawn from the true-detective magazines. The collections bear titles such as *Cult Killers, Serial Murderers, Spree Killers,* and *Medical Murderers* (Lucas 1992; Crockett 1990, 1991; Linedecker 1990a; Mandelsberg 1991, 1992; Linedecker and Burt 1990; compare Lane 1991). At any given time in a typical American chain bookstore, it would not be difficult to find forty or fifty different titles (fact or fiction) dealing with serial homicide as the central theme, and the great majority appear from the most important publishing houses.

Of the book-length studies, several were "instant reaction" accounts, relating cases that had attracted much media attention. There were no less than five studies of Jeffrey Dahmer's case, three each on Andrei Chikatilo and Aileen Wuornos, as well as others on nationally publicized cases such as Westley Alan Dodd, Arthur Shawcross, and the Green River Killer (see Table 4.4).

Other books covered far more obscure figures, whose cases had attracted chiefly local attention at the time of the initial arrest or trial. In this category, we find the books on Wayne Nance (from Montana), Dayton Rogers (Oregon), and Robert Hansen (Alaska). Ginsburg's *Shadow of Death* (1993) discusses a still unsolved series of killings in New England that have attracted virtually no attention outside the local area. In terms of the quality of writing or investigation, these books are by no means inferior to the level of the genre, but the choice of such relatively obscure cases may indicate that publishers and authors were actively seeking out incidents that had not hitherto been described, in order to satisfy a perceived public appetite.

This is confirmed by the increasing tendency to publish books on cases that were by no means fresh in the public mind, either reprints of earlier studies or else new discussions of cases that were of historical interest by this time. The question of reprints is interesting, as prior to the late 1980s true-crime studies had been viewed as ephemera that went quickly out of print, and they were virtually never reprinted. Among studies of older cases, we now find new or reprinted books on offenders of the 1960s or 1970s, such as Antone Costa, Richard Speck, Edmund Kemper, Richard Cottingham, Richard Trenton Chase, and Randy Kraft. Several other books chose subjects whose arrests had occurred five or ten years earlier, like Henry Lee Lucas (arrested in 1983: two books), Christopher Wilder (died in 1984), Robert Hansen (convicted in 1984), and Richard Ramirez (arrested in 1985). The suggestion that publishers were going far afield to find true-life cases may explain the intense interest in the case of Andrei Chikatilo, the first overseas case in decades to attract comparable attention, and one of the first from a country other than England.

MAKING MONSTERS

Portrayals of serial killers grew sharply in number, but they also changed fundamentally in character. In the middle years of the century,

Table 4.4. True-Crime Studies of Serial Homicide, 1990–1993[a]

Subject	Author (date)	Title
David Carpenter	Graysmith ([1981] 1990)	*The Sleeping Lady*
Antone Costa	Damore (1990)	*In His Garden*
Green River Killer	Smith and Guillen (1990)	*The Search for the Green River Killer*
Matamoros case	Linedecker (1990b)	*Hell Ranch*
Dorothea Puente	Blackburn (1990)	*Human Harvest*
Christopher Wilder	Gibney (1990)	*The Beauty Queen Killer*
Richard Ramirez	Linedecker (1991)	*Night Stalker*
Clifford Olson	Mulgrew (1991)	*Final Payoff*
The Neelleys	Cook (1991)	*Early Graves*
Robert Hansen	Gilmour and Hale (1991)	*Butcher Baker*
Richard Cottingham	Leith (1991)	*The Torso Killer*
Jeffrey Dahmer	Baumann (1991)	*Step Into My Parlor*
Jeffrey Dahmer	Davis (1991)	*The Milwaukee Murders*
Jeffrey Dahmer	Dvorchak and Holewa (1991)	*Milwaukee Massacre*
Henry Lee Lucas	Cox (1991)	*The Confessions of Henry Lee Lucas*
Henry Lee Lucas	Norris (1991)	*Henry Lee Lucas*
Judias Buenoano	Anderson and McGehee (1992)	*Bodies of Evidence*
Robert Berdella	Jackman and Cole (1992)	*Rites of Burial*
Richard Trenton Chase	Biondi and Hecox (1992)	*The Dracula Killer*
Andrei Chikatilo	Conradi (1992)	*The Red Ripper*
Jeffrey Dahmer	Norris (1992b)	*Jeffrey Dahmer*
Jeffrey Dahmer	Schwartz (1992)	*The Man Who Could Not Kill Enough*
Larry Eyler	Kolarik and Klatt (1992)	*Freed to Kill*
Randy Kraft	McDougal (1992)	*Angel of Darkness*
Dayton Rogers	King (1992)	*Blood Lust*
Wayne Nance	Coston (1992)	*To Kill and Kill Again*
Douglas Clark	Farr (1992)	*The Sunset Murders*
Aileen Wuornos	Reynolds (1992)	*Dead-Ends*
Aileen Wuornos	S. Russell (1992)	*Damsel of Death*
Aileen Wuornos	Kennedy (1992)	*On a Killing Day*
Arthur Shawcross	Norris (1992a)	*Arthur Shawcross*
Arthur Shawcross	Olsen (1993)	*The Misbegotten Son*
The Copelands	Miller (1993)	*The Copeland Killings*
Unknown (New England)	Ginsburg (1993)	*Shadow of Death*
Robert Hansen	DuClos (1993)	*Fair Game*
Andrei Chikatilo	Lourie (1993)	*Hunting the Devil*
Andrei Chikatilo	Cullen (1993)	*The Killer Department*
Andrei Chikatilo	Krivich and Ol'gin (1993)	*Comrade Chikatilo*
Robert Berdella	Clark and Morley (1993)	*Murder in Mind*

(continued)

Table 4.4. (*Continued*)

Subject	Author (date)	Title
Westley Alan Dodd	G. King (1993)	*Driven To Kill*
Richard Speck	Breo and Martin (1993)	*The Crime of the Century*
Randy Roth	Smith (1993)	*Fatal Charm*
Catherine Wood and Gwendolyn Graham	Cauffiel (1993)	*Forever and Five Days*
Gerald E. Stano	Flowers (1993)	*Blind Fury*
Joel Rifkin	Eftimiades (1993)	*Garden of Graves*

aDates refer to U.S. paperback editions where available.

there had been a wide range of available images and stereotypes, from the monstrous lunatics of the comic books or detective magazines to the far more complex images of some of the films. However, the prevailing image in the more serious works tended to emphasize the individual pathology of the killer, who is usually depicted as sick and inadequate rather than evil. This is certainly true of *M*, and the midcentury cinema was heavily influenced by Freudian interpretations of the roots of crime. In Bloch's *The Scarf*, the killer David Morley is clearly motivated by feelings of revenge against a brutal and sexually repressive mother, emotions reinforced by a disastrous early sexual experience with a middle-aged teacher.

This psychoanalytic approach reached its apogee in *The Sniper* (1952), which addressed the topic of serial murder with a sophisticated and sympathetic awareness of contemporary criminological theories. The film is heavily Freudian in nature, depicting a disturbed young man constantly seeking revenge against his mother (see Chapter 2). The compulsive nature of the sniper's violence also bears an explicit resemblance to the William Heirens case, which formed the basis of *While the City Sleeps* (1956). This tradition continued in Hitchcock's 1960 film *Psycho*, in the conclusion to which a psychiatrist interprets Norman Bates's violence in terms of his relationship to his mother, and in effect suggests that Norman should not be blamed for his crimes. In the British *Peeping Tom* (1960), similarly, the killer is presented as a severely disturbed psychiatric case. Other 1960s films like *The Boston Strangler* and *In Cold Blood* reinforced the image of the killer as an inadequate who was the slave of his upbringing and environment. In fiction, broadly psychoanalytic (and mother-oriented) themes predominated in ripper books of the 1950s like Simenon's *Maigret Sets a Trap* and Colin Wilson's *Ritual in the Dark*.

From the early 1970s, the complex psychological analyses of the earlier films began to give way to new attitudes and emphases, and the changes often reflected shifts in more general public attitudes toward the etiology of crime. Above all, the more therapeutic views of the 1950s were transformed into law and order perspectives, which emphasized the guilt and moral depravity of the individual offender. One of the most successful instances was *Dirty Harry*, which returned to the basic plot of *Sniper*, reproduced the original San Francisco setting, and used many of the same visual images, but with a radically different ideological twist. In the later film, the killer is depicted as a creature of pure evil, who cynically takes shelter behind psychiatric diagnoses of his alleged sickness. Moreover, the film criticizes the gullible and soft-hearted courts and media that permit such imposture. The same theme emerged in other hard-boiled thrillers like Charles Bronson's *Ten to Midnight* (1983), in which a Bundy-influenced killer announces that he will escape punishment by feigning an insanity defense. The audience is clearly meant to support the Bronson character's instant decision to kill him without trial.

In terms of the causation of serial murder, the films of the 1980s offered explanations that often verged on the supernatural, or overtly portrayed superhuman monsters, representatives of total, incomprehensible evil. It is instructive to contrast the psychoanalytic approach of *Sniper* or *Psycho* with a film like *Halloween*, in which no serious attempt is made to explain Michael Myers's wrongdoing in secular or psychological terms. In contrast to *Psycho*, in *Halloween* it is the psychiatrist character who agrees that Michael Myers is, in fact, the bogeyman.

As in so much else, *Halloween* shaped the genre, and serial killers were increasingly portrayed as monsters. This derived partly from the common device of the villain's resurrection after apparent death. In commercial terms, this near invincibility left open the possibility of future sequels; but it also reflected crossover from the supernaturally oriented gore genre to which these films were so closely related. In the context of the slasher films, such resurrections tended to promote increasingly inhuman interpretations of the killer's origin and powers.

In 1978, Michael Myers was certainly intended to represent a human villain, and so initially was the derivative Jason of *Friday the Thirteenth*; but by the mid-1980s, Jason had become so immune to normal rules of human behavior to be brought back from the dead by a lightning bolt, in a manner reminiscent of older Frankenstein or Dracula films. This trend reached its height with the *Nightmare on Elm Street* series, which began in 1984, in which the serial child killer Freddie Krueger appears only as a supernatural figure seeking revenge on the families of those responsible for his death, and kills his teenage victims in their dreams. By the late 1980s, Jason and Freddie had firmly established themselves among the more traditional figures of supernatural evil who provided themes for Halloween costumes, characters such as Dracula and the Mummy.

The theme of the serial killer as possessed by supernatural evil also occurred in Stanley Kubrick's *The Shining*, another 1980 film, which can scarcely be placed in the same category as the slasher movies. After the Gainesville murders of 1990, the media speculated that the crime scenes included features copied from the recent film *Exorcist III*, which depicts a demonically possessed serial killer. The same year, the television series "Twin Peaks" used a parody of such a possession theme to explain the serial murders at the heart of the plot, involving a demonic figure known as Bob.

A similar transition to the superhuman occurred in literature, most notably in the work of Thomas Harris, who drew so heavily on real-life cases. However, he takes considerable artistic license with these characters, especially in portraying killers like Hannibal Lecter as uncontrollable monsters little different from the most savage wild animals, who must at all times be restrained in captivity to prevent them from making savage attacks on guards or visitors. In reality, serial killers appear much more able to restrain their violent instincts. However, this portrait of the multiple killer as a monster in human form was influential on subsequent depictions. Similar stereotypes also occur frequently in the emerging genre of *splatterpunk*, short stories of extreme graphic horror strongly influenced by the gore films. Inevitably in such a context, serial killers are depicted in the most monstrous and nonhuman guise, reflecting trends in both the novel and the cinema (see, for example, Gorman and Greenberg 1993; Sammon 1990; Laymon 1989).

THE IMPACT ON POLICY

It is scarcely too much to describe multiple murder in the last decade as a cultural industry in its own right, with serial killers as a pervasive theme in television, the cinema, and the publishing world. Fictional and true-crime depictions also had a clear impact on changing perceptions of real world offenders, which would be significant for shaping debates over policy, and in every case the emerging view reflected the ideas proposed by federal law enforcement agencies in the early 1980s. This affected the popular view of the scale of the crime, the nature of the offender, and the appropriate antidote to the evil.

First, the intensity of the coverage clearly supported charges that serial murder was a vast menace. The popular books and articles on the topic naturally tended to report inflated statistics, but there was also the impressionistic effect based on the sheer volume of easily available serial murder books. Multiple murder therefore acquired high public visibility, which in turn increased the likelihood that the news media would report on relevant stories. In terms of law enforcement priorities, the prominence of serial murder made it likely that prestige and rewards would be won by successful interventions in this area, and therefore the offense would attract resources.

Moreover, the specific type of multiple murder that gained visibility was very much that of the extreme sexual sadist or psychopath. There was a cyclical effect, in which the media tended to focus on crimes that most resembled available public stereotypes: sex killers like Bundy, cannibals like Hannibal. In turn, reporting of those specific cases reinforced awareness of these stereotypes. This reinforced the idea that the real serial killer was a ripper or sexual killer, rather than a medical murderer or a woman killing members of her family or intimate circle.

Finally, the popular culture depictions of the problem placed massive emphasis on the heroic role of the (federal) mind-hunters, rather than the ordinary police officers and detectives from local agencies, who are virtually always responsible when serial killers are apprehended. Van Arman's *Just Killing Time* features as hero "the head of the federal agency that hunts the most dangerous criminal alive—the serial killer." The unit was needed because serial killings were "types of assault local enforcement had little chance of solving without help" ([1992] 1993:33). One true-crime book claims that murderer Robert Hansen was pursued and arrested with the assistance of "VICAP, the FBI unit made famous in *The Silence of the Lambs*" (Du Clos 1993).

Taken together, these cultural trends established a public expectation that the federal experts in fact possessed the highest expertise in such cases, and that it was normal or even essential to seek their advice when murders were not solved rapidly. This tended to promote the view that serial murder cases were almost ipso facto federal in nature, exactly the view that the Justice Department had been at such pains to cultivate in the early 1980s.

APPENDIX: RECENT FICTION DEALING
WITH SERIAL MURDER

It is freely admitted that this listing is impressionistic rather than comprehensive, and it certainly understates the number of relevant texts from the 1970s. However, there is no doubt of the rapid expansion of the serial murder theme in novels from the late 1980s onwards. I have also excluded books on the original Jack the Ripper case, which represent a distinct subgenre. In each case, the first date cited refers to a book's first publication. The second date indicates the edition consulted here.

Author	Date	Title
I. 1972–1987		
Sanders, Lawrence	([1972] 1980)	*The First Deadly Sin*
Campbell, Ramsey	([1979] 1985)	*The Face That Must Die*
Kienzle, William	([1979] 1989)	*The Rosary Murders*
Stevens, Shane	([1979] 1990)	*By Reason of Insanity*
Harris, Thomas	([1981] 1990)	*Red Dragon*
Sanders, Lawrence	([1981] 1982)	*The Third Deadly Sin*
Woods, Stuart	([1981] 1987)	*Chiefs*
Rule, Ann	([1983] 1984)	*Possession*
Slade, Michael	([1984] 1986)	*Headhunter*
McBain, Ed	([1984] 1985)	*Lightning*
Ackroyd, Peter	(1985)	*Hawksmoor*
Eckert, Allan W.	([1985] 1986)	*The Scarlet Mansion*
Ellroy, James,	(1986)	*Silent Terror*
Schutz, Benjamin	(1986)	*Embrace the Wolf*
Kellerman, Jonathan	(1987)	*Over the Edge*
Clark, Mark	([1987] 1989)	*Ripper*
Slade, Michael	([1987] 1989)	*Ghoul*
II. 1988–1993		
Harris, Thomas	([1988] 1989)	*The Silence of the Lambs*
Izzi, Eugene	(1988)	*The Eighth Victim*
James, P. D.	([1988] 1989)	*Devices and Desires*
Kellerman, Jonathan	([1988] 1989)	*The Butcher's Theater*
Montecino, Marcel	([1988] 1989)	*The Cross-Killer*
Parker, Robert B.	(1988)	*Crimson Joy*
Pearson, Ridley	([1988] 1989)	*Undercurrents*
Straub, Peter	([1988] 1989)	*Koko*
Duncan, Robert L.	([1989] 1990)	*The Serpent's Mark*
Harvey, James Neal	([1989] 1990)	*By Reason of Insanity*
Lieberman, Herbert	([1989] 1990)	*Shadow Dancers*
Sandford, John	([1989] 1990)	*Rules of Prey*
Cornwell, Patricia	([1990] 1991)	*Post-Mortem*
Dorner, Marjorie	([1990] 1992)	*Freeze Frame*
Lindsey, David L.	([1990] 1991)	*Mercy*
Pearson, Ridley	([1990] 1991)	*Probable Cause*
Sandford, John	([1990] 1991)	*Shadow Prey*
Straub, Peter	([1990] 1991)	*Mystery*
Caunitz, William J.	([1991] 1992)	*Exceptional Clearance*
Ellis, Bret Easton	(1991)	*American Psycho*
Goldberg, Leonard S.	([1991] 1992)	*Deadly Medicine*
Harvey, James Neal	([1991] 1992)	*Painted Ladies*

(continued)

Author	Date	Title
Kane, Larry	(1991)	*Naked Prey*
LaPlante, Lynda	([1991] 1993)	*Prime Suspect*
Sandford, John	1992	*Eyes of Prey*
Martin, David	(1991)	*Lie To Me*
Wiltse, David	([1991] 1992)	*Prayer for the Dead*
Clark, Mary Higgins	(1992)	*Loves Music, Loves to Dance*
Coram, Robert	([1992] 1993)	*Running Dead*
Cornwell, Patricia D.	([1992] 1993)	*All That Remains*
Craig, Kit	(1992)	*Gone*
De Noux, O'Neil	(1992)	*Crescent City Kills*
Kerr, Philip	([1992] 1993)	*A Philosophical Investigation*
King, Charles	([1992] 1993)	*Mama's Boy*
McAllister, Casey	([1992] 1993)	*Catch Me If You Can*
Papazoglou, Orania	([1992] 1993)	*Charisma*
Patti, Paul	(1992)	*Death Mate*
Pearson, Ridley	([1992] 1993)	*The Angel Maker*
Perry, Michael R.	(1992)	*The Stranger Returns*
Sandford, John	([1992] 1993)	*Silent Prey*
Van Arman, Derek	([1992] 1993)	*Just Killing Time*
Walker, Robert W.	(1992)	*Killer Instinct*
Wetlaufer, Suzy	([1992] 1993)	*Judgment Call*
Blake, Sterling	(1993)	*Chiller*
Cornwell, Patricia D.	(1993)	*Cruel and Unusual*
Girard, James Preston	(1993)	*The Late Man*
Heffernan, William	(1993)	*Scarred*
Hill, Carol DeChellis	(1993)	*Henry James' Midnight Song*
Hunter, Jessie Prichard	(1993)	*Blood Music*
Kimball, Stephen	(1993)	*Red Days*
Koontz, Dean	(1993)	*Dragon Tears*
LaPlante, Lynda	(1993)	*Prime Suspect 2*
Lindsey, David L.	(1993)	*Body of Truth*
Margolin, Phillip	(1993)	*Gone But Not Forgotten*
Martini, Steve	(1993)	*Prime Witness*
McGuire, Christine	(1993)	*Until Proven Guilty*
Monninger, Joe	(1993)	*Razor's Song*
Parker, T. Jefferson	(1993)	*Summer of Fear*
Patterson, James	(1993)	*Along Came a Spider*
Pearson, Ridley	(1993)	*The Angel Maker*
Sandford, John	(1993)	*Winter Prey*
Straub, Peter	(1993)	*The Throat*
Weaver, Michael	(1993)	*Impulse*
Huebner, Frederick D.	(1994)	*Methods of Evaluation*

Chapter 5

Serial Murder as Modern Mythology

Good versus evil. Heroes trapping monsters.
This isn't fantasy. It's life.
Capture a Pinnacle True Crime today
—Advertising slogan for Pinnacle Books

The appeal of serial murder stories is not difficult to understand. A true-life case is likely to offer what is generally recognized as the material of high drama, with a peculiarly vicious and dangerous villain being pursued and (usually) apprehended by the forces of order (Lesser 1993). An offender can be characterized in various ways, as representing either objective moral evil or an extreme pathological condition, but in either instance a writer or journalist can explore extreme states of thought and existence. Accounts of the crimes can be taken at various levels. They offer a certain amount of intellectual interest, in terms of a psychological case study and an authentic police procedural; but in addition, cases have a great potential for emotional popular appeal, as they depict at the most basic level Manichaean conflicts between good and evil.

Other aspects of the appeal of such books and films are more controversial, and more disturbing. There have long been controversies about the violent and sexually sadistic nature of the material, and the degree to which both fact and fiction depict or even extol violence against women. The serial murder theme does owe some of its success to its sexual and sensationalistic content, but it also reflects ideas and mythological images that long predate the recognition of the phenomenon of multiple homicide. Serial murder can in fact be presented as a remarkably rich system of contemporary mythology in which the killers fulfill the symbolic roles that would in earlier societies have been taken by a wide variety of imaginary villains and folk-devils. This chapter will discuss the images and stereotypes that permeate contemporary depictions of serial murder.

THE APPEAL OF THE GENRE: THE SEXUAL ELEMENT

The sexual component of both fact and fiction about serial murder has given rise to considerable public debate and concern, and it has been charged that the obvious focus on sexually oriented violence appeals to a prurient interest in bizarre sexuality, and perhaps even reflects a concealed or sublimated desire to participate in such activities. The use of the cinematic "I-camera" to witness the crimes through the killer's eyes suggests that men in the audience are being invited to identify with the criminal (though this simplistic view has been effectively challenged by Clover, 1992).

In the early 1980s, one theory was that the films reflected male desires for vicarious revenge against women, who had attained such significant social and political gains during recent years. Psychoanalytic critics argue that fears of "sex pollution" are especially likely to be manifested in eras when male dominance seems under the greatest threat, and that extreme violence may be a predictable response to such unease (Modleski 1988:111). Such a position is especially attractive when dealing with work from the early part of the century, and the ripper figure in early German culture often serves as a manifestation of revenge against the unchecked and aggressive sexuality of Lulu, the liberated bisexual woman (Green and Swan 1993:6–7, 33–34, 140–42, 197–98). In Hitchcock's original *Lodger*, the ripper is renamed the Avenger. In the slasher films of the 1980s, the women who fell victim to the masked killer were usually those who had been depicted as the most promiscuous, with the implication that their deaths represented condign punishment.

The slasher films were all the more contentious because these works were specifically targeted at teenagers, with the audience usually indicated by the use of a phrase in the title suggesting school or teenage activities, such as Halloween, graduation day, slumber party, Valentine party, or hell night. The stories also capitalized on themes and folktales popular among the young, and recounted familiar urban legends and campfire stories about escaped maniacs, bad or haunted places, and vengeful spirits (Goode 1992:303–43; Brunvand 1981, 1984). For young people, the films were said to be attractive because they offered a dare, an opportunity to demonstrate the courage to view such a frightening work. For couples, the popular assumption was that such films offered the opportunity for the girl to seek protection and reassurance from her date.

The appeal to the young probably contributed to one of the most controversial aspects of the genre: the almost invariable association between violence and sexual activity or nudity. In commercial terms, this largely arose from an accident of the film rating system. For a slasher film, it was vital to have an R (restricted) rating, which indicated a considerable degree of violence and sexual activity, but not enough to earn an X, which by 1980 invariably denoted a hard-core pornographic work. R films were widely shown and attractive to a large audience, while X releases were increasingly restricted to specialized adult cinemas, often confined to major metropolitan areas. Ironically, X films by this date were almost entirely free of violence.

Even more damaging than an X or no rating was the simple PG (parental guidance), indicating that a film was suitable for young teenagers and most children. A PG film was unlikely to be frightening, and thus would not attract an older audience. However, there was a guaranteed technique of obtaining an R rating, as censors were flexible about the amount of violence that might be acceptable for a PG film, but were relatively strict about allowing no nudity. In other words, nudity was a guaranteed way of assuring that a film would attract an R, even if the actual violence would not do so of itself. The consequence was that any violent film seeking commercial success was obliged to include sexual content to obtain the necessary rating.

But the equation between violence and sexuality was disturbing, especially for feminist theorists who suggested that such fictional works contributed to real-life crimes against women. In England, there were feminist demonstrations against the showing of *Dressed to Kill* and *The Shining*, both of which were relatively serious contributions. Virtually all the victims depicted in slasher movies were young, and while male victims were shown, the most dramatic set-piece incidents always involved young women, generally in a state of undress. It is noteworthy that slasher films never depict a killer who chooses children or elderly people as victims, never a homosexual killer attacking young men, or a skid row slasher targeting vagrants. Supposedly such a theme would appear too unacceptably perverted or sordid for the presumed audience, while the attacks on teenage girls would be seen as exciting. One 1980 film, *Cruising*, did indeed depict a gay serial killer, but this was radically different from the slasher genre. In addition, the mode of killing in most of the films usually involved slashing or stabbing, which is commonly seen as a surrogate for sexual activity.

In this context, it is useful to compare the slasher films of the early 1980s with *Henry: Portrait of a Serial Killer* (made in 1986, released in 1990), a heavily fictionalized version of the Henry Lee Lucas affair. In *Henry*, the murderer kills in a variety of ways, but one of the methods most commonly seen in the film involves breaking the neck of the victim. The work involves quite as much nudity and extreme violence as a slasher film, but it attracted none of the same youthful audience, who were said to be repelled by the grimly serious tone of the story, and the unglamorous methods of the violence. Significantly, the makers of *Henry* had to struggle to avoid an X rating, which would have been commercially disastrous. The corollary would appear to be that the earlier R-rated films had been attractive because of their sexy or exciting qualities, and even because of their lighthearted attitude to the violence.

The most egregious commercial use of sexual violence occurs in the detective magazines, which generally treat multiple sexual homicide as their topic of major concern. A survey of magazine covers suggested that "the most common image . . . was that of a woman in an inferior or submissive position. . . . [O]ther repetitive cover imagery included violent struggles, brassieres, guns, accentuated breasts, strangulation, corpses, blood and knives or other cutting instruments" (Dietz et al. 1986:199). Such magazines "juxtapose conventionally erotic imagery . . . with images of violence and suffering" (p. 207). These magazines can serve as what Dietz et al. have described as "pornography for sexual sadists" (p. 197).

"Lovely Victims"

Similar remarks can be made about the appeal of true-crime books. Of course, these vary greatly in tone and content, and there certainly are well-written accounts that seek to be scholarly and analytical. Some of them are among the most valuable resources available on the issue of serial homicide (see, for example, Cauffiel 1993; Olsen 1993; McDougal 1992). In terms of the genre, however, the tone of the audience appeal is almost always sensationalistic and prurient, rather than serious or academic, and this is most evident from the cover blurbs, which are intended to attract the interest of prospective purchasers. It might well be that the authors themselves have little sympathy for the way in which publishers emphasize these elements of the cases, but it can scarcely be denied that this cover material reflects the assumed interests of the market.

The vast majority of such books appear in cheap paperback editions, usually with a similar physical appearance. Red and black predominate for cover illustration, and the content of the work is suggested by titles incorporating a word related to death, evil, or darkness: *Rites of Burial*, *Dracula Killer*, *Red Ripper*, *Blood Lust*, and so on (see Table 4.4). Most books include photographs of offenders and victims, and generally include crime scene pictures, often of murder victims.

Particularly instructive here are the cover blurbs, which almost invariably promise accounts of extreme horror, with a particular emphasis on sexual atrocities, and on the youth and attractiveness of the victims.

With few exceptions, the crimes are presented as "brutal" or "sadistic," while the victims are "lovely" or "stunning," a choice of words that is curious unless the account is in some way intended to provide a degree of sexual excitement. Typical here is *The Beauty Queen Killer*, an account of Christopher Wilder. The cover announces, "To the stunning young model, the innocent college girl, the police captain's beautiful daughter and all the others, he didn't look like a killer. . . . They were all attractive, vulnerable and ambitious" (Gibney 1990). The cover of *To Kill and Kill Again*, a study of Montana killer Wayne Nance, similarly focuses on the youth and beauty of the victims: "A young girl's battered body . . . a preacher's wife brutally raped and murdered . . . a pretty teenage hitchhiker mysteriously missing . . . unspeakable acts of sexual depravity and sadistic murder" (Coston 1992).

The cover to the 1988 edition of Ann Rule's *Lust Killer* begins, "One by one the young women vanished without a trace," and then itemizes the victims, giving each a "sexy" epithet such as "pretty Linda Slawson" or "lovely college girl Jan Whitney." One victim is a "beautiful pre-med honor student," another is "stunningly attractive." Ted Bundy's victims "were all young, bright and beautiful" (Rule 1980). *In His Garden* tells the story of a series of murders in the 1960s on Cape Cod, and the front cover promises "the chilling truth about the charming serial killer and four lovely victims" (Damore [1981] 1990). The cover of *Mortal Remains* tells of the discovery of "the first victim . . . the petite teenage girl was bound at the wrists and ankles with fishing twine. She'd been stabbed and bludgeoned" (Scammell 1992). *True Detective* typically reported the 1966 murders committed by Richard Speck under the title "Eight girls, all pretty, all nurses, all slain."

The blurb to *Fair Game*, an account of Robert Hansen, includes all the common key words. The victims are "young and naive," "terrified." Hansen is "twisted," "the savage hunter," "depraved," "notorious": "He terrorized his hapless prey, then raped and murdered them." The situation is a "nightmare," "shocking." The cover matter of *Blood Lust* tells how Dayton Leroy Rogers "abducted women, forced them into sadistic bondage games, and thrilled in their pain and mutilation" (King 1992). The various themes are neatly epitomized by the cover advertising an account of the Hillside Stranglers: "Young . . . beautiful . . . dead. Twelve women violated and brutally murdered" (O'Brien 1987).

It might be argued that all the statements offered here are literally true, in that the killers were indeed sadistic, the crimes did involve rape and mutilation, and the women victims might have been lovely or beautiful; but this does not entirely explain why these themes are so strongly emphasized. In this context, it is instructive to compare these accounts of heterosexual killers and rapists with books on homosexual serial murderers or child-killers. There are works on these individuals, but it is inconceivable that such an account would emphasize that the young male victims were handsome, tall, or brilliant, still less "lovely."

The only adjectives used consistently for these victims refer to age, like the "twenty-nine teenage boys, all brutally tortured, violated and strangled" by John Wayne Gacy (Cahill 1986) or the "seventeen young men" killed by Jeffrey Dahmer (Dvorchak and Holewa 1991). One rare exception to this is the study of Randy Kraft, which describes his "dozens of innocent victims"; but there is no hint on the cover that the victims were in fact all male (McDougal 1992). In such a homosexual context, the emphasis shifts from the victims to the nature of the bizarre atrocities committed by killers like Dahmer: "body parts in the freezer . . . twisted sexuality . . . torture . . . cannibalism" (Dvorchak and Holewa 1991).

THE MANIPULATION OF FEAR

However, the appeal of serial murder is far more complex than simple prurience. Even if we make the crude and questionable assumption that the books and films invite identification with the killer, it is still necessary to explain why these works place so much emphasis on stimulating and manipulating the fears of the audience, and why, moreover, the most commercially successful works are exactly those which provide the greatest scares. The covers of these books generally use laudatory quotes from reviews, suggesting that the work is "genuinely frightening" (*By Reason of Insanity*), "cold sweat chills . . . delicious shudders" (*Shadow Dancers*), "thoroughly chilling" (*The Serpent's Mark*), offering an experience "more profound than terror" (*The Silence of the Lambs*). The paradox of such a marketing appeal is epitomized by the sign that appears at the start of the film of *The Silence of the Lambs*, in which FBI trainees are exhorted with the words, "Hurt, Agony, Pain—Love It" (compare Clover 1992).

Both books and films on the theme of serial murder are obviously intended to evoke fear. This appeal has given rise to much scholarly discussion, chiefly in the context of fictional works of horror or suspense, and it is useful here to compare the true-crime accounts with the many supernaturally oriented stories of horror or fantasy that have enjoyed such great popularity since the late 1970s. Horror stories provide the reader with the opportunity to explore extreme states of behavior or consciousness, but usually with the certainty that the events portrayed cannot happen. In a sense, the reader takes an intellectual vacation in the fantasy created by the author, in the knowledge that the process of return is easy and secure. The required suspension of disbelief is temporary and reversible.

The true-crime books, in contrast, provide no such assurance that the horror cannot occur, and the fear generated is meant to be all the more intense because it approximates more closely to real life and thus could potentially happen. These books emphasize quite unsubtly that the threats are real and can strike at any time. A book on Westley Alan Dodd concluded with this passage:

> Meanwhile, until such time that predators like Dodd can be effectively removed from our midst, society *must* remain aware that there are other Westley Alan Dodds out there at this very moment, lurking in the shadows and waiting for just the right moment to strike. (King 1993:333)

The "lurking" threat was all the more terrifying because the enemy was not easily recognized by obvious warning signs such as a wild or demented expression. Especially during the panic of the mid-1980s, the emphasis was repeatedly on the apparent normality of such killers, who could easily be a person one knew well, without ever realizing their intrinsic evil. Van Arman's novel *Just Killing Time* ([1992] 1993) warns that serial killers "are the people you meet at the PTA or Little League. They ride the bus with you, your children play with their children, they may even break bread with you at family gatherings" (p. 19). Advertising material for the True Crime Book Club begins with the words: "A blood-chilling scream in the night. Your quiet neighbor arrested for murder. Why? Find the fascinating answers inside."

The language of concealed evil recurs frequently. Ted Bundy, for example, was *The Stranger Beside Me*, while a 1984 film tells of *The Boys Next Door* who were serial killers. In the television documentary *Murder: No Apparent Motive*, David Berkowitz was "an ordinary-looking postal worker"; Wayne Williams was "a soft-spoken business man"; Albert De Salvo was "a married man with two children"; "all normal looking—all men." They are "like your next door neighbor—people you would not suspect." They are "Monsters Like Us," to use the title of a recent CNN documentary series. A new collection of sketches of such killers is aptly entitled *Murder Next Door* (Baumann and O'Brien 1993).

The appeal to fear appears paradoxical, but it can be explained if it is placed in the context of what we might call the underlying mythology of the genre. The books postulate the existence of extremely dangerous and threatening individuals who undertake the worst crimes imaginable; but there are also factors that make these crimes perhaps less threatening than everyday crime, and that counteract their threat potential. Violent crime in this context is linked to a handful of very evil individuals, and understanding this menace is perhaps less difficult than comprehending the diverse factors (social, economic, educational) that drive the faceless robbers and murderers of real life. Crime can thus be personalized in the form of a Westley Alan Dodd or a Ted Bundy. Once such an individual has been identified, he can be fought, defeated, and captured, by whatever means are appropriate. As Bundy himself remarked, "For that matter, for people to want to condemn someone, to dehumanize someone like me, is a very popular and effective way of dealing with a fear and a threat that is just incomprehensible" ("Condemned Killer" 1986).

Moreover, in these works multiple homicide can be comprehended with a certainty that is lacking in real life. There are very few authentic cases where it can be said with certainty that we know the exact number of killings associated with a particular offender, or if in fact a genuine series even existed. In contrast, readers of a novel or true-crime study are permitted the illusion that they can observe the actions of the killer from within, so that there is never serious doubt about matters like an individual's guilt or the scale of his or her crimes. Portraying the evil of a serial killer thus makes the conceptualization of crime more manageable, simpler, and perhaps ultimately less rather than more frightening. This is especially true with potentially complex phenomena such as the disappearance or maltreatment of children, which are far easier to comprehend if they can be visualized in terms of the depredations of a few (or even a few hundred) pedophile serial killers.

Moreover, virtually all the books and films on serial murder portray not only the actions of the villains themselves, but also of the heroic police, detectives, or criminologists who pursue and (almost invariably) apprehend them. Where the greatest villains are involved, it is only natural that the agents of society should be presented as uniquely able, courageous, and skilled, an idealization that is most apparent in recent accounts of the mind-hunters of the BSU. Even with books that address unsolved cases, the emphasis is still on the complex mechanics of the process of detection, and the ways in which the forces of rationality and law repeatedly approach their criminal quarry (see, for example, Ginsburg 1993; Smith and Guillen 1990; McIntyre 1988). In terms of the genre, one of the many sins committed by the extraordinary film *Henry: Portrait of a Serial Killer* was the failure to provide any suggestion that the villain would or could be apprehended. There was no good or rational character to provide a point of identification for the viewer, and it was this amorality that was cited by video stores and cinemas that refused to rent or show this film, even though they were prepared to accept the casual slaughter of a *Friday the Thirteenth* installment.

Nor does the vast majority of serial murder fiction pay attention to the element of pure chance that continues to play an enormous role in the apprehension of serial killers. Years after VICAP became operational, the typical case is still usually discovered by luck, and through arrests made by officers who have no idea they are dealing with a serious offender. A characteristic instance occurred on Long Island in 1993, when Joel Rifkin was stopped by police for driving without a license plate. The car was found to be carrying the decomposing remains of one of his estimated seventeen victims, a series hitherto unrecognized by law enforcement. Erratic driving led to Randy Kraft being detained by California Highway Patrol officers. The body they observed in his passenger seat was the last of forty or more victims. In 1992, William Lester Suff was detained in California for making an illegal U-turn, then found to be wanted for a parole violation. Further investigation linked him to some of the nineteen unsolved murders in Riverside County. Cases like those of Jeffrey Dahmer or Gary Heidnik were uncovered fortuitously when neighbors complained about noise and smell emanating from their properties.

Forensic skills and behavioral science play no role in such authentic cases, though they might be useful in the retroactive reconstruction of the crimes. In contrast, serial murder fiction almost invariably depicts the chesslike intellectual pursuit by which a killer is gradually identified and apprehended, and little is left to accidental discovery. Nor, of course, do the films or novels reflect the real-life instances where forensic and behavioral analyses have simply been misleading or utterly wrong. To acknowledge such exceptions would be to subvert the discourse of rationality on which the fiction depends, and through which order is imposed upon an otherwise inexplicable world.

CROSSING BOUNDARIES

"Between us and you there is a great gulf fixed" (Luke 16:26).

With few exceptions, serial murder books or films should be more properly described as studies of the suppression and control of serial murder, the triumph of reason and courage over chaos and evil. The conflict fits very naturally into a Freudian interpretation, with serial killers being portrayed in terms of the unchecked, lustful, and destructive qualities of the id, while the heroes who challenge and suppress them epitomize the controlled and rational forces of the superego. The triumph of rationality and the discourse of science is at its clearest in the case of Thomas Harris's mind-hunters, who perform tasks that fit well into the roles traditionally assigned to heroes and shamans in storytelling and mythmaking. They are agents of justice and science, but they gain wisdom by venturing into the cells of multiple killers, the hostile domain dominated by the rival forces of irrational violence and savagery. They do this in order to gain critical knowledge that will permit them to comprehend and defeat the forces of chaos still at large.

The process of boundary crossing is fundamental to many mythic systems, not least that of the American Western, of which Slotkin has written:

> The American must cross the border into Indian country and experience a regression to a more primitive and natural condition of life so that the false values of the "metropolis" can be purged and a new, purified, social contract enacted. . . . The heroes of this myth-historical quest must therefore be "men (or women) who know Indians"—characters whose experiences, sympathies and even allegiances fall on both sides of the frontier. . . . [T]hey are mediators of a double kind who can teach civilized men to defeat savagery on its native grounds—the natural wilderness, and the wilderness of the human soul. (Slotkin 1992:14)

Such journeys into Indian territory are often undertaken with the purpose of rescuing abducted captives, another point of resemblance between the Western and the serial murder genre.

In Thomas Harris's books and the related films, the boundaries between rationality and savagery are given literal form through the glass walls or metal cages used to restrain Hannibal Lecter, and to prevent him from attacking prison guards or hospital staff. In recent television news reports on serial murder, one of the most frequently employed visual images shows the caged Lecter in conversation with FBI agent Clarice Starling, the two being divided by the impenetrable glass wall. Even so, Sterling succeeds in forming a bond with Lecter, a link symbolized by the single physical contact of their hands. By her act of border crossing, she shows that she is what Slotkin terms a "woman who knows Indians," and therefore a fit heroine for this mythological scheme. Her achievement also fits her to rescue a captive who has fallen into the hands of the enemy. Conversely, the two guards who venture into Lecter's cell without the appropriate skill and preparation are killed and mutilated.

The same ideas of boundary emerge in a recent book on the FBI's BSU: "They think like a serial killer. They know his habits and his twisted fantasies. They walk the edge between good and evil, sanity and insanity" (Jeffers 1992). Detectives and mind-hunters undertake some personal risk by undertaking such interviews, in terms of physical violence, but also more subtly in the contamination they might acquire from the values and characters of such alien beings; and this ambiguity adds to the interest and complexity of the heroic figures.

The dangers of border crossing are a major theme in the interviews with the imprisoned Ted Bundy, and they helped make the book *The Only Living Witness* (Michaud and Aynesworth 1983) one of the most read works of true crime. Stephen Michaud remarks on Bundy's apparently separate personalities and notes that seeing the killer personality ("the hunchback") was like "the sight of a shark behind aquarium glass." The most frightening moments were those of unnatural rapport, as when Bundy declared, "You too, Steve, could make a successful mass killer. I really think you have it in you!" (p. 13).

Apart from *The Silence of the Lambs*, many works make use of such ambiguous heroes whose careers take them sufficiently into the realm of the insane villains to partake of their nature. The publicity for the film of Harris's *Manhunter* invites, "Enter the mind of a killer. You might never return." In *Cruising* (1980), it is implied that the detective hero who solves the murders has been so contaminated by his contacts with the violent underworld into which he has crossed that he himself has become an irrational killer. *Tightrope* (1984) follows a similar theme by suggesting throughout that the detective played by Clint Eastwood may himself be the multiple sex killer sought by police. The detective hero of Sandford's *Rules of Prey* ([1989] 1990) has in fact claimed more victims than the serial killer he defeats and kills, though unlike his opponent, he has always operated under the mask of legality. Such morally ambiguous depictions emphasize the extremely alien and dangerous quality of the enemy realm inhabited by the killers, and the iron reality of the frontier dividing the two worlds.

SERIAL MURDER AS MYTHIC SYSTEM

Serial murder fiction thus reduces a quite complex social and behavioral problem to a personalized, almost gladiatorial conflict between individual heroes and villains, and both sides are presented in accordance with very traditional images and stereotypes. If the hero is the border crosser, the virtuous avenger, then villains are usually represented in the most frightening and threatening manner conceivable, as totally other as can be imagined. In achieving such monstrous images, contemporary constructions of the serial murder phenomenon have much in common with mythological types from many different societies and eras.

These depictions evoke such profound responses because the image resonates as a universal and perhaps mythic symbol. In fact, the "highly ritualized and formulaic character" of serial murder fiction contributes to its "folk-tale" quality, "a set of fixed tale types that generate an endless stream of what are in effect variants: sequels, remakes and ripoffs" (Clover 1992:9–10; compare Hawkins 1993). Serial murder stories are so successful because they appeal to what are universal nightmares and fears, and (like all horror tales) they succeed because of an "engagement of repressed fears and desires and its re-enactment of the residual conflict surrounding those fears" (Clover 1992:11). This universality goes far toward explaining the success of the frightening imagery surrounding serial killers in contemporary culture (Stevens 1992; Goode 1992).

The concept of myth is useful in comprehending these patterns, using myth according to the definition of Alan Watts, as a symbolic story that demonstrates "the inner meaning of the universe and of human life." Such stories are created to explain the otherwise inexplicable phenomena of everyday life, and they thus tell us a great deal about the society that creates the mythology: its concerns and fears, its areas of knowledge and ignorance. In turn, the myths can have a huge influence in the real world, as the stories are repeatedly told and retold in order to reaffirm values and social solidarity.

Myths often supply ideal statements of what society should be, and generally serve a didactic purpose. For scholars like Durkheim or Dumézil, they represent an idealized commentary on social values and institutions, which are projected into a metaphysical realm. However, other myths present frightening or threatening images, which enhance social cohesion by warning of the dangers that will befall people if they fall short of correct values and ideals. Myths are especially likely to emerge or develop at times of perceived social crisis or strain, when social solidarity may be reinforced or restored by formulating heroic images to which society can aspire, or frightening folk-devils against which it can unite (Erikson 1966). Times of extreme crisis are likely to call forth the most stark and threatening constructions of the mythical Other. These dangerous outsiders fulfill a critical social function in defining conventional morality and behavior by providing a *ne plus ultra*, against which normal society readily finds common ground.

Moreover, such enemy or devil figures tend to follow similar patterns in the way they are constructed by cultures in many different times and places, so that they are sometimes viewed as archetypal. The exact nature of this Other changes according to time and place, and common devil-figures involve the night-hag, the ritual child-eater, or the predatory band of killers. In contemporary American culture, however, serial killers appear to have most of the characteristics generally ascribed to such external enemies. They provide a means for society to project its worst nightmares and fantasies, images that in other eras or other regions might well be fastened onto supernatural or imaginary folk-devils—vampires, werewolves, witches, evil sorcerers, conspiratorial Jews.

CRIMINALS, SAVAGES, AND APES

In constructing the characteristics of dangerous outsiders, tales and legends usually focus on their supposed inversion of normal culture, for example, in supposing that the out-group deliberately chooses to eat and drink the substances generally believed to be most noxious and revolting, and indulges in forms of sexual expression that normal people find most outrageous (Ginzburg 1991; Kuhn 1990; Hsia 1988; Cohn 1975; Erikson 1966). These nightmares are diverse in character, but one of the most persistent themes concerns what is perceived as the atavistic reversion to savagery or primitivism (Douglas 1993).

This atavistic response is a powerful theme that also appears in many human cultures during times of turmoil or insurrection. Such protests often draw on the symbolic vocabulary of inversion, of reversed behaviors such as transvestism or ritualized cannibalism and mutilation, actions by which the protagonists seek to show that the natural and just order has been subverted and nullified by injustice or corruption (Thompson 1991; Stam 1989:122–56; MacAloon 1984).

Images of primitivism, savagery, and the jungle (which often have powerful racial overtones) are frequently symbolized by the theme of cannibalism, which pervades the literature on serial murder. As Arens has discussed, "there is no more universally common way of distancing oneself from other people than to call them cannibals. It is one of the ultimate insults, one of the definitive signs of nonhumanity" (Arens 1979: quoted in Trinkaus and Shipman 1992: 105). It is commonly used as a rhetorical tactic for justifying the use of armed force against the group so stigmatized.

The Other is par excellence a cannibal, and the threat of reversion to this state was a common literary theme in stories of the European encounters with the outside world, from *Robinson Crusoe* to the Donner Party and the tales of wrecked sailors celebrated in Poe's *Narrative of Arthur Gordon Pym*, to the more recent tales of airline survivors in the Andes (Read 1979; Simpson 1984). The suggestion is that civilized behavior is only a thin veneer, which is all too readily abandoned once symbolic and geographic boundaries are crossed. Cannibalism was in its day the "ultimate evil," and the idea of reversion was a central theme of

Conrad's significantly entitled *The Heart of Darkness*, no less than Upton Sinclair's *The Jungle* (the term *heart of darkness* often occurs in accounts of serial murder, as in Drukteinis 1992).

The cannibal myth recurs in many different times and places—from the early Christians who were accused of incest and ritualized cannibalism, through the anti-Jewish blood-libel of the middle ages, and the purported deeds of witch-groups, whether European, African, or Chinese. In each case, children frequently feature as victims (Victor 1993:276–90; Hsia 1988, 1992; Eilberg-Schwartz 1990:37–41; Kuhn 1990; Cohn 1975). From a psychoanalytic perspective, it is customary to see such images as projections of repressed inner desires, for example, in the case of medieval legends of animalistic wild men and werewolves: "The wild man, both brutal and erotic, was a perfect projection of the repressed libidinous impulses of medieval man" (quoted in Lopez 1978:229). Historically, such figures were seen as denizens of the distant jungle or wilderness, but as each wilderness "was brought under control, the idea of the Wild Man was progressively despatialized. This despatialization was attended by a compensatory process of psychic interiorization" (Hayden White, quoted in Eilberg-Schwartz 1990:22).

Similar savage concepts have also been used for murderers and other conventional criminals, albeit veiled in the language of science. In the 1870s, Cesare Lombroso developed a highly influential theory explaining criminality through literal atavism, reversion to a prehuman state (Rennie 1978). He attempted to resolve

> the problem of the nature of the criminal—an atavistic being who reproduces in his person the ferocious instincts of primitive humanity and the inferior animals. Thus were explained anatomically the enormous jaws, high cheek bones, prominent superciliary arches, solitary lines in the palms, extreme size of the orbits, handle shaped ears found in criminals, savages and apes, insensibility to pain, extremely acute sight, tattooing, excessive idleness, love of orgies, and the irresponsible craving of evil for its own sake, the desire not only to extinguish life in the victim, but to mutilate the corpse, tear its flesh and drink its blood. (Lombroso, quoted in Gould 1981:124)

Such a creature was literally a monster who could be dealt with only by implacable social warfare. Criminals were "fierce and lubricious orangutans with human faces" (Hippolyte Taine, quoted in Gould 1981:139).

Atavism became a central theme in early-twentieth-century racial theory, when the nonwhite races were identified with the primitive qualities lurking inside the apparently civilized as a "heritage of our human, and even our prehuman, past. The Underman may be buried deep in the recesses of our being; but he is there, and psychoanalysis informs us of his latent power." Racial theorist Theodore L. Stoddard argued in the 1920s that this "primitive animality" was especially to be found in "the pauper, criminal and degenerate elements," but it might be expressed anywhere in a "distinct resurgence to the brute and the savage" (quoted in Slotkin 1992:200).

More recently, the most powerful and recurrent images of contemporary satanist atrocities include the cannibalism attributed to serial killers like Ottis Toole, and the boiling cauldrons of human remains allegedly left by the homicidal drug cult active at Matamoros, Mexico. The theme recalls the stereotypical cannibals encountered by missionaries in nineteenth-century Africa and featured in cartoons and comic books until quite recent years.

The Matamoros case offered an extraordinary powerful range of symbols and associations, which fully explains its tremendous national impact (see Chapter 10). The incident involved the abduction of a normal and innocent young American to be carried across the literal and metaphorical border into a realm of cannibalism and primitive paganism (Linedecker 1990b; Schutze 1989). In fact, one of the earliest true-crime studies of the case is simply entitled *Across the Border* (Provost 1989; for the enduring symbolic significances of the Mexican border, see Slotkin 1992). The incorrect description of the alien rites as voodoo indicates the profound ethnic and racial tensions implicit in the affair (Green 1991). Quite similar images emerged from the Dahmer case, with its tales of boiling skulls, and hearts extracted for consumption. This affair even involved alleged attempts to turn victims into zombies, a term that again evokes images of voodoo and jungle rituals (Stingl 1992; compare Tallant 1946).

WOLVES AND LAMBS

Outside the ritual domain, these images pervade those murder cases that have had the deepest social impact in terms of the number of legends, rumors, and jokes they have evoked: the case of Ed Gein in the 1950s, Jeffrey Dahmer in the 1990s. The Gein story generated literally hundreds of jokes ("Gein-ers"), with the focus overwhelmingly on the cannibalistic aspects. Typical examples include the alleged remark of Gein to the sheriff who arrested him: "Have a heart"; or the saying that Gein "could not operate his farm, as all he had left was a skeleton crew" (Gollmar 1989:203–6). Within days of the discovery of the Dahmer case, very similar jokes proliferated, and there was a lively commerce in these lines on electronic mail and computer networks. ("Jeffrey Dahmer got bail—but it cost him an arm and a leg"; "roommate wanted—some assembly required"). However, this sort of joke is recorded in many other instances of multiple murder, and a version of the "arm and a leg" joke had been told about Antone Costa in the late 1960s (Vonnegut 1975).

Such a humorous response is a measure of the disquiet caused by such a case, and it reflects the deeply felt need to release fears and tensions inspired by the collective horror, feelings that would otherwise have been repressed with pernicious consequences. Moreover, the jokes occur in a communal aspect:

> An alliance is formed between those who laugh and the laughter becomes a group situation. . . . This unifying pact strengthens the tie between the people, but at the same time, the controlling and inhibiting function of the individual can become restricted or loosened. Thus in the identification with the group and with the common aggression, grim humor can be released under the support of group sanction. (Arndt, in Gollmar 1981:210)

Exactly the same analysis can be offered for the adoption of grotesque cases into children's rhymes and folksongs, which have at various times celebrated Jack the Ripper and Fritz Haarmann [Fritz would "make you into red chopped meat" (Plant 1986:48)]. In rumor and urban legend, the cannibal threat is often presented as a collective danger, so that the stereotypical "they" are plotting to drain "our" blood or eat "our" flesh, the groups in conflict often being presented in racial terms. Turner (1993) points out how frequently "blood-draining" or blood contamination motifs feature in black urban legends, for example, in the context of the Atlanta Child Murders (see Chapter 8).

The cannibal theme is regularly suggested by nicknames or titles bestowed upon killers, such as butcher (Gilmour and Hale 1991) and of course ripper. Both Clifford Olson and Robert Hansen have been dubbed butchers. Primitivism is here used to suggest a thorough dehumanization on the part of both the perpetrator who becomes atavistic savage, and the victim, who is reduced to meat-animal. The alleged victims of Dorothea Puente constituted a *Human Harvest*. The serial killer "selects his [or her] victims like ripe tomatoes in a grocery store . . . [he or she] devours, savors and digests each victim before reaching out to pluck up another" (McDougal 1992:xii). By inviting the reader to participate in a masochistic fantasy of utter passivity and powerlessness, this language greatly enhances the fear and danger inherent in the offense.

In the cinema, butchery for the purposes of cannibalism is hinted at in the influential *Texas Chainsaw Massacre*, and made explicit in the second film in that series. In 1973, the German film *Tenderness of the Wolves* appeared, which depicted 1920s serial killer Fritz Haarmann as even worse than a wolf: He was "a human vampire who picked up boys, molested them sexually and drained their blood. He then used their bones in soup and sold their flesh to a local butcher shop for sausage meat" (Russo 1981:239). Some critics stress the subtler but nevertheless potent elements of symbolic cannibalism in other films about serial murder, especially Hitchcock's *Frenzy*, where it is connected to other disturbing sexual themes (Modleski 1988:106–9).

The human butchery theme is suggested by the title of *The Silence of the Lambs*. The phrase has quite complex origins in terms of the narrative, but at least one level of meaning evokes the lamblike passivity of the (female) victims assailed by the wolflike killers Hannibal Lecter and Buffalo Bill; and Bill draws heavily on the real-life Ed Gein. The title has been repeatedly imitated, for example, in a recent study of a British pedophile murder ring, where the child victims become *Lambs to the Slaughter* (Oliver and Smith 1993). A multiple–child murder case in Michigan is studied in the book *Wolf in Sheep's Clothing* (McIntyre 1988). Of course, the innocence of the lambs or sheep also has inevitable religious connotations, in which the predators acquire diabolic associations. In terms of gender issues, it might be suggested that this predator/prey theme goes far toward explaining the recurring theme of the (male) killer assailing the female victim: "The functions of monster and hero are far more frequently represented by males and the function of victim far more garishly by females" (Clover 1992:12).

Concepts of primitivism and animal savagery pervade the literature on serial murder, most strikingly in the imagery of predation and hunting commonly found in book titles and blurbs. The phrase *hunting humans* was coined by the mass killer James Huberty, but it has since become the title of two books on the theme of serial murder (Leyton 1986; Newton 1990). One account of Alaska serial killer Robert Hansen is entitled *Fair Game*, and the book describes the offender "snaring his quarry and gunning them down" (DuClos 1993). The souvenirs which many killers retain of their victims are often described as trophies, and Norman Bates's taxidermic interests derived from the real-life Ed Gein (compare Goleman 1991). *Stalk* is another potent word, as in the case of Californian serial killer Richard Ramirez, the Night Stalker. In the early 1990s, there was intense media and political concern about the perceived threat from irrational men who relentlessly pursued women, the chase often culminating in acts of murder. The response was to be found in so-called stalker legislation.

This animalistic theme is often quite overt, suggested, for example, by the superhuman sense of smell evinced by Hannibal Lecter; and Hawkins (1993) points out the origins of the Lecter/Starling relationship in the prototypical fairy tale "Beauty and the Beast." A serial killer is a "beast," or "subhuman": the original Jack the Ripper was a "nameless reprobate, half-beast, half-man" (quoted in Walkowitz 1982). These images were freely applied to individuals such as Peter Sutcliffe, the Yorkshire Ripper, who "like the marauding animal he was, he needed a fresh killing" (Bland 1992:250). Modern serial killers *are* beasts of prey, in the most precise sense. They stalk through modern cities like a hungry tiger, completely indifferent to the fear and suffering of their victims" (Wilson 1988:405–6, emphasis in original). Killers, like wild beasts, go on rampages.

Conversely, such predatory monsters must be hunted down, and we read of investigators being engaged in *Mindhunting the Serial Killers* (Clark and Morley 1993), *The Hunt for a Serial Killer* (Ginsburg 1993), and even *Hunting the Devil* (Lourie 1993). This imagery is often taken to remarkable pseudoscientific lengths, so that one supporter of a draconian law against sexual predators wrote,

> Chronic sexual predators have crossed an osmotic membrane. They can't step back to the other side—our side. And they don't want to. If we don't kill them or release them, we have but one choice. Call them monsters and isolate them. . . . I've spoken to many predators over the years. They always exhibit amazement that we do not hunt them. And that when we capture them, we eventually let them go. Our attitude is a deliberate interference with Darwinism—an endangerment of our species. (Andrew Vachss 1993)

These concepts culminate in the term *monster*, a word that still retains something of its original implications of supernatural origins. The memoirs of the FBI's serial murder expert Robert Ressler are entitled *Whoever Fights Monsters*, while Jerry Brudos "killed like a sadistic monster" (Rule 1983a). In 1981, the *New York Post* headlined the arrest of Wayne Williams with the words "Atlanta Monster Seized"; in 1993, the same paper offered a "Portrait of a Monster," in this case, Joel Rifkin. This usage reached a remarkable climax in 1992, when PBS's quality documentary series "Frontline" gave the title "Monsters among Us" to a study of sexually violent offenders like Westley Dodd.

SUPERNATURAL INTERPRETATIONS OF SERIAL MURDER

The only hyperbole that lies beyond *monster* is a supernaturally oriented term like *demon* or *devil*, which occurs, for example, in the context of "the demon brothers of LA" (Crockett 1990:430). The image recurs frequently: "the specter of serial killers traveling from city to city to stalk prostitutes" (Squitieri 1990); Charlie Hatcher was "the incarnation of pure evil" (Ganey 1989).

This terminology pervades the literature of both fact and fiction, often in association with concepts such as possession. In terms of the fictional accounts, demonological ideas often result from the familiar device of telling the story through the voice of the killer, and presenting his delusions in a first-person narrative. These often take a religious form, and the book therefore emphasizes supernatural and demonological themes. In *Red Dragon*, for instance, we constantly see the killer through his own perspective as a supernatural creature identified with a figure in the Book of Revelation.

Supernatural interpretations are also likely given the common literary device of portraying a fictional killer through his multiple personalities, none of which are fully known to the conscious ego. This device was pioneered in Hogg's classic *Confessions of a Justified Sinner*, and has more recently been used in novels such as *Ghoul*, *Ripper* and *Shadow Dancers*, as well as Stephen King's story "Strawberry Spring," and of course the film *Psycho*. The key to the plot is thus the killer's psychopathology, but the story line lends itself easily to the interpretation of the homicidal personality as a form of demonic possession, the theme employed by Hogg. This idea is present in Bloch's *The Scarf* (1947), in which the killer knows, "Something was waiting, watching there inside him, something of which he never dared be unaware."

Some recent accounts even take this suggestion of diabolism or possession literally, and at this stage we can speak quite literally of the lethal outsiders as folk-devils. By the 1980s, the traditional demon images had become thoroughly assimilated to their modern counterparts, so that serial killer Richard Trenton Chase was termed the Dracula Killer, while Wayne Boden became the Vampire Rapist. A review prominently quoted (in red type on black background) on the back cover of a book on Randy Kraft remarks, "To open this book is to open a peephole into Hell" (McDougal 1992). Kraft is given the sobriquet, the Angel of Darkness; Donald Harvey had been the Angel of Death.

It is perhaps inevitable that the concept of serial murder is now being employed retroactively to construct and explain menaces and monsters from earlier history that had once been dismissed as purely supernatural (Douglas 1993). There have been scholarly attempts to assess "the historical similarity of twentieth century serial sexual homicide to pre-twentieth century occurrences of vampirism" (Brown 1991b). The notion that werewolf tales may trace their origin to the activities of serial killers was suggested by Russell (1978), and it has been widely accepted; but many recent accounts accept these accounts of the early trials of such demon figures without due recognition of the extensive torture and leading questioning required to elucidate these confessions of brutality and cannibalism (Douglas 1993; Oates 1988). The linkage remains uncertain, though a major television news documentary on serial murder shown in 1993 suggested strongly that historical accounts of werewolves and vampires originated with mistaken interpretations of the work of serial killers (CNN, *Murder by Number*, January 1993). If serial killers were not literally monsters, they were as close to the reality as could be conceived within the intellectual framework of a scientific age.

The cultural imagery applied to serial killers from the late 1970s had decisively shifted toward portrayals of monsters, savage animalistic beings at war with society. As such, they had come to represent an evil force that was at best difficult to comprehend, and that could be dealt with only by forceful policing and constant vigilance. They were depicted as the purest conceivable examples of moral evil, and as such could be employed as a powerful recurrent theme in contemporary social and political rhetoric.

Chapter 6

The Social Critique:
"The Kind of Society We Have Now"

Richard Slotkin has suggested how social and political mythology is often encapsulated in highly charged phrases, such as *the Frontier* or *Pearl Harbor*:

> Over time, through frequent retellings and deployments as a source of interpretive metaphors, the original mythic story is increasingly conventionalized and abstracted until it is reduced to a deeply encoded and resonant set of symbols, "icons," "keywords" or historical cliches. In this form, myth becomes a basic constituent of linguistic meaning and of the processes of both personal and social "remembering." Each of these mythic icons is in effect a poetic construction of tremendous economy and compression and a mnemonic device capable of evoking a complex system of historical associations by a single image or phrase. (Slotkin 1992:5–6)

Individuals or criminal cases can also carry such associations, and names like Ted Bundy or Matamoros can thus have an ideological or mythic significance far beyond their real importance. This chapter will suggest some of the ways in which such images have been employed by various political perspectives and interest groups as symbolic weapons in their particular cause.

In the 1980s, serial murder came to symbolize the worst manifestations of human behavior, which might be regarded either as a matter of extreme social or psychological dysfunction or else a form of simple moral evil. Whatever the causation, there was an overwhelming consensus that a behavior so aberrant and so threatening represented an absolute form of evil with which it was impossible to sympathize. It could also be argued plausibly that there must be something wrong with a society that could produce such a gross breakdown of generally accepted behavior as that evoked by a name like Ted Bundy, and there was speculation as to how social changes might have contributed to creating this phenomenon. The question asked is, in effect, What kind of society are we? or What kind of society have we become? and the various solutions offered have provided great rhetorical opportunities for claims-makers in a variety of causes.

It might be suggested, for example, that the offense occurs in consequence of a general social change or perceived social evil that the claims-maker wishes to stigmatize. Many claims-makers use this type of crime as a moral exemplar, a didactic tool that can be employed against a diverse range of phenomena. All acquire an added and threatening significance by being mapped together with serial homicide, thus presenting a moral critic with the opportunity to excoriate contemporary social abuses. The offense thus becomes a potent weapon against these abuses, which can somehow be blamed for inciting the violence of the offender, or for creating the conditions that made his or her actions possible. And in each case, a specific remedy is often advocated.

However, this is by no means the only strategy in which serial murder can be utilized. It is also possible to suggest that multiple homicide reflects a major flaw in the mechanisms of police and law enforcement, perhaps a systematic failure to protect a particular ethnic group or other category of victims. In this perspective, the rhetoric might well be deployed against the government and official agencies, and provide the basis for a radical political critique.

THE CRITIQUE OF SOCIAL CHANGE

In establishing a problem, it is desirable to emphasize the scale of the current phenomenon, its epidemic or plague quality usually being substantiated by attempts to provide a framework that is statistical, social scientific, and thus (apparently) objective. It is also critical to establish that such a problem is indeed new and modern, a phenomenon that has arisen within very recent memory, perhaps as a new importation from some alien society—a "growing menace" (Levin and Fox 1985). If serial murder is acknowledged to have a lengthy pedigree in a particular society, then it is implausible to attempt to blame it on recent developments. A certain amount of historical amnesia is necessary, if only as a rhetorical stance. If earlier incidents of this type of crime are acknowledged, then the author will commonly draw a sharp distinction in number and scale between such murders and the contemporary epidemic, a common theme in the American panic of 1983–1985 (Lindsey 1984a; see Chapter 3).

Once the epidemic has been established as genuine, it is possible to explore its rhetorical consequences, which might be either radical or conservative. In both cases, a common theme is that the offense results from social changes that have had a detrimental effect on traditional community values and structures. Multiple homicide is thus presented as a manifestation of the callous and depersonalized nature of the present age, which is contrasted with the supposed harmony and tranquility of bygone days. In this view, we have become a society of strangers.

One of the central homiletic themes is that a particular society under-values the lives and safety of some or all of its citizens, and has given preference to some alternative goal, perhaps material goods, personal liberty, or personal fulfillment. In Japan, a recent child murder case was followed by what has been described in the media as "national soul-searching": "Some point to the growing division of Japanese society into haves and have-nots. Others blame the flamboyant self-indulgence of the new consumer culture" ("In the Land" 1989). After a South Korean case in which eight young women were mutilated by a serial killer, the *New York Times* headlined, "A new era comes to Korea, followed by crime . . . [T]he nation asks what happened to its values" (Weisman 1990).

Mutatis mutandis, the same themes occur in a wide variety of societies. This is suggested by the remarks of the Austrian newspaper *Die Presse* following the 1991 trial of a group of medical personnel guilty of killing over forty patients:

> The most recent investigations into what is "holy" to the Austrians showed it quite clearly: Their own health is most important to the individual, but the general protection of human life—in the narrow as well as the broadest sense—ranked behind protecting material goods. To damage an auto appears to be much worse than visiting injustice or harm on one's fellow man. (quoted in Protzman 1991)

In the United States, Ann Rule used the same analogy to argue for the VICAP program:

> We realized that if you lost your boat or your car, there was a central information spot where you could see if anybody had found it, but if you lost your child or your spouse, there was no place, no central clearing house. (CNN, *Murder by Number*, 1993)

The moral is that boats and cars are worth more than people, who are disposable.

Social goals have fallen prey to crass materialism, the transformation of human beings into expendable commodities, and the rise of serial murder reflects these themes of lost community and declining values. In fact, these ideas are cited so commonly that they have become clichéd. When in 1977 the "Doonesbury" comic strip parodied news coverage of the Son of Sam case, the imaginary killer repeatedly presented the same hack-neyed themes, for example, that his "is a story of hopelessness and shattered dreams in the city they call New York."

Serial Murder and the Conservative Critique

In the United States during the 1980s, similar themes dominated the prevailing discourse surrounding serial homicide, as well as other concur-rent problems involving child abuse, missing children, and satanism. In each case, the rhetorical construction of the problem must be understood in the broader context of contemporary ideological attitudes, and espe-cially the conservative revival. In this conservative worldview, it was natural for serial murder, like threats to children, to be interpreted as one among many symptoms of social dislocation that ultimately found its roots in sexual permissiveness and family breakdown, the weakening of moral standards in the previous two decades. The critique of changing values, social decay, and general depersonalization was thus appropri-ated by New Right conservatism.

Throughout the various panics of the early 1980s, the New Right sought to contrast the virtues of traditional society with contemporary degrada-tion and demoralization. This implied using a rhetoric of jeremiad that sought and indeed required examples of extreme violence and sexual exploitation, preferably with stereotypes of sexual predators as bizarre and frightening as possible. In this historical vision, the alleged wave of serial murder since about 1966 fit perfectly, and monsters like Bundy or Gacy could be presented as concrete and memorable examples of the gross and unrestrained sexual excess to which liberal morality had offered so little discouragement. Sexually motivated multiple homicide was a bitter consequence of society's approval of easy access to pornography, increased media violence, and the weakening of community ties, which allowed killers to procure so many apparently disposable victims.

Such conservative views were often expressed in an overtly partisan context, but they appear in the serial murder literature in the guise of objective expert comment. Moreover, they are accepted and depicted in this way in media sources that are generally viewed as politically liberal in tone, such as the *New York Times* or *Washington Post*. This neglect of the ideological implications of these interpretations suggests the thorough command that the Justice Department's experts had obtained over the field of serial murder, and the degree to which their opinions were regarded as authoritative.

In 1984, several *New York Times* stories on serial killers quoted favorably the view that exposure to sexually explicit and sadomasochistic materials tended to arouse the violent instincts of individuals already prone to extreme acts by an abusive upbringing. The implication was that serial murder resulted from excessive social liberalism. The article cited several (mainly federal) law enforcement experts for the view that the surge of serial murder "is linked somehow [*sic*] to the sweeping changes in attitudes regarding sexuality that have occurred in the past twenty years" (Lindsey 1984a). The "apparent increase" may have arisen from legal changes, "greater tolerance of prostitution and pornography, including some pornography that depicts violent attacks upon women, or children engaged in sexual acts" (Lindsey 1984b).

However, changing sexuality was only part of the cause, which was to be found in broad trends in contemporary American society. "The rising incidence of family breakup which can be crushing to the children involved . . . increased mobility and dispersion" (Lindsey 1984b). One *New York Times* story concluded with the words of Pierce Brooks, the original advocate of VICAP: " 'We are becoming more of a society of strangers,' he said, and the stresses that result may contribute to the growth of multiple murders" (Berger 1984).

Newsweek remarked that

> the transient character of modern American life creates the perfect environment for serial murderers Some suggest that sexual permissiveness has unleashed deviant drives; others contend that a whole generation has been numbed by watching thousands of TV murders in which victims do not appear to suffer. (Starr et al. 1984)

A *Washington Post* column asserted that the sexually motivated serial killer

> is the price we pay for slavish devotion to individualism, mobility, the right to buy smut, the right to ignore one's neighbors even when they seem weird. He can come through town and no one will ask him any questions. This is the way it is going to be, as long as this remains a nation of strangers. (Achenbach 1991)

The role of media violence was often cited. Two law enforcement officers were quoted in the *New York Times* as believing that the rise in attacks by men against women was due "at least partly to an increase in movies that depict sexual violence uncritically and may encourage it" (Lindsey 1984a). The consequence was a general dehumanization, so that "Murder is like going down to the store and getting a Popsicle" (quoted in Berger 1984). Ann Rule asserted that sadistic pornography was "partly to blame" for the rise in serial murder (Berger 1984). As FBI agent John Douglas remarked, "It becomes easy when they decide to kill. It's like throwing away a piece of garbage" (Squitieri 1990). In turn, the popular celebrity of serial killers in fiction and cinema was a tragic symptom of social decline: "The psychos and loonies of today are perfectly cast for an age inured to intense violence" (James 1991).

The Threat to Children

Children were presented as the greatest victims of America's supposedly selfish hedonism of the liberal 1970s. Conservatives argued that the quest for individual pleasure and fulfillment had created a world in which children's interests were largely ignored in matters like divorce, while children were exploited through child abuse and pornography. The motif of the disposable child pervades the policy debates of the early 1980s, finding a sharp focus in the problem of missing and runaway children (Best 1990).

This rhetoric also permitted the denunciation as deviant or immoral actions that might otherwise be viewed as consensual and largely harmless. There were in the 1970s groups who wished to denounce and stigmatize what to them were moral offenses such as homosexuality or the sale of pornography, or religious deviations such as satanism. They could achieve little support for these views in the prevailing moral climate, which emphasized the freedom of consenting adults to determine their private moral conduct. However, shifting the focus to children's involvement fundamentally changed the moral and legal environment, as by definition children could not legally give informed consent to sexual activities. Adding children to the picture made it impossible to claim that actions were moral, victimless, or consensual.

Thus attention turned to types of exploitation such as child pornography, child murder and child abuse, and it will be argued that the emphasis on children often sought to appeal to antihomosexual sentiment. Especially by citing cases where boys had been victimized, claims-makers were drawing attention to the widely credited link between homosexuality, pedophilia, and violent crime, and seeking to stigmatize the overt homosexual movement, which was one of the aspects of contemporary "permissiveness" most detested by social conservatives (see Chapter 10). Given the political context of these years, it is not surprising that the antiabortion "prolife" movement would also exploit the idea of a threat to children, and the term *serial killer* was frequently applied to doctors and others who performed abortions (see, for example, the CBS's "48 Hours" report, "Choosing Sides," August 11, 1993).

In the context of serial murder, there was an invaluable reciprocal relationship between claims-makers in the areas of serial murder and child exploitation. For the child abuse activists, the emphasis on serial murder proved that the problem might lead to real and indeed lethal harm, so that the abuse issue could be personalized in the threatening form of a Corll or Gacy. Both were male killers preying on boys and could be seen as uniting the stereotypes of aggressive homosexual and pedophile killer. Conversely, the serial murder activists (especially in the federal law enforcement bureaucracy) stood to benefit from the perceived vulnerability of children to this type of homicide, as the emphasis on young and innocent victims would justify the expansion of official powers to meet the alleged threat.

Virtually all the major congressional hearings that did so much to publicize the serial murder menace were ostensibly concerned with children's issues and threats to children, and the leading activists tended also to be concerned with children's rights. The examples of John Walsh and Paula Hawkins have already been mentioned, but also active in the 1984 hearings was television producer Kenneth Wooden. He was throughout the decade a prominent advocate of the need to protect children from violent crime, as well as from sinister cults and devil worshippers (Wooden 1976, 1981, 1988). The tone of Wooden's congressional evidence is suggested by his remark, "Children in America are treated like garbage. Raped and killed, their young bodies are disposed of in plastic bags, in trash trucks, and left in city dumps." His views gained importance from his role in television news, where he was frequently involved in stories publicizing threats against children. In early 1984, for example, he produced an item on the ABC news magazine "20/20" on the theme of child murders and disappearances, citing serial killers as a major culprit. This led to a major public campaign in which pamphlets were distributed warning of the "child lures" used by killers to entice their young prey.

This emphasis could be traced throughout the campaigns of the early 1980s. Pierce Brooks opined that if his VICAP scheme had been in operation in the 1970s, then Bundy could have been apprehended, "stopped at the pass" in Utah, and many lives would have been saved. As a powerful exemplar, he specifically mentioned "the little thirteen-year-old" killed in Florida, who might have survived to become a happy young bride, instead of "mouldering in a grave" somewhere (interview on *Murder: No Apparent Motive*). Brooks asserted, "They're not just killing pretty young ladies, they're killing kids too, by the thousands" (Lindsey 1984b). The consequence of VICAP would be, "We're going to save a lot of lives" ("FBI Launches Frontal Attack" 1984). Another Justice Department official, Alfred Regnery, supported VICAP because serial murder "often involves torture, sexual assault and mutilation, occurs in widely scattered areas, and more often than not, victimizes children" ("Thirty-Five Murderers of Many People" 1983).

Serial Murder and Child Abuse

Serial killers were an extreme threat to children, while they exemplified in their own characters the effects of child abuse, reinforcing yet again the potentially catastrophic consequences of this type of victimization. When John Crewdson in *By Silence Betrayed* wished to establish the link between children being abused and the same individuals subsequently growing up to become abusers themselves, the example he chose to illustrate such a transition was John Wayne Gacy (Crewdson 1988:66–67). Of course, he did not suggest that any significant proportion of abused children develop in such an extreme way, but there is a clear rhetorical effect of amplification. By maltreating children, it seems, society is creating the monsters of the next generation. When asked what could be done to prevent multiple killers, psychiatrist Park Dietz stated, "Parents should stop torturing their children" (interview on *Murder: No Apparent Motive*).

The theme of child abuse recurs frequently in the true-crime literature. A few killers like Lucas, Shawcross, and Gacy have asserted that they were the victims of extreme sexual and physical abuse over many years, and Lucas in particular has recounted the most harrowing tales of savage violence (Norris 1991, 1992a). He was allegedly "beaten, knocked unconscious and repeatedly injured by his mother and her pimp" (Norris 1988:235). Others, however, were subjected to abuse in far more subtle senses, which would scarcely have merited the term before the growth of modern sensibilities about child maltreatment (Best 1990). Bobby Joe Long claims that his mother was "cruel in her disregard for his needs," and devoted too much attention to her dog (Norris 1988:235).

The impact of emotional abuse is often associated with family dysfunction. Many commentators have suggested that serial killers tend disproportionately to derive from nontraditional families: They resulted from unwanted pregnancies, they were illegitimate and/or adopted, they were raised in broken homes or state institutions (Norris 1988; Ressler et al. 1988). Leyton remarks that they typically tend to fall into one of four categories: "adopted, illegitimate, institutionalized in childhood or adolescence, or with mothers who have married three or more times" (Leyton 1986:291). Though writers are usually careful to specify that such environments do not necessarily produce such baleful consequences, the repeated assertion naturally supports conservative arguments about the virtues of the traditional nuclear family.

The idea that serial murder was a consequence of child abuse became a commonplace of the 1980s, in part because the doctrine was useful to so many groups. The value for children's rights advocates is self-evident, while therapists benefited by having the problem brought within the area of their particular expertise. It was especially significant for the growing body of psychiatrists who had come to accept the reality of Multiple Personality Disorder, a syndrome that was believed to stem from gross abuse during childhood. A number of serial killers claimed to be in dissociative states at the time of committing their crimes, and the ensuing trials offered expert witnesses a prominent platform from which to demonstrate the truth of their opinions. Moreover, the killers themselves were often anxious to assert such a "multiple" defense, as this offered the chance of an insanity verdict, which could not be obtained on the basis of a condition like sexual sadism or psychopathy. Multiple defenses were offered during the trials of Kenneth Bianchi, John Wayne Gacy and Arthur Shawcross, though unsuccessfully in each case.

CRIME AS MORAL EVIL

The cultural imagery of serial murder offers a stark contrast between the unfathomable evil of the predatory killer and the simple innocence of his or her prey, who are often children, and this is a powerful device for enlisting support in a war against these external monsters. In terms of practical policy, such a dichotomy can be used to justify the most extreme measures of social defense against the alleged culprits. Moreover, this perception has crucial implications for the locus of intervention. If it is suggested that crime or violence arises because of social or environmental factors, then it is essential to change the underlying conditions, and the individual responsibility of the offender becomes almost irrelevant. On the other hand, concentrating on the individual moral characteristics of the offender provides an ideological basis for wars on crime, and draconian law and order policies.

In the contemporary American context, such attitudes tend to favor strongly conservative political views, and it is not surprising to find them advocated at the height of the first Reagan administration. The shift from seeing killers as misunderstood psychiatric anomalies to creatures of pure evil exactly suited the broader anticrime rhetoric of those years. The language of war permeated the serial murder literature almost as thoroughly as that of plague and epidemic. An Associated Press account of the inauguration of the NCAVC in 1984 was headlined "FBI Launches Frontal Attack on Serial Killers."

Nor is this sort of shift a new trend in criminological theory. There is a classic study of how the predominantly social and environmental theories of crime causation in the nineteenth century were overturned by the revolutionary and individualistic theories of Lombroso (Lindesmith and Levin 1937; see Chapter 5). In criminological thought, such a biomedical perspective prevailed for half a century, and all but eclipsed the previously thriving sociological school, to the benefit of conservative political ideologies. This intellectual transformation has been described in a passage that seems quite apposite to recent views of the serial killer:

> It may well be that the theory of the born criminal offered a convenient rationalization of the failure of preventive effort and an escape from the implications of the dangerous doctrine that crime is an essential product of our social organization. It may well be that a public which had been nagged for centuries by reformers welcomed the opportunity to slough off its responsibilities for this vexing problem. (Lindesmith and Levin 1937:670)

Contemporary views of serial murder have not quite espoused Lombrosan or biomedical beliefs, although Norris (1988) has ventured some distance in this direction.

Stasio (1989) has remarked how frequently moralistic and law-and-order themes occur in recent novels on serial murder, where police characters in particular use the offense as a vehicle for attacks on rehabilitation, social theories of crime, and moral relativism in general. In *The Silence of the Lambs*, it is Hannibal Lecter himself who rejects Clarice Starling's attempts to find what made him a killer: "Nothing happened to me Officer Starling. *I* happened. You can't reduce me to a set of influences. You've given up good and evil for behaviorism, Officer Starling. You've got everybody in moral dignity pants—nothing is ever anybody's fault. Look at me Officer Starling. Can you stand to say I'm evil? Am I evil?" (p. 21).

The implications of this moralistic approach are suggested by the response of conservative columnist Cal Thomas to the Dahmer case (Thomas 1991). Thomas, a leader of the Moral Majority, drew an extended comparison between the recent event and the Corll affair, which he had covered as a journalist in 1973. His basic theme was reflected in his title, which asserted, "Serial murders underscore evil's presence." Such affairs illustrated the role of genuine spiritual evil in crime causation, "not an admission that our sophisticated culture usually accepts." Evil implied individual responsibility and theories of punishment based on retribution and deterrence. Reform and rehabilitation were essentially mythical, and "that is why we need prisons and capital punishment—to protect us from evil." "A better case for the death penalty could hardly be found" than Jeffrey Dahmer. Though there is no explicit reference here to the homosexual content of both cases, Thomas's writings have long denounced homosexual activities and organized gay rights movements, and it is likely that readers are meant to draw the conclusion that this is one critical aspect of the evil he denounces.

Restoring the Death Penalty

The practical applications of this approach are exemplified by the role of serial murder in the capital punishment debates of the 1980s. The restoration of capital punishment was contentious for many reasons, but one of the most powerful abolitionist arguments concerned the poor and minority populations from which death row inmates were usually drawn. In Thurgood Marshall's phrase, the institution represented an "ultimate form of racial discrimination." The several states that reinstituted the death penalty in the decade after 1978 had much discretion about which inmates to execute first, and virtually all chose offenders who both were white and had been sentenced for singularly heinous crimes. This tended to maximize support for capital punishment, by showing that the penalty was a necessary response to extreme moral evil and social danger, while publicizing such extreme cases also appeared to show the futility of rehabilitative efforts (Cartwright 1992).

This explains why serial killers were often among the first to be executed in restorationist states, including Steven Judy in Indiana (1981: guilty of "a string of bodies" across the United States), Velma Barfield in North Carolina (1984: four victims), Carroll Cole in Nevada (1985: thirteen victims), or Steven Pennell in Delaware (1992: four victims). There were perhaps fifteen other such examples between 1980 and 1993. Cole's execution "immediately paved the way for others in the Western states" (Newton 1990:70).

Ted Bundy's execution in Florida in 1989 was greeted by widespread public celebrations in what can only be termed a party atmosphere, and only the most dedicated opponents of the death penalty criticized the decision to kill him. Linedecker writes of this incident,

> Private citizens were sending a blunt message that the men and women in the ponderously muddled justice system didn't seem to grasp: dealing with serial killers isn't a silly game for a few venal lawyers and misguided do-gooders to play out in the nation's court-rooms. Punishment should fit the crime! (Linedecker 1990a:xiii)

Executing serial killers created a public consensus for the legitimacy of what had previously been regarded as a reactionary and even racist form of punishment. (Incidentally, no less an expert than Robert Ressler opposes the death penalty for serial killers: Ressler and Schachtman 1992:247.)

Especially during 1984, the rhetoric of both official statements and media coverage of serial murder tended to reflect politically and morally conservative themes, although it might well be that neither journalists nor authorities quoted espoused a particular partisan agenda. However, it is notable that many such articles appeared during the lead-in to the 1984 campaign, in which Ronald Reagan overwhelmed Walter Mondale. The key issues of this campaign concerned the reassertion of traditional standards and what a later president termed family values, in addition to the familiar Republican issue of being tough on crime. One of the speakers at the White House news conference announcing the opening of the NCAVC was Vice President George Bush, who remarked, "I'm not suggesting that our opponents are soft on crime, but our record is out there" (Anderson 1984). Support for the mind-hunters implied adherence to a detailed ideological agenda about the causation of criminality and the stern measures needed to combat it.

THE CRITIQUE OF AUTHORITY

The particular construction of serial murder that emerged in the 1980s therefore had conservative undertones, but this was neither inevitable nor indeed the only possible reaction to the issue. For example, the theme can be used to denounce extreme violence committed by states or official agents, whether or not they are acting under the cover of legal authority. This makes the point that military or police actions might well be indistinguishable from regular criminality. Cambodian dictator Pol Pot has been described as a serial killer (Kernan 1993), while a forensic pathologist used the same terminology to attack the atrocities carried out by the Argentine regime during the repression of the 1970s so-called dirty war:

> It was serial murder with X thousands of victims. Those generals were in the same league, as far as I'm concerned, as Ted Bundy or John Gacy. . . . In fact, those two guys missed their opportunity. If they'd gone to Argentina, they would probably be brigadier generals. They would have fit right in. (Michaud 1987)

Even the destruction of American Indian tribes in the pioneer era has been stigmatized as serial murder (Randall 1992).

Serial murder can also be employed to draw attention to specific social issues and conflicts. Even in the 1980s, there were alternative constructions of the problem, with important subtexts that were potentially far more radical than the orthodoxy of the war against monsters. This is apparent if the emphasis of the murder problem is shifted from the nature of the offender to the broader circumstances of the act. What all serial murders have in common is that on several occasions, an individual was murdered, and that the police either failed to detect it or else could not apprehend the killer. It is then possible to ask about the offenders, How are they getting away with it? Several answers are possible, each of which implies a criticism of bureaucratic agencies and official priorities.

One common suggestion is that the killers are preying on a group who are especially vulnerable because of their extreme poverty or isolation, and that the crimes should draw attention to underlying social injustice. This idea emerged strongly in the original Jack the Ripper case of 1888, when the murders were widely used to focus attention on the problems of multiple deprivation in the East London communities where the crimes occurred. One much reproduced cartoon of the era depicts a ghostlike figure wandering the streets with a butcher's knife. The caption reads,

> There floats a phantom on the slum's foul air
> Shaping, to eyes which have the gift of seeing
> Into the specter of that loathly air.
> Face it—for vain is fleeing!
> Red-handed, ruthless, furtive, unerect,
> 'Tis murderous crime—the nemesis of neglect!
>
> (Rumbelow 1988)

The ripper murders are the consequence of overwhelming poverty, "the nemesis of neglect."

Similar social critiques have often recurred during this century. In 1974, for example, Calvin Jackson killed eleven poor and elderly people over a six-month period in a welfare hotel in New York City. The official neglect that apparently led to these crimes scarcely being noticed was extensively denounced in the media. One socialist observer wrote:

> What kind of community is it that can have this happen in its midst and not know about it? . . . [This is] a microcosm of New York City. What happened here is happening all over the city: cynicism, neglect, bureaucratic bungling, failure of the authorities to fulfill their obligations. (Wilson 1974)

When in 1971 the murders of over twenty itinerant farm workers were attributed to Juan Corona, a California state senator remarked,

> It is a biting commentary on our morals, that it takes the murder of twenty men, and the attention of the world's press, to point up the existence of this sorrowful subculture which we use—and abuse—to produce the food we eat. (quoted in Bézard 1992:38)

In 1987, a pair of Paris serial killers targeted elderly women. In response, the newspaper *Le Monde* remarked of the solitary old:

> These old women gradually recede into an accepted peripheral existence . . . And when a prowler in search of cash batters one of them to death in

her home for a few francs, neighbors do not even notice it. They die as they
have lived, without a sound. (Ambroise-Rendu 1987)

The solution to a problem phrased thus would lie less in devoting resources to law enforcement than to enhancing social services and
strengthening local communities; and such analyses did emerge in the
United States during the 1980s.

The rhetorical theme is that society is guilty for the crimes and so, by
extension, are all its individual members who have failed to curb these
abuses (Rosenbaum 1933b). In 1967, Harlan Ellison wrote of Jack the
Ripper,

> The Jack I present is the Jack in all of us, of course. The Jack that tells us to
> stand and watch as a Catherine Genovese gets knifed, the Jack that con-
> dones Vietnam because we don't care to get involved, the Jack that we need.
> We are a culture that needs its monsters . . . That is the message of the story.
> *You* are the monsters. (Ellison 1974:Vol. 1, p. 226, emphasis in original)

The suggestion is also made that people who fall victim to serial killers
do so because they are undervalued by society and official agencies. Even
if they are not actually persecuted or discriminated against, they are
regarded as disposable in a dehumanized contemporary society (compare
Best 1990:22–44). In Britain, this theme emerged strongly in media reports
on a series of child murders. The London *Sunday Times* published an
article on the "slaughter of the lambs," claiming that:

> thousands upon thousands of children, some in the 10–13 age group,
> vanished from their homes each year, often heading for London . . . [A]t
> the moment nobody knows how many young boys and girls—known to
> pimps and pedophiles alike as "mysteries"—have been swallowed up in
> large cities such as London in the last decade. Nobody knows how many
> . . . have come to the attention of men who regard them as free-range
> products on the hoof to be either bought for pleasure or taken by force, used
> and disposed of in shallow graves. . . . That's the kind of society we have
> now. (Dalrymple 1991)

Serial murder thus arises in a society that dehumanizes and devalues its
citizens, and treats its children as commodities, "free-range products on
the hoof," "mysteries." Children are "swallowed up" in the megalopolis;
its elderly "die without a sound"; it places more value on material goods
than human life.

The same themes also occur in literary and fictional accounts of serial
murder, where the bizarre and violent actions of killers are seen as a
reflection of social tendencies: modernization, urbanization, industrial-
ization, and consequent *anomie*. Colin Wilson and Patricia Pitman argue:

The bigger and more centralized a society becomes, the more of these socially irresponsible individuals it creates. The impersonality of society produces either revolt or contemptuous indifference. Hence the age of centralization is also the age of the juvenile delinquent and the sex maniac. (Wilson and Pitman 1984:33)

Elliott Leyton argues similarly that multiple murder arises from the conditions within the "dehumanized industrial system," and comments,

If we were charged with the responsibility for designing a society in which all structural and cultural mechanisms leaned towards the creation of the killers of strangers, we could do no better than to present the purchaser with the shape of modern America. (Leyton 1986:295)

Dehumanization is a central idea of Bret Easton Ellis's novel *American Psycho* (1991), in which the frequent use of expensive consumer brand names indicates the unchecked snobbery and materialism of yuppie New York in the 1980s. The culture and attitudes thus created permit the killer Patrick Bateman to treat his women victims as simple commodities or consumer goods, who can be killed or tortured purely for entertainment. The multiple murders are a logical extension of the normal violence and depravity of the city: "strangled models, babies thrown from tenement rooftops, kids killed in the subway, a Communist rally, Mafia boss wiped out, Nazis" (p. 4). Meanwhile, the cynicism and violence of political life are suggested by the poster of Oliver North that Bateman keeps on his wall (p. 339). The opening line of the book clearly identifies contemporary New York with Dante's *Inferno*, while the very title reinforces this element of cultural criticism, suggesting that the killer is a distinctly *American* psycho, whose behavior reflects American conditions. The book cannot be identified with any partisan agenda, but the critique is clearly directed against the conservative America of the 1980s rather than the supposed decadence of earlier years. For Ellis, as for Wilson or Leyton, the solution to contemporary serial murder lies in social changes far more profound than the nostrums of the federal justice agencies.

The Attack on the Police

The rhetorical use of the serial murder theme often has an implicitly radical character because of the central role of the police in investigations, which often leads to claims that law enforcement agencies have been guilty of serious error or misconduct. Such charges may be unwarranted in that cases of this sort are often difficult and time-consuming, but the mere fact that murders continue over a lengthy period of time is likely to lead to a searching critique of police methods and priorities.

Different types of investigations tend to elicit different public re-sponses. Some series of murders are in effect discovered only at their conclusion, with the discovery of bodies and the apprehension of an offender. In this case, the investigation reconstruct the career of the killer largely in retrospect, as occurred in the Jeffrey Dahmer incident of 1991 or the Joel Rifkin case in 1993. On other occasions, it is known for some time that a multiple killer is active, but the investigation fails to identify or apprehend the offender. Public knowledge of such an ongoing case may last for weeks, months, or even for several years, as in the Atlanta Child Murders or Seattle's Green River killings.

Of the two types, it is the former that perhaps should be more damning to police prestige, as the murders occurred without formal recognition that a crime series had been in progress and often without knowledge that a person had died or even disappeared. Paradoxically though, it is the latter sort of long-running cases that do the most damage to official reputations. These cases are likely to attract different kinds of rumor and speculation, which may initially focus on law enforcement. It may be suggested that the police should be able to prevent further crimes, but that for some reason they are unable or unwilling to do so.

When a case lasts for some time, it is common to suggest that the offender might in fact be a police officer. Such an individual would thus have special inside knowledge of the investigation and perhaps the tacit support of friends within an agency (see, for example, the speculations surrounding the Green River investigation in Washington state; Smith and Guillen 1990). This suspicion is made plausible by the numerous true-life serial killers who have impersonated police officers at some stage during their career, usually to win the confidence of potential victims.

"Something Failed"

It might also be suggested that the lack of police success reflects the low priority accorded to the protection of particular categories of victim—prostitutes, homosexuals, ethnic minorities, the elderly, and so on. Such victims are seen as "less dead" or perhaps "less human," lacking in full human status. This is illustrated by a series of killings of poor homeless women that occurred in northeast Philadelphia during the late 1980s. These have been aptly described as "The Nobody Murders" (Mallowe 1990). Even in the local Philadelphia press, the individual crimes received very little attention until after several killings had been recorded, and what coverage there was occurred in the popular *Philadelphia Daily News* rather than the more prestigious *Philadelphia Inquirer*. In consequence, the story remained virtually unknown outside the city. With so little public concern or awareness, the police felt little pressure to attach a high priority to the case and even refused to declare that a serial killer was at work, ostensibly to avoid creating panic (Sanginiti 1990). Not until 1990, five years after the first killing, did the case (the Frankford Slayings) become a major concern of police and media. Arrests followed shortly afterwards.

Such instances are far more common than the legendary series associated with a Dahmer or Gacy; and in these obscure cases, the police are likely to be criticized for failing to take notice of the victims' disappearances, or to devote adequate resources to investigating the crimes. This reinforces the theme that the victim group is brutalized and exploited, and implicates official agencies with the continuing violence. It also supports the idea that members of that victim group cannot seek help from officialdom and must find it elsewhere, either through autonomous political action or lobbying for political and social change.

The impact of such racial and populist rhetoric can be observed from a case that occurred in late 1990 in the South Bronx, in New York City, when a cabdriver was suspected in the murders of five girls and young women. Initial police reaction was to reject charges that the crimes were linked, and police stated at one point, "There is no serial killer and there is no linkage between these cases." They also specifically rejected local rumors that the cabdriver, Alejandro Henriquez, was a suspect in any of the attacks (McKinley 1990). However, the victims' friends and relatives formed a support group, which acted as a highly efficient source of political pressure on the police and city authorities, urging that the case be made a high priority and that police pursue possible links between the crimes. The group's rhetoric repeatedly emphasized that perceived official racism had led to the alleged lack of police action. One member of the support group remarked, "Something didn't work because it took five children to be killed . . . whether it's because we're Spanish, poor, or live in the South Bronx—for whatever reason, something failed" (Gonzalez and Lorch 1991). The community activism succeeded to the extent that Henriquez was arrested, and charged in the alleged series of murders.

Serial murder thus offers a powerful rhetorical device for minority groups. African-Americans have perhaps made most use of this tactic of citing unequal protection, but other minorities have also been affected (see Chapter 8). In 1993, a series of thirteen unsolved murders of Yakima Indians in Washington state led to charges that federal authorities placed a very low priority on the defense of Indian lives:

> People here think that because it is on an Indian reservation and involves Indian people, the FBI just doesn't care. . . . [T]he attitude among the FBI is "They're just Indians, just alcoholics, so who cares?" and dismiss it. . . . A feeling persists among many on this reservation that if the victims had been

the daughters of prominent local white citizens, the federal response would have been different (Egan 1993).

SUMMARY

In such cases, the focus of attention shifts dramatically from the character of the individual monster to the nature of the broader transaction: the group to which both perpetrators and victims belong, and the social environment that permits such a crime to occur. In such cases, it is common to view both offender and victim as representatives of particular social categories and to suggest that this type of violence is somehow characteristic of relationships between those groups. The crime can thus be framed as typical of violence by men against women, by whites against blacks (or vice versa), or by homosexuals against a variety of targets.

What gives the serial murder issue its undoubted power and popularity is that there is little or no need to argue for the reality and severity of the harm associated with the behavior. That is taken for granted by virtually all groups and shades of political opinion. The question then arises of how this weapon can be used, which groups or behaviors can be stigmatized by association with this undoubted evil, and how plausibly this juxtaposition can be undertaken. The next chapter will describe how serial murder has been enlisted as an ideological weapon for many groups and causes, including feminists and religious groups, both advocates and opponents of the rights of homosexuals and ethnic minorities.

Chapter 7

Everyman: Serial Murder as "Femicide"

The phenomenon of serial murder is often employed to illustrate the dehumanization of a particular group and the extreme social dysfunction indicated by the prevalence of this crime. In recent literature, these ideas have been applied most systematically from the feminist viewpoint, which commonly asserts that serial murder is a subset of male sexual aggression toward women. Some have sought to coin neologisms like *gynocide* or *femicide* for this type of activity (Quindlen 1993; Radford and Russell 1992). Some feminists argue that in serial murder both killer and victim are in a sense representative of broader categories in the wider society, with gender as a principal determinant. Since the late 1970s, this interpretation of serial murder as the ultimate manifestation of sexual abuse has become a significant component of feminist theory.

This approach also provides justification for extreme or militant action in response to that injustice, by suggesting that multiple homicide is the natural extrapolation, the logical end of the spectrum of problems perceived in everyday life, a spectrum that includes rape and child abuse as well as sexual harassment and the sale of pornography. In the face of such a menace to life and limb, this view justifies extralegal activities such as vigilantism or restricting the right of access to sexually explicit materials.

Closely linked to the theme of persecution and neglect is the idea that savage violence is characteristic of the group to which the offender belongs. The serial sex-killer is depicted as representative of the broader category of all men, or at least men living within a patriarchal culture. Though it is not implied that all men are actual rapists or sexual killers, all are portrayed as having this potential, and pathological violence is a logical extrapolation of what is otherwise seen as harmless or minor behavior, for example, involving pornography or sexual harassment. Such activities are thus stigmatized by association with the far higher threshold of multiple homicide. This chapter will describe the construction of serial homicide as part of the larger sexual violence problem and will consider how feminist theorists take account of apparently contradictory evidence, above all the existence of numerous female serial killers.

CONSTRUCTING SEXUAL VIOLENCE

The concept of sexual violence as a generalized and systematic assault upon women and girls originated with the antirape movements that emerged in the United States in the early 1970s, as part of the wider feminist movement. Work written from this perspective drew attention to sexual murder as one extreme form of exploitation, and this served rhetorically to emphasize the real harm associated with sexual assault. It was thus an antidote to the idea that women might be asking for the rape they experienced. These ideas provided British feminists with an influential model for interpreting the Yorkshire Ripper case of 1975–1981, when Peter Sutcliffe killed thirteen women in northern English towns such as Bradford and Halifax (Bland 1992:233–52; Doney 1990; Burn 1984; Beattie 1981; Cross 1981). This case caused a radical rethinking of feminist attitudes in Great Britain, and there is abundant evidence that activists enjoyed great public success in propagating their expansive view of the newly constructed "sexual violence problem." The wide publicity accorded to this case permitted radical feminists to use the rhetorical technique of convergence to assimilate other less serious issues to the immensely threatening theme of sadistic serial homicide (Jenkins 1992a).

This construction of the Yorkshire Ripper case went far toward defining British perceptions of multiple homicide over the next decade, and the image of Sutcliffe pervades the pioneering feminist work on serial murder, *The Lust to Kill*, published in England in 1987 (Cameron and Frazer 1987). In the United States, no one incident had anything like the same impact, and in fact American theorists like Jane Caputi sometimes drew on the Sutcliffe case and the British literature on sexual violence. Her 1987 book *The Age of Sex Crime* became one of the most frequently cited works in the feminist literature on violence against women, and she often returned to the topic (see, for example, Caputi 1989, 1990a, 1990b). However, the general theme of serial murder was also used by most of the leading feminist theorists, including Phyllis Chesler, Andrea Dworkin, Catherine MacKinnon, Robin Morgan, Diana E. H. Russell, and Judith Walkowitz.

By the late 1980s, there was growing interest in the theme of femicide, or women being killed as part of generalized misogynist terrorism, the misogynist killing of women by men. This ranged from analyses of witch persecutions in early modern Europe through modern occurrences of battering and murder in marriage, female infanticide, and, of course, serial murder, "serial femicide" (Bart and Moran 1993). The category has even been expanded to include deaths from botched abortions, and the transmission of AIDS by rapists (Radford 1992:7). In 1989 a northern California feminist group formed a Clearinghouse on Femicide.

Interest in femicide intensified during 1989 following the mass killing of fourteen female students in Montreal by Marc Lepine, who had denounced his victims as "fucking feminists" prior to shooting them. The Montreal massacre proved a traumatic event, which was widely discussed in print and on film, and also called forth demonstrations in both Canada and the United States to protest violence against women. The incident was often referred to by feminist speakers, and Robin Morgan would begin her public presentations by reading the names of the Montreal victims and asking, "Why do men hate women so?" By 1990, a substantial literature was developing on the theme of femicide. This was the subject of a major article by Jane Caputi in *MS.* magazine (1990b), and there were accounts in feminist publications such as *Off Our Backs* and *Trouble and Strife.* An important collection of articles appeared in book form in 1992 (Radford and Russell 1992).

The Scale of Femicide

Feminist writers invariably suggest that violence against women is a pervasive social danger. In order to substantiate this argument, it is essential to focus on the most extreme manifestations of the behavior and to select those statistics that emphasize widespread victimization. Serial femicide is presented as a very common occurrence, and feminists continue to use the very high Justice Department estimates for the scale of multiple murder. This is due in large measure to the citation of these figures by the influential Jane Caputi, the leading "serial murder expert" from the feminist point of view (Radford 1992:11; Caputi 1987:117). Jill Radford writes:

> There is clearer evidence from the United States to suggest that serial killings of women and girls have become more frequent. Although precise figures are unavailable, law enforcement experts estimate that "as many as two thirds [or 3,500] of the estimated 5000 unsolved homicides in the nation each year may be committed by serial murderers." Jane Caputi reports that by the mid-1980s police officials estimate the total number of serial killings had risen to four thousand per year. While some serial

murderers kill males, most experts agree that the vast majority of the victims are female. (Radford and Russell 1992:11)

The 3,500 figure is taken from the 1984 *Newsweek* article written at the height of the murder panic (Starr et al. 1984; discussed in Chapter 3), but it is here repeated in a 1992 account, long after it should have been known to be dubious.

The problems with this statistic were, or should have been, apparent. If, in fact, 3,500 females fell victim to serial killers each year during the mid-1980s, this would have accounted for some 70 percent of *all* murders of women and girls. Apart from being implausible as it stands, this figure would also leave little room for the domestic murders that, according to the femicide literature, are believed to be so endemic a problem.

The feminist literature thus continues to circulate extraordinarily high and inaccurate estimates of serial murder activity long after they have been discredited elsewhere and to suggest moreover that the pace of activity is continuing to accelerate: "A surge in serial murder activity . . . is recognized by criminologists to have begun in the 1950s and has become a characteristic phenomenon of the late twentieth century in the United States" (Caputi and Russell 1992:17). The *MS* article quoted Robert Heck's claim that serial murders were not only becoming more numerous, but also more vicious, with more extreme torture and mutilation. To support this claim, the authors cite serial murder cases like that of Gary Heidnik, Roy Norris, and Lawrence Bittaker (p. 17; Russell 1992:166–68).

Serial Murder as Gender Terrorism

Throughout feminist accounts of serial murder, the emphasis is naturally on the sexual and misogynist motivation of the crime and its association with sexual exploitation. In 1981, for example, Marin County in northern California was the scene of several murders by the Trailside Slayer, a serial killer later identified as David Carpenter (Graysmith 1990). Feminist Diana Russell organized a protest demonstration against what she terms "these and other femicides" (Radford and Russell 1992:xiv). In the subsequent literature, known serial killers are also quoted to present their extreme misogyny, which (it is suggested) caused or contributed to their murders.

In addition, it is a central theme in this literature that serial murder is chiefly an offense committed by men against women that, "serial killers are almost always white men, and that ninety percent of the people they kill are women or girls" (Domingo 1992:196). Detective novelist Sara

Paretsky writes, "With one or two exceptions, serial killers are always men. Their victims are always women, children or homosexual men" (Paretsky 1991). Places in which killings occur are "areas terrorized by male Rippers acting out the ultimate male fantasies of a violent male sexual culture," the origin of the problem being made explicit by the multiple repetition of the adjective *male* (*New Statesman*, January 23, 1981). The offense is thus framed as a gender-based crime in which one part of the population engages in behavior systematically intended to subdue and repress another part, a concept that stems from Brown-miller's (1975) classic formulation of rape as a "conscious process of intimidation by which *all* men keep *all* women in a state of fear." Analogies with terrorism are often drawn, so that femicide becomes "sexist terrorism against women."

The analysis thus places the blame for the offense firmly on masculine characteristics, claiming that such behavior is formed within the structures of a male-dominated society. The feminist literature thus employs serial murder as an ideological weapon not so much against men as a category, but against the patriarchal society they are believed to dominate. Serial murder is thus typified neither as a problem for law enforcement nor mental health, but as a political problem par excellence, an issue of the relative power held by different groups. This argument is used to criticize every aspect of mainstream society, from government and law enforcement agencies to academic and therapeutic sources, as well as the "official" media. All are attacked for treating serial murder in a way that appears to accept and even legitimize its misogynist foundations, so that in a sense, the media become accomplices to the crimes they affect to condemn. To quote Catherine MacKinnon, this is a "social world that wants—even loves—women dead."

Serial murder is thus systemic, rather than the product of individual pathology. As the British *Feminist Review* argued in 1981, even the ultimate conviction of the Yorkshire Ripper was effectively a whitewash because it failed to consider broader social factors within patriarchy:

> Sutcliffe's trial demonstrated men's collaboration with other men in the oppression of women. . . . The trial refused to recognize the way in which Sutcliffe's acts were an expression—albeit an extreme one—of the construction of an aggressive masculine sexuality and of women as its objects. This cover-up exonerates men in general even when one man is found guilty. (Holloway 1984:14)

Sutcliffe claimed to have been driven by voices,

> but the voice that Sutcliffe obeyed was the voice not of God or delusion, but of the hoardings on the streets, of newspaper stands, of porn displays

and of films. It is the voice which addresses every man in our society and to that extent, as the feminist slogan claims, all men are potential rapists. (p. 22)

The Ripper case was used to indict the whole structure of government and media in a patriarchal society.

Serial murder is seen as a powerful weapon in the political suppression of women, and the ideologies surrounding the offense are considered almost as damaging as the behavior itself. Feminists suggest that the offense is constructed to provide support for patriarchal ideology, a pattern that can be traced back to the early case of Jack the Ripper. For Walkowitz, the Ripper myth has been an extraordinarily valuable component of patriarchal ideology:

> The Ripper has materially contributed to women's sense of vulnerability in modern urban culture. Over the past hundred years, the Ripper murders have achieved the status of a modern myth of male violence against women, a story whose details have become vague and generalized, but whose moral message is clear: the city is a dangerous place for women, when they transgress the narrow boundaries of home and hearth and dare to enter public space (1982:543)

In this view, official and patriarchal sources invariably tend to glamorize or romanticize criminals such as Jack the Ripper or Ted Bundy (Walkowitz 1982). As early as 1975, Susan Brownmiller's *Against Our Will* used the legend of Jack to criticize "the myth of the heroic rapist" in academic and journalistic circles, and she quotes descriptions of the killer as "the hero of horror in Victorian times" (Brownmiller 1975:294–96). In the 1970s, a British stage production of *Jack the Ripper* was advertised as offering "Scenes of Fun, Terror, Song and Dance" (Rumbelow 1988). Charges of trivialization were especially popular in England during 1988, the year that saw the centenary of the Ripper case and a further contribution to the already considerable tourist industry surrounding the affair (Cameron 1992:184–88). However, such heroic approaches also extend to more commonplace offenders, and Caputi and others have stressed the hunting and even sporting rhetoric employed by the mass media to depict serial killers (as when a pair of linked killings is termed a "doubleheader"; see, for example, Newton 1990:230).

The glorification of the killer is linked to attempts to make him appear as threatening and destructive as possible, on the lines familiar from the monster or cannibal mythology discussed in Chapter 5. Lucy Bland writes, "The myth of this murderer as a beast or monster was and is necessary to men in particular if they are to *distance* themselves from him and separate this form of violence toward women from other forms of male-female relationships" (1992:250–51, emphasis in original). For feminist writers, such a process of externalization denies the fundamental connection between such extreme behavior and the everyday violence of battering and domestic abuse.

While glamorizing the offender, official ideologies are believed to trivialize and neglect women victims of offenses such as sex murder. It has been suggested that while the Atlanta Child Murders were in progress, dozens of unsolved murders of adult women occurred in the same city, but with little or no official notice (almost forty such cases between 1978 and 1982; Dettlinger and Prugh 1983:354). It is argued that gender determines the relative significance accorded a victim and that female victims possess a low degree of importance (Russell and Ellis 1992:161–62). In violent acts like the serial murders of Texas killer Kenneth McDuff, "women are stalked as prey or treated as disposable commodities" (Pederson 1992). It is also remarked that the victims who are discussed attract public attention because there is something sexy or mysterious about them (compare Chapter 5). Brownmiller notes that the first few victims of the Boston Strangler were entirely neglected by the media because they were black or elderly, while mass coverage only began when the Strangler claimed a young white woman in her twenties (1975:200–6).

The exaltation of offenders over victims extends to attempts to interpret serial murder activity in a way that blames the victim, that is, it seeks to make the women responsible for a quintessentially masculine offense. Radford denounces those who explain male violence in terms of the inadequate mothering experienced by offenders like Marc Lepine, whose guilt is thus attributed to a woman (Radford 1992:5–6). Others criticize psychiatric attempts to attribute Peter Sutcliffe's violent actions in some measure to frustration with his wife, Sonia.

In the cinema, the Norman Bates of *Psycho* and the Jason of *Friday the Thirteenth* both owe their murderous characters to their repressive mothers: Norman Bates's mother was a "clinging, demanding woman," Jason's was a killer herself. Ann Rule has attributed the sexual murder of prostitutes to this kind of antifemale revenge, arguing that the killer "is usually controlled by the mother, usually a woman who is sexually promiscuous" (quoted in Squitieri 1990). In the feminist literature, this sort of explanation is seen as an attempt to evade blame by the male gender, while other nonfeminist explanations for the offense are seen as at best a form of collective male denial.

Policy Agendas

This interpretation extends to policy responses, and the suggested solutions to the serial murder problem were to be found not in the arrest or punishment of any given individual, but in broad social changes to enhance the equal rights and safety of women. Feminist writers suggest that men and the society they dominate are to blame for serial murder, and yet official responses almost invariably call for women to restrict their freedom of action by taking extra security measures, "the familiar female choice between freedom of movement and safety" (Radford and Russell 1992:xiv). Feminists thus challenge the implication that "public space is men's space and women's presence in it is conditional on male approval. Woman's place, according to patriarchal ideologies, is in the home" (Radford 1992:7). Feminist responses to serial murder incidents often take the form of attacking such restrictions, to assert the collective strength of women to move and travel as they wish despite intimidation. Thus a multiple-murder case might provide the opportunity for direct action campaigns and grass roots organizing.

In the late 1970s, for example, there were "reclaim the night" and antipornography demonstrations in the English cities that were the scenes of the Yorkshire Ripper's crimes. Feminists thus symbolically struck back at serial murder by attacking those cultural elements that were believed to promote the behavior, above all pornography. In 1979, there was an apparent series of thirteen murders of (mainly black) women in the Boston area, and here too the response was the formation of a feminist self-help organization, based in the Combahee River Collective (Grant 1992:145–60). The group succeeded in mobilizing hundreds of women in protest marches against perceived male violence.

The Green River Killings evoked a similar response, organized through the Women's Coalition to Stop the Green River Murders. By 1984, the group was organizing marches in Seattle, in which "women will mobilize to take back the night and to claim our rights to live after sunset" (Smith and Guillen 247-249). The group suggested that the crimes reflected bias and neglect on the part of the male-dominated society: The prostitute victims were "victims of a sexist society. Violence against women is an all-American sport." The police were subject to particular criticism because of the "farce" of their investigation, which by that point had been in progress for two years without locating a plausible suspect. This failure resulted from the low priority accorded to victims: "If fifty-two white, middle class college girls were missing or dead, there would be an entirely different response" (pp. 247–49). Almost identical arguments were employed during the Southside Slayings case, which occurred in Los Angeles shortly afterwards, and throughout 1986 feminist groups organized weekly vigils outside police headquarters. In September, the group Take Back the Night announced that the first anniversary of the discovery of the murder series would be commemorated by a candlelight vigil (*Los Angeles Times*, September 24, 1986).

Apart from grass roots political organization, feminists have used the threat of sexual violence to argue for extensive legal changes to enhance the safety of women. In the early 1990s, a federal bill proposed by U.S. Senator Joseph Biden (Democrat from Delaware) attempted to include violence against women, "gender-based assaults," in the category of hate or bias crimes, for which special legal remedies would be available under civil rights law, in addition to expanding funding for programs to reduce crimes of sexual violence (U.S. Senate 1993; compare "Silent Suffering" 1992).

Sexual violence and especially serial murder have been used rhetorically to stigmatize other behaviors that lack the prima facie harmfulness required to justify campaigns of control or suppression. This is done by the technique of problem convergence or guilt by association, suggesting that other apparently trivial actions are in reality stages on the road toward the very serious harm wrought by rape and multiple homicide. One of the most sweeping examples of this tactic was provided by lesbian activist Sheila Jeffreys, writing in the British radical magazine *The Leveller*:

> All men are potential rapists. . . . Every man benefits from the actions of every rapist. . . . The spectrum of violence by men toward women, all aspects of which serve the twin purpose of male gratification and political control of women, includes: wife-beating, sexual abuse of children, frotteurism (rubbing the penis against part of a woman's body—common at Wimbledon tennis matches and in the tube), voyeurism (often reconnoitering for a rape victim), obscene remarks, pornography, touching up, Boston Strangler and Bradford Ripper, wife-murder, obscene telephone calls, father-daughter incest and rape. (Jeffreys 1979)

There are many specific examples of such convergence, suggesting that a given problem is really a subset of the serial murder issue. Diana Russell discusses the case of Gary Heidnik, who imprisoned several women in his Philadelphia cellar, as part of the general theme of slavery and femicide. Heidnik's crimes become only one manifestation of the broader theme of female sexual slavery, a term that encompasses so-called white slavery, forced prostitution, and a great deal of what would normally be regarded as consensual prostitution (D. Russell 1992:167–69).

In 1977 and 1978, feminists organized protests against the Hillside Strangler killings in Los Angeles and placed the crimes in the context of the rape and child abuse believed to be in progress in the city, though receiving less media attention (Lacy 1992:316–24). This protest "connected this seemingly random incident of violence in Los Angeles with the greater picture of nationwide violence toward women" (p. 323). The domain of the serial murder problem thus expanded immensely and so did the range of possible legal intervention.

Serial Murder and Pornography

As a rhetorical theme, serial murder has been most important in feminists' attempts to condemn pornography, based on the claim that sexually explicit material often depicts the subordination of women and thus extols aggressive male sexuality (Jeffreys 1990; though see Altimore 1991). However, the counterargument has been made that themes of male dominance and brutality represent only a very small proportion of commercially available erotica, while most bondage and domination material depicts men as sexually subordinate to women. Feminist activists counter that *any* pornographic picture that focuses solely on female breasts or genitals presents the woman as a dehumanized tool for sexual pleasure. The disembodied parts thus depicted are accordingly parallel to the mutilated remains of the victim of a ripper (Caputi 1987).

Jane Caputi has used the same criticisms against advertising materials that similarly employ disembodied legs, heads, or breasts, which to the feminist critic signify "dismemberment and necrophilic rape" (Caputi 1992:203–21). Describing one such advertisement for Yves St. Laurent stockings, Caputi writes, "The intent and meaning of all such symbolic dismemberments can best be understood by listening to an actual sex killer describe the meanings of his actions," and she then reproduces an excerpt from such an interview with an offender (p. 213). The juxtaposition is intended to place the advertisement in the realm of propaganda for femicide and sexual mutilation.

Associations with the known or assumed characteristics of serial killers are employed to consummate the argument. For example, it is argued that pornography incites sexual violence. To substantiate this, a typical passage notes that "such notorious killers as Edmund Kemper (the Coed Killer), Ted Bundy, David Berkowitz (the 'Son of Sam') and Kenneth Bianchi and Angelo Buono (the Hillside Stranglers) were all heavy pornography consumers" (Caputi and Russell 1992:19). (Of course, it remains open to question how many other consumers engaged in no violent behavior whatever). Further evidence used to support this linkage derives from the classic FBI study of thirty-six convicted sex-killers, a large majority of whom were found to rate pornography as one of their highest sexual interests (the finding is repeatedly cited by,

for example, Caputi 1992:204, 215). In this context, one of the r
examples of the link between misogyny, pornography, and sᴄᵣᵢₐₗ ₐₐₐₐ
der is Ted Bundy, who prior to his execution in 1989 asserted that he had
often been stimulated to commit violent acts by the influence of pornography, though in this case it usually involved very soft-core material.

Feminists thus seek to condemn the makers and users of pornography
by linking them symbolically with serial killers. Chris Domingo argues,

> Not only is femicide ignored by mainstream news and discourse, it is
> joked about and used as grist in the R-rated movie mill. Serial murder is
> actually *enjoyed*—not only by the woman haters who commit the murders,
> as evidenced by the usual presence of semen at the crime scenes—but by a
> large percentage of the male population, as evidenced by attendance at
> slasher films and the popularity of photographs in which women are
> victims of violence. (Radford and Russell 1992:196)

This passage implies a linkage between the perverted aggressive urges
of the killer himself and those of the audience who consume fictional
works related to male domination, as both are rhetorically united in a
common masturbatory enjoyment of female suffering and death.

If pornography promotes sexual violence, this provides an effective
justification for the censorship or suppression of literary or cinematic
works that can be interpreted in this light. During 1980 and 1981, feminist protests over the Trailside Slayer case in California were partly
expressed in antipornography movements, campaigns against adult
magazines like *Hustler* and *Penthouse*, and the destruction of photographs that were claimed to "eroticize the murder of women" (Craft
1992:325–45). In the following years, there were extensive legal conflicts
in midwestern cities that attempted to restrict pornography as a violation of women's civil rights and an encouragement to sexual assault and
murder (Downs 1989). The campaign achieved national impact with the
testimony before the Meese Commission of 1985–1986, the Attorney
General's Commission on Pornography and Obscenity (U.S. Attorney
General 1986).

Patrick Bateman and Hannibal Lecter

The experience of real-life serial murder cases was cited in the debate
over mainstream works that depicted the murder or torture of women,
and criticisms reached new heights in 1990 and 1991. The new controversy began with a controversy over the novel *American Psycho*, by Bret
Easton Ellis, a well-known author whose work was generally reviewed
in serious literary circles. The book tells the story of the fictional serial
killer Patrick Bateman, an articulate yuppie modeled closely on Ted Bun-

dy. The work was under contract to the publishing house Simon and
Schuster, but women staff members took great exception to extremely
violent and sadistic passages in which Bateman was depicted torturing
and mutilating women with pliers, electrocuting victims, and placing a
live rat inside a woman's vagina. The National Organization for Women
threatened to boycott all books published by Simon and Schuster, except
for those by feminist authors; and in November 1990, one month before
the scheduled release date, the firm took the unusual step of announcing that it would not be publishing the novel (Manguel 1991; O'Brien
1990; Rosenblatt 1990). *American Psycho* eventually appeared from Vintage in March 1991.

Ellis's work naturally attracted criticism from feminist circles, but it was
also attacked in quite mainstream publications oriented toward women.
The Canadian *Chatelaine* described Ellis's novel as "a walk on the vile side"
(Scott 1991), while *Working Woman* used the Ellis affair to lambast the
alleged corporate irresponsibility that permitted the publication of "offen-
sively tasteless" works (Collins 1991). *Mademoiselle* denounced the "best-
seller from Hell" (Harrison 1991). Even *US News and World Report* argued
that everything short of actual censorship should be employed to prevent
the publication of works of this sort, which promoted violence against
women (Leo 1990). However, there were also charges that Simon and
Schuster was permitting censorship, while several libraries encountered
criticism due to their decision either to stock or reject the book (Birkerts et
al. 1991; Flagg 1991). The feminist role in attacking the book was constructed as part of the wider problem of "political correctness," the
alleged tendency of academics and intellectuals to suppress views that
were not liberal or feminist in tone (Iannone 1991).

While the *American Psycho* controversy was at its height, the film of *The
Silence of the Lambs* appeared in February 1991, and the two works were
linked in critical writing over the next few months (Halberstam 1991). It
was suggested that these represented part of a general trend depicting
women in lethal danger, and that this reflected a broad masculine hostility against women in general, and specifically against the social advances that women had made in the past two decades. This type of film
might even represent a new genre in motion pictures (Rapping 1991).
Mademoiselle offered a critical review of *The Silence of the Lambs* under the
significant title, "The Evil Movies Do" (Rosenbaum 1991).

WOMEN AS SERIAL KILLERS

The feminist construction of serial murder was based on a number of
specific and questionable assumptions, both about the scale of activity

and the nature of perpetrators and victims. It was assumed that the normal serial killer was a man killing women or girls for sexual pleasure, and cases involving women offenders were all but ignored. In 1987, for example, Cameron and Frazer published their "feminist investigation of serial murder," which "began from a simple observation: there has never been a female Peter Sutcliffe" (1987:1).

This statement must be examined critically in light of the undoubted existence of numerous women through history who have murdered repeatedly. Perhaps 10 to 15 percent of known American serial killers are women (see Chapter 2), while in nineteenth-century England, the multiple-murder cases involving the largest number of known victims all involved women offenders. Jack the Ripper earned worldwide notoriety with his five victims, but there may have been twenty deaths in each of the cases of his contemporaries Mary Ann Cotton (executed in 1873) and Amelia Dyer (executed in 1896; Gaute and Odell 1979). In the United States, Lydia Sherman poisoned at least a dozen victims in the 1870s, and Amy Archer-Gilligan may have been the most prolific serial killer in the nation's history (see Chapter 2). The legendary Belle Gunness was linked to dozens of deaths before her activities were discovered in 1908 (Langlois 1985; De La Torre 1955). One recent "encyclopedia" of female multiple killers offers accounts of over eighty cases, many of which involved in excess of ten or twenty victims (Segrave 1992).

Women multiple killers exist, and there are many readily available published accounts (Newton 1993b; Nash 1981). In recent years, there have been case studies of women who have killed numerous children and family members (Anderson and McGehee 1992; Egginton 1990; Ann Rule 1988; Kuncl and Einstein 1985; Barfield 1985), and of female nurses and other "medical murderers" who kill patients or others in their care (Cauffiel 1993; Davies 1993; Askill and Sharpe 1993; Linedecker and Burt 1990; Elkind 1989). There are also accounts of women who participated in killings alongside male partners (Miller 1993; Farr 1992; Cook 1992; Ritchie 1988).

In addition, the theme of the female serial killer is quite well known in literature and fiction, and real-life cases have influenced portrayals like the homicidal nurse in Stephen King's novel *Misery* (1987). Other works have often employed a woman villain for a deliberate surprise ending, on the assumption that the audience will not expect the culprit to be female. The device has been used in various Jack the Ripper works, such as the 1971 film *Hands of the Ripper*. This was the plot twist in the original *Friday the Thirteenth*, as well as in books like Sanders's *Third Deadly Sin* ([1981] 1982), Lindsey's *Mercy* ([1990] 1991) and Slade's *Headhunter* ([1984] 1986). In fact this shock ending has now been used so frequently as to have become commonplace. There are even a handful of treatments of the woman as sex-killer, as in the popular 1992 film *Basic Instinct*.

Feminists therefore faced some difficulties in defending the simple equation between multiple killers and male rippers, but they tended to confront these problems by employing one of four rhetorical approaches, that might be summarized as follows:

- There are no female multiple killers.
- Female multiple killers are manipulated by men.
- Female multiple killers do not kill for sexual motives.
- Female multiple killers act for rational political or economic motives.

Women might be *multiple* killers, but *serial* killers were invariably male.

The simplest tactic was to assert that there were no female multiple killers, usually by the simple device of neglecting to mention cases. The second method was to argue that many known women killers were largely passive accomplices who had been manipulated or dominated by their men, prominent examples including Myra Hindley or Judith Neelley.

The third approach was more complex, as it accepted the existence of women who killed multiply, but denied that such a person was a serial killer because she did not act out of sexual motivation. Women might kill frequently, but they did not do so out of the impulses that drove a Bundy or a Dahmer. Critics thus argue that the vast majority of known cases involving women killers do not form part of the serial murder problem as they are defining it. During the 1983 hearings before the Senate Committee on Juvenile Justice, Arlen Specter pointed out that in fact there were numerous women multiple killers, but Ann Rule responded that these scarcely counted as serial murderers because they were generally poisoners operating within the family. The distinction is by no means obvious, and she did not attempt to substantiate it.

Finally, one could justify the actions of female multiple killers by arguing that their actions had rational self-defense or loosely economic motives. It is also significant that so many of the women killers were attacking those who were supposed to be in their care, so that their behavior might be seen as quasi-political in nature:

> Traditionally the female role in our society is to be a nurturer, caregiver, nurse, cook, food server and so on. . . . Perhaps these females are rebelling at some level against their role as an inferior. As they went on their murderous way, were they mocking their place, sending up their role in a particularly gruesome manner? Were they striking back at a male-dominated world that gave them little opportunity except as breeding machines and quasi-servants or servants in fact? (Segrave 1992:4)

This postulated element of feminist political protest was supported by the ambiguous sexuality of the killers, many of whom were lesbians or bisexuals (see, for example, Cauffiel 1993; Segrave 1992). The women who killed were linked by their "immense and intense hatred of men. . . . These women despised men, and they got even" (Segrave 1992:7). However, this is a sensitive point in feminist theory, as it would be undesirable to bolster a supposed linkage between lesbianism and homicidal violence (Suggs 1992). In 1992, both feminists and gay rights activists organized protests against the film *Basic Instinct* over precisely this issue.

Virtually every feminist writer denies that women could be serial killers: "Only a handful of the women profiled employed more typically "male" methods of aggressive murder; the few women who worked with men in some fashion also tended to use "male" methods. . . . There are no female counterparts to a Bundy or a Gacy, to whom sex or sexual violence is a part of the murder pattern" (Segrave 1992:4–5).

Framing Aileen Wuornos

Such an interpretation was challenged by a well-publicized case that came to light at the end of 1990, when it was reported that two women were hitchhiking along the roads of Florida, killing the middle-aged men who picked them up. In January 1991, Aileen Wuornos was arrested and charged in seven deaths (her partner and lesbian lover Tyria Moore was not charged). This was presented as a major story, and one *CBS News* account of the case was introduced by Dan Rather declaring that Wuornos was "America's first female serial killer" (compare MacPherson 1991). Interest was maintained through the following year by repeated coverage of the trial on the cable channel Court TV, as well as by features and interviews on news magazine programs like NBC's *Dateline*. Television movies and feature film projects soon followed, including the CBS production *Overkill: the Aileen Wuornos Story*, broadcast in November 1992. There was also an independent documentary film, Nick Bromefield's *Aileen Wuornos: the Selling of a Serial Killer*.

It is likely that one reason for the publicity was the recent success of the film *Thelma and Louise*, which depicted two women forced to go on the run after killing a man who had attempted to rape one of them. The film presented the two sympathetically as feminist rebels who had been exploited and abused by a succession of men, and it was widely reviewed in feminist circles as "empowering". It also prepared the ground for media accounts of the Florida women who allegedly killed men who picked them up for sex, and analogies with the fictional killers were often drawn. This was "a dark version of *Thelma and Louise*" (Mac-Namara 1991).

The Wuornos case appeared to represent a significant departure from stereotypes and challenged the idea that only men could commit multiple random homicides or could be "thrill-killers." In response, feminists asserted that Wuornos's crimes were caused by the abuse she claimed to have suffered through the years. They employed the case as a means of denouncing other male crimes, including sexual abuse of children and physical brutality toward prostitutes like Wuornos. She herself claimed to have been raped during childhood, and her father was a convicted child molester.

In this perspective, it was common to quote sympathetically Wuornos's claim that she had been raped repeatedly, and "just got sick of it" (St. George 1991; Reynolds 1992; Kennedy 1992; Russell 1992). "I was raped—tormented—badly. And I'm sitting on Death Row for defending myself—justifiable homicide. . . . Anyone who rapes, to me, is a sick deranged piece of puke that doesn't deserve to live" (NBC *Dateline*, August 25, 1992). Therefore, "They all deserved it. They all asked for it. Everything I did was in self-defense" (MacNamara 1991). Clearly, "asking for it" was not a defense that would have been tolerated for a second if applied to a male serial killer, and certainly not one who preyed on women.

The self-defense argument gained substance from the reporting on the NBC news program "Dateline," which presented two substantial segments during 1992. The first, "Confessions of a Serial Killer" (August 25) initially presented Wuornos as a reversal of the normal stereotype of a man killing female prostitutes. During the interview, she repeatedly refused to express contrition for her crimes and described the various killings as the consequence of attempted rape or violence by the men involved. She absolutely rejected the label of murderer, still less serial killer. When asked if she ever realized she had been out of control, she angrily responded, "Those men were out of control. I'm sick and tired of those men out there thinking they can control us and do whatever they damn well please with our bodies and think they can get away with it because this is a male-dominated society."

From a feminist point of view, such a presentation was plausible and even attractive, even if few would sympathize with the actual violence. However, "Dateline" presented other aspects of the case in a still more sympathetic light, suggesting that Wuornos's death sentence had been obtained through improper prosecutorial behavior. It was argued that the conviction and death sentence might never have been obtained if the jury had been allowed to hear the early confessions in which Wuornos had asserted self-defense, and this position was strengthened by a still more favorable report on the same program the following November ("What the Jury Never Heard," November 10, 1992). This focused on Wuornos' first victim, whom she alleged to have been a violent sexual sadist who threatened her with torture and dismemberment. "Dateline" discovered evidence that the man in question did indeed have a lengthy record of violent sexual offenses, which made her defense plausible. Moreover, neither this nor other relevant evidence had been introduced at the trial, and it was argued that a retrial was justified. The new segment became an aggressive critique of the Florida prosecutors.

The NBC report made a strong case for arguing that one specific trial had been flawed, though it is very likely that convictions would still have been obtained in the six other deaths. However, the new construction of the case fitted well into feminist theories about the pervasive danger of male sexual violence, and the need for courts to take account of such behavior as an extenuating circumstance for women resisting rape or assault. Increasingly, Aileen Wuornos was framed as a martyr to the patriarchal injustice of the legal system. As she remarked, "You've already put me on the cross, and I'm dying a slow death." She was also a militant heroine in the fight against sexual violence, who had literally taken up arms to resist a rapist. Her assertions drew heavily on feminist rhetoric, as when she argued, "Society didn't care, did they? They framed me for political purposes." While she made this statement, the camera focused on the NBC interviewer Michele Gillen nodding in apparent sympathy with the "so-called serial killer" [*sic*].

The Wuornos case was widely discussed in radical feminist circles. In the lesbian magazine *Frighten the Horses*, editor Cris Gutierrez declared, "The night I saw Aileen Wuornos . . . on "Dateline," she became my instant hero. . . . After hearing her defend her actions, defiantly stating that she only killed men who would have killed her, I wanted to join her fan club. . . . I consider her a feminist role model" (1993:7). The article presented Wuornos as an example of female self-defense and showed a cartoon of a heavily armed woman seeking revenge against the "pig who prosecuted Aileen Wuornos" (p. 9). Both the article and the issue in which it appeared were also illustrated by photographs of women holding handguns.

The new view of Wuornos also supported the arguments of those who regarded serial murder as an exclusively male behavior. In an op-ed piece published in the *New York Times* in January 1992, Phyllis Chesler simply stated that a serial murderer was by definition a male sex-killer, and that therefore Wuornos (who was merely "on trial as a serial killer") could not have fallen into this category. For Chesler, as for most of the femicide theorists, "most serial killers, like Mr. Bundy, are white male drifters who hate women and are obsessed with pornography. They often rape their victims, either before or after killing them. In many cases, these men were abused by their fathers as children" (Chesler 1992a). Wuornos apparently fits none of these categories, did not victimize women, children, or homosexuals, and claimed self-defense. If this analysis were correct, then it was unjust to treat Wuornos as a serial killer, and Chesler compared her allegedly harsh treatment with the mild conditions accorded to another Florida criminal, Ted Bundy, prior to his execution. Wuornos's case exemplified the sufferings of women in patriarchal society, and specifically within the justice system (Chesler 1992b). It also showed the need to restructure the legal right of self-defense to take account of the special needs and interests of women (Chesler 1993).

Assessing Claims

Phyllis Chesler's sympathetic account of Aileen Wuornos epitomizes two decades of feminist writing on serial murder, which is viewed as a male act committed by men against the less powerful, generally women or children. Moreover, the act itself could be traced to the behavior of other males (abusive fathers) and to a violent male sexual culture. In analyzing this picture, it must be said that the stereotype of the killer fits poorly with the evidence, just as there is little substance to the quantitative claims made about the prevalence of the behavior.

The stereotypical serial killer is usually believed to prey on women, and most of the celebrated cases involve the victimization of white women, often in their teens and twenties. These crimes are often placed in the context of what appears to be a common danger to women from sexually motivated assailants and murderers. In reality, women and especially white women are by far the least likely segment of the population to fall victim to homicide. For Americans in the 1990s, the lifetime chance of becoming a murder victim is about 1 in 150, but this ranges from a high of 1 in 21 for black men to 1 in 104 for black women, one in 131 for white men, and 1 in 369 for white women. By these admittedly crude figures, white American women are almost eighteen times less likely to be murdered than their Black male counterparts. In response, feminist activists suggest that very few of the men are killed solely because of their gender, in contrast to female victims; but this rhetorical ploy seems disingenuous at best (Radford 1992:10).

However, if the analysis lacks scholarly merit, there is no doubt that the theories presented during these years have been of immense ideological value. For feminists in the last decade, serial murder has been as valuable a rhetorical device as rape was in the 1970s, in confirming that the wrongs suffered by women were quite comparable to the physical atrocities inflicted upon other minorities or relatively powerless groups. Rape and serial murder have been for the women's movement cultural images quite as threatening and powerful as lynching was for blacks in the civil rights movement, and like lynching these offenses have promoted unity and cohesion within the movement. They have also added a crucial sense of urgency to the feminist agenda and have helped promulgate feminist constructions of the origins and scale of sexual violence.

Chapter 8

The Racial Dimension:
Serial Murder as Bias Crime

THE VICTIM GROUP AS TARGET OF PERSECUTION

The feminist critique of serial murder focuses on the structural injustices that are said to give rise to the crime. This interpretation can be used to buttress the ideological position that any particular group is subject to extreme persecution because of deep-rooted structural factors within the society. Serial murder is thus framed as a crime arising from hatred or bias, though the nature of the persecuted victim population is highly mutable. Cases like those of Peter Sutcliffe or Ted Bundy involved the victimization of women, but racial factors have been prominent in other cases.

Race and ethnicity have long been considered significant factors in both the academic discussion of crime and, perhaps more important, in the symbolic politics surrounding "law and order." It has been charged that anticrime campaigns often contain a thinly disguised agenda of racial hostility and fear, while ethnic conflict has been claimed as the underlying agenda in most American campaigns to restrict or control drugs or alcohol (Goode 1989, 1993; Musto 1987). It is not surprising that race should play a role in as major an area of public concern as serial murder, but the nature of racial discourse in this area is radically different from that found in discussions over street crime or illicit drug dealing. In serial murder, the underlying assumption is that blacks and other racial minorities are massively *under*represented among offenders or even altogether absent, so that this is a type of violent crime that appears to characterize whites rather than blacks. This perception has provided much rhetorical ammunition in recent debates over crime, though it will be suggested that the argument rests on foundations that are fundamentally flawed.

This chapter will discuss the ways in which the concept of serial murder has been employed as a weapon in racial politics, with a particular emphasis on two of the best-known incidents, the Atlanta Child Murders of 1979–1981, and the crimes of Jeffrey Dahmer in Milwaukee a decade later. It will then examine the assumptions about the racial composition of offenders, and suggest how perceptions are shaped by the ideological assumptions of both law enforcement agencies and the mass media.

For centuries, the lives of African-Americans have been blighted by negative stereotypes, which frequently associate them with crime and violence (Lynch and Patterson 1992; Rose and McClain 1990; Hawkins 1986). This chapter will consider an area where stereotypes imply a diametrically opposite image, and blacks appear disproportionately free of involvement in the most serious of crimes. However, this image is false; and this apparently favorable stereotype is both as inaccurate and as pernicious as any of the more familiar racial slurs. The very failure to draw attention to black serial killers might in itself arise from a form of bias within the media and law enforcement.

SERIAL MURDER AS RACIAL PERSECUTION

When an offender of one race regularly targets victims of another, it is not difficult to understand why this should be interpreted as part of a generalized or systematic hostility, especially if there is a long previous record of hatred and violence between the two races. In American history, there are remarkably few real-life serial murder cases that have involved killing across racial lines, but the handful of incidents have incited enormous fear and anger (Hickey 1991). Occasionally, blacks have been culpable, with Whites portrayed as the victims of racial persecution. During 1977 and 1978, Columbus, Georgia, witnessed a series of murders of elderly White women by a black Stocking Strangler, subsequently identified as Carlton Gary. His crimes were viewed in the community as racially motivated assaults, and the murders touched off intense local controversy, leading to threats of vengeance against black individuals. Conversely, the racial murders of blacks by Neal B. Long brought the city of Dayton, Ohio, "toward the brink of racial war" in 1974–1975 (Newton 1990:210).

It has also been charged that such attacks formed part of organized conspiracies. A series of murders of Whites by blacks in California in 1973–1974 (the Zebra Murders) was believed to have been associated with a splinter of the Black Muslim movement, a clandestine organization known as the Death Angels, which is said to have claimed hundreds of White victims across the United States (Howard 1980). Moreover, the movement was said to survive under other guises, and there have been several instances where the murders of Whites by blacks have been interpreted as the work of the putative Death Angels or cognate groups. These cases have included De Mau Mau murders in Chicago in 1978, and it has been suggested that the cult was linked to the Yahweh group active in Florida into the 1990s (Newton 1992:32).

Newton fully accepts the reality of the menace, and further suggests that the Death Angels are "still at large. Still hunting (1990:348)." The truth of such charges remains quite uncertain, and the report of an organized terrorist group or movement is particularly difficult to credit. However, the existence of such traditions or legends is indicative of the tendency to see interracial violence as symptomatic of more general racial conflicts. Though the Death Angels story has not yet achieved widespread public knowledge or acceptance, it is likely that the story might gain popularity in circumstances of increased racial confrontation, especially following a hypothetical series of widely reported interracial attacks on Whites.

In recent decades, the victimization theme has especially been used to depict blacks as the innocent victims of crimes committed either by White offenders or (more subtly) by White society as a whole. In this latter view, the actual race of the offender is not crucial to the interpretation of the action as a direct manifestation of bias, as it is claimed that the crimes are made possible by the systematic racism built into contemporary social arrangements, and the extreme violence of a serial killer is depicted as the culmination or logical outcome of the more routine racial bias encountered in everyday life. As in the case of violence against women, the victimization of blacks is thus mapped together with a group of behaviors that would not by themselves be seen as gravely threatening.

The Atlanta Child Murders

In the contemporary United States, the Atlanta Child Murders provide perhaps the clearest demonstration of the rhetorical use of serial murder to stigmatize racial bias and exploitation. Between 1979 and 1981, it was postulated that a racially motivated killer had been targeting black children and teenagers and had claimed up to thirty "missing and murdered children" before an arrest was made (Keppel 1989). Some researchers have questioned not only the guilt of the accused killer, Wayne Williams, but also whether there were linkages within the perceived wave of killings and disappearances (Fischer 1991; Dettlinger and Prugh 1983). Particular attention has been directed to the compiling of "the list," the official enumeration of the victims believed to have been claimed by one killer. It has been argued that several of these individuals might have died in unrelated incidents through causes other than murder. Meanwhile, equally plausible grounds can be cited for including over sixty other individuals as possible serial murder victims, and some of these attacks occurred after the detention of Wayne Williams. In this view, the whole investigation was shaped by political pressures, and the definition of the scale of the problem was decided by political and racial factors (Turner 1993:78–82; Boles and Davis 1988; Headley 1986).

In the early stages of the case, during 1980, black community activists charged that the authorities were displaying racial bias through their unwillingness to see connections between the murders or disappearances of possible victims. The key activist was Camille Bell of the Stop the Murders Mothers Committee, who denounced police neglect of the victims. James Baldwin remarks that even after several killings, "Authority and/or bureaucracy responded at its usual snail-like pace: the missing children were for a while lumped together as runaways or hustlers" (1985:49). In contrast, the state was swift to condemn Bell's committee for its private endeavors to pursue the investigation, again suggesting that the victims were of little account.

However, the activists soon succeeded in posing the problem as one of serial homicide, possibly with a racial motivation, and at this point city and state agencies became very active and probably tended to go to the opposite extreme by claiming linkages between crimes that may not have possessed common elements. "The state of Georgia had never before exhibited so intense an interest in Black life or Black death" (Baldwin 1985:58). The crimes attracted worldwide attention and were frequently discussed as a manifestation of black suffering and injustice. This was the theme emphasized not only by local activists, but by national news media, including all the nightly network news shows, as well as ABC's "20/20." The case attracted numerous national celebrities to the city, to offer support or advice to the black community or to draw attention to other causes. These personalities included black leaders like Muhammad Ali, Coretta Scott King, and Jesse Jackson, as well as activist groups like the Communist Workers' Party and the Guardian Angels, and show business figures like Burt Reynolds. Even former Ku Klux Klan leader David Duke attempted to get involved, ostensibly to forestall retaliatory violence against white people (Linedecker 1988:168). Across the nation, it became fashionable for people of radical or liberal inclination to wear red ribbons to show support and sympathy for Atlanta's black community.

As the perceived racial element of the crisis came to the forefront in 1980 and 1981, the Atlanta affair became a focus of national organization and campaigning by black groups and leaders, who cited it as paradigmatic of the pain and violence of the black experience in the United States. Jesse Jackson declared that "the killings were racially motivated, no matter what race the killer might turn out to be" (Dettlinger and Prugh 1983:186). However, the great majority of black leaders left little doubt that the crimes were the work of a white killer or killers. The Reverend Joseph Lowery of the Southern Christian Leadership Conference simply stated, "Black people don't kill their children," while the Communist Workers' Party asserted, "There never has been a black mass murderer" (pp. 186–87). The tone of the racial rhetoric heightened steadily as time progressed and the murders remained unsolved. Sentiment may have been aggravated by the Republican victory in the 1980 presidential election and consequent fears that black social gains might be halted or reversed.

The Atlanta crimes were increasingly contextualized as part of general antiblack violence:

> Meanwhile, against the background of the shooting of National Urban League president Vernon Jordan in Fort Wayne, Indiana, and the horrible slayings of black men in Buffalo—where hearts were actually cut out of chests—and the then unexplained slayings of blacks in Salt Lake City, Atlanta's troubles in 1980 spawned rumors and speculation of a national conspiracy of genocide against blacks. (Dettlinger and Prugh 1983:157; see also Turner 1993:123–27)

Conspiracy charges also focused on allegations that blacks were the subjects of bizarre medical or scientific experiments, an idea promoted by comedian and conspiracy theorist Dick Gregory (Turner 1993:144–51). One widely retold story linked the crimes to the presence of the federal Center for Disease Control in Atlanta, and suggested that white scientists were seeking to "harvest" interferon and other biological substances from the genitals of black men, in order to promote the life and health of wealthy white patients (Dettlinger and Prugh 1983:59–60. The origins of the story can be precisely located in Norman Spinrad's science fiction novel, *Bug Jack Barron* (1969), which has not only the same plotline as the Atlanta rumors, but the same southern black setting.

The tale gained credence from the scandal of the "Tuskegee syphilis experiment," which became the subject of media controversy in 1972. In this case, scientists had permitted syphilis to rage unchecked for de-

cades in a rural black population, a story that was modified in the retell-
ing to suggest that white doctors themselves had deliberately infected
the black men. The Tuskegee legend has since been cited in connection
with alleged plots to exterminate blacks through AIDS and a variety of
public health schemes (Junod 1993; Turner 1993:151-163). Some of these
tales involve multiple homicide for the sake of medical research, and a
Baltimore variant implicated Johns Hopkins University: "At Hopkins,
they snatch children off the street and experiment on them at night in
the basement" (St. George 1993). Similar stories are recorded about the
research hospitals connected with Columbia University in New York
City, and the University of Pennsylvania in Philadelphia. The Atlanta
tales thus fitted into a growing tradition of urban legend-making that
became powerful among African-American communities (Turner 1993).

In Atlanta itself, conspiracy charges faded somewhat after the arrest
and conviction of Wayne Williams, but many activists remained uncon-
vinced. Years afterwards, Camille Bell would warn "her brothers and
sisters to prepare for the day when 'they' come to put 'us' into 'concen-
tration camps'" (quoted in Dettlinger and Prugh 1983:97). The Williams
defense team also continues to assert that the murders were the work of
a Ku Klux Klan group, while popular rumor implicated the FBI directly
in the killings (Turner 1993:123–27).

However, even if Williams were the sole perpetrator, this would not
remove the Atlanta incident from the records of perceived racial injustice, and the most sophisticated presentation of this argument did not
appear until 1985, years after Williams's incarceration. James Baldwin's
book *The Evidence of Things Not Seen* fully acknowledges the doubts about
Williams's guilt, but the identity of the perpetrator is perhaps less important than the racial injustices that the cases illustrate. The murders are
viewed as characteristic of the African-American experience within the
white-dominated society of the United States, "the situation of the black
man in the American inferno" (Baldwin 1985:20). The murders collec-
tively become "the Terror" (p. 27), "racial terror" (p. 79), part of the
ongoing assault upon black communities committed successively (he
argues) in the name of segregation, desegregation, and integration
(p. 120).

The crimes are explicitly compared to the lynchings and other racial
persecutions of the early twentieth century, the memory of which forms
so potent an element in modern American political culture. Baldwin
draws parallels between the murder of Clifford Jones, which brought the
Atlanta attacks to public attention, and the 1955 lynching of Emmett Till,
a notorious atrocity that did much to galvanize the civil rights movement: This is "a comparison I wish neither to force nor avoid" (p. 40).
The Atlanta Child Murders are thus mapped together with perceived

racial injustices through history, including the anti-Semitic policies of tsarist Russia or Nazi Germany, until the child murders become "this latest pogrom" (p. 79). Even Williams himself becomes a victim of systematic oppression, and "must be added to the list of Atlanta's slaughtered black children" (p. 125).

The Theme Develops

The Atlanta affair was only the best-known of a group of similar incidents about this time, in all of which black activists attributed the career of a serial killer to his choosing low-priority victims, with the suggestion that the police deliberately undervalued black lives. Activists commonly suggested that the deaths continued as a consequence of police bias and neglect and that those murdered were victims of racism as surely as if they had been lynched. In the Boston area in 1979, local black feminists remarked that "one of the things that most galled people was that in the beginning, the first reports of the murders had been buried in the back of the *Boston Globe* with the racing reports. It was not news" (Grant 1992:150). Without media pressure, police were slow to intervene to prevent further killings.

These were common criticisms during what was described as the Southside Slayer case in Los Angeles, which was a prominent news story from early 1985 though the summer of 1987. It was alleged (questionably) that one man was responsible for up to twenty killings of street prostitutes, mainly of black and Hispanic origin (see Chapter 2). During the summer of 1986, a campaign against police neglect was led by community activist Margaret Prescod, of the Black Coalition, which urged local residents to involve themselves in the investigation to make up for official shortcomings. Central to Prescod's rhetoric was the theme of unequal justice: "We know if the victims were white residents of Santa Monica it would be handled in a different way" (quoted in *Los Angeles Times,* July 27, 1986): "If the South Side victims had been married women from Beverly Hills or young women attending the University of California at Los Angeles, the lack of police progress would be a scandal . . . What kind of moral judgment is being made about the value of people's lives?" (quoted in Bigelow 1986).

Though her activism was predominantly based on racial concerns, Prescod suggested that police indifference arose from both race and gender factors, and she cooperated with the feminist group Take Back the Night. In her view, the victims were undervalued not only because they were black, but also because they were prostitutes, who were depicted as betraying their appropriate sexual role and obligations (see

Chapter 7). In contrast, she emphasized the humanity of the victims: "These women are more than just a police record. They have left behind loved ones" (quoted in *Los Angeles Times* March 5, 1986). Though the importance of Prescod's campaign was denied by police, her activities were widely reported, and this probably contributed to the dramatic expansion of the personnel and resources available to the special police task force during 1986.

The Dahmer Case

There are obvious parallels between these incidents and the more recent Jeffrey Dahmer case, in which a white male killed up to seventeen men and boys, who were predominantly drawn from African-Americans and other ethnic minorities (Baumann 1991; Davis 1991; Dvorchak and Holewa 1991; Klein 1992; Norris 1992b; Schwartz 1992). This led to the case being framed as an instance of racial bias and exploitation, and local community groups used the affair to mobilize support for protests and marches against official racism. Such interpretations were all the more likely given the time and place in which the offenses occurred. The murders were discovered in July 1991, a few months after the initial broadcasting of the videotape of Rodney King being beaten by Los Angeles police officers. In Milwaukee itself, there had for some years been activism by black groups who alleged that resources were unfairly targeted toward white areas and business districts, to the exclusion of black communities. In 1990, one local alderman had earned national notoriety by threatening to form an armed black militia unless more action were taken to promote social justice and equity, and his demands were the subject of a "60 Minutes" report.

In Milwaukee, the local impact of the Dahmer affair was epitomized by the newspaper headline, "Serial Murder Case Exposes Deep Milwaukee Tensions" (Terry 1991b) One black minister stated, "Milwaukee is a sick town and it's been swept under the carpet for years . . . But this has lifted up the carpet and the whole world can see the dirt" (quoted in Terry 1991b). It was implied that the persecution of minority people by Dahmer was related or equivalent to police abuse of the same groups over the years: "We want changes made. There has been a great deal of blood spilled" (quoted in Terry 1991a).

Particularly controversial was an incident in which police had been called to rescue a teenage boy who had been found bleeding in the street. Officers determined that he was in fact a boyfriend of Dahmer's who was fleeing after a "domestic quarrel between homosexuals," and so they returned the boy to Dahmer's apartment, where he was killed shortly afterwards. Race entered into this transaction in several ways: the complaining neighbors who reported seeing the boy were black, while the victim himself was of Laotian origin. The suggestion was that the white officers had placed little weight on the word of either complainants or victim, while accepting the word of (the white) Dahmer, an instance of apparent bias that had directly resulted in murder. The affair earned national notoriety, while within Milwaukee itself, it was cited as symptomatic of police racism. One community spokesman was the Reverend Leharve Buck, who remarked, "If that boy had been white, he'd be alive today. People felt completely sold out by the police after that" (quoted in Terry 1991b).

A local rap musician, Top Dog, issued a song about Dahmer, demanding why he had not yet received the death penalty and suggesting that "'Cause he's white, they'll never treat that man rough/ If he was black they'll beat him down with handcuffs/. . . . See, the system is a trip" (quoted by Tim Cuprisin in *Milwaukee Journal*, January 28, 1992). A black police officer stated, "If you're poor, black, hispanic, gay or lesbian, then in the eyes of the Milwaukee Police Department, you are engaging in deviant behavior" (quoted in Terry 1991b). As the relative of one victim remarked, "The police don't give a damn when bad things happen in poor areas" (quoted in Terry 1991a). Community activist Queen Hyler stated, "This is a very racist city. You have a white guy killing people weekly, with bodies stacking up in a building occupied mostly by blacks, but the cops are too busy riding shotgun on the black community to pay any attention" (quoted in Dvorchak and Holewa 1991:166). As in Atlanta, the murders were believed to reflect the lesser value that the authorities placed on the lives of minority citizens.

In the Dahmer case, however, there was the added element that a white perpetrator had indubitably been responsible for a series of grotesque crimes, and this led to emphasis on the alleged fact that serial killers are always white males. This was not entirely a new idea, and the notion that blacks never became serial killers had been expressed in the Atlanta controversies. This theme was often asserted in the numerous media talk shows and interviews in the months following the exposure of the Dahmer case.

Inverting Racial Stereotypes

Both experts and members of the public claimed that serial murder was an offense committed by white men, and that one seldom heard of serial killers who were African-American or drawn from other minority groups. This idea, effectively symbolized by the terrifying figure of

Jeffrey Dahmer, has played a significant role in the rhetoric of minority protest, where it has been employed to challenge stereotypes that minorities are especially prone to violence. In one form or another, jungle and cannibal images have been used to denigrate blacks for centuries, but the concept of (white) serial killers as monsters, the ultimate subhuman savages, provides a form of ideological rebuttal.

For example, during the 1992–1993 debate over the federal funding for biomedical research into violence, it was argued that such an investigation would inevitably contain a covert racist agenda, which would exclude the violence of the most brutal offenders. In one much-quoted passage, Dr. Frederick Goodwin, head of the federal Alcohol, Drug Abuse and Mental Health Administration, discussed recent findings about aggression and crowding in primate populations, especially among adolescent males. He continued, "That is the natural way of it for males, to knock each other off. . . . [M]aybe it isn't just the careless use of the word when people call certain areas of certain cities 'jungles.'" These remarks were felt to constitute a major ethnic slur, a direct comparison between "sexed-up, aggressive male rhesus monkeys" and "inner-city men," who were predominantly black. The resulting debacle forced Goodwin to resign (Renseberger 1992). In response, critics suggested that "Jeffrey Dahmer killed seventeen people, chopped them up and ate them. No one said, 'Let's look at his genetic make-up'" ("Ambitious Federal Plan," 1992).

Charges of gross violence are thereby redirected toward the majority ethnic community, while the supposed white predominance in serial murder activity is felt to counterbalance the overrepresentation of black offenders in conventional violent crimes. This notion appeared in popular culture, for instance, in a video by the rap group X-Clan ("Fire and Earth"), which attacks negative stereotypes of blacks. The singer refers to the times he has been "called an animal," but meanwhile, "in Milwaukee, there's a cannibal."

The view has also been reported in the community at large. In 1992, the *Philadelphia Inquirer* presented a series of interviews with young men, mainly black, who had been convicted of murder. In virtually all cases, the offenders rejected any blame for the incident, attributed the violence to the victim, and were puzzled or outraged that they had received prison sentences. The central theme was that none of the group saw himself as a real murderer or serious criminal. In one typical instance, a convict remarked, "I didn't execute nobody or cut them up. I could see if somebody kill six, seven people—then they deserve life. . . . It's not like I'm no serial killer. I didn't kill *a lot* of people" (Marder 1992, emphasis in original).

AFRICAN-AMERICANS AND SERIAL HOMICIDE

This point about racial disparity among serial killers has been accepted by many scholars: Leyton, for example, writes that modern serial killers "were almost never drawn from the ranks of the truly oppressed: there are few women, blacks or native Americans in our files" (1986:288). However, the assertion can readily be disputed, and while African-American serial killers have left little impression in the collective memory, they undoubtedly exist. In his study of American serial murder from the 1790s to the 1980s, Eric Hickey has suggested that about 13 percent of known cases can be associated with African-Americans (1991:133–34, 169–70). This is comparable to the findings of Michael Newton, who finds that 16 percent of American cases during the present century involved black offenders (1992:49). The question then arises why such a considerable presence has been neglected so that the normal stereotype of the serial killer almost wholly omits blacks. The reasons may reflect the force of different kinds of ethnic prejudice, both in determining law enforcement attitudes to cases involving different races and the way in which such incidents are reported and preserved by the media.

African-Americans have been well represented in the history of serial murder in the United States, and in the mid–twentieth century, black offenders were among those claiming the largest number of victims. During the 1930s and 1940s, there was a group of such cases including Jarvis Catoe, Jake Bird, and Clarence Hill, all of which can be described as fitting the classic stereotypes of serial murder (Jenkins 1989, 1994; see Chapter 2).

From the late 1960s, the scale and frequency of serial homicide activity in this country accelerated dramatically, and the number of African-American cases grew proportionately. Accurate figures are difficult to come by, but one method of proceeding is to focus on extreme serial cases, those offenders claiming eight or more victims during their careers. Such spectacular cases are likely to be widely reported, and will therefore be found in national media. Between 1971 and 1990, there were approximately a hundred such cases in the United States. Of these, about thirteen involved African-American offenders. This again confirms the estimates of Hickey and Newton, and suggests that the percentage of black serial killers is closely comparable to the proportion of blacks in the U.S. population as a whole (see Table 8.1).

Note that Table 8.1 includes several cases that remain unsolved, and it is naturally difficult to assert the racial origins of an individual not yet apprehended. It is also possible that some of these cases might not in fact represent true series—both the Atlanta and Southside Slayer cases

Table 8.1. Cases of Extreme Serial Homicide (Eight or More Victims) by Black
        Offenders, 1971–1990

Offender	Where active	Dates
Nathaniel R. Code	Louisiana	1984–1987
Alton Coleman and Debra Brown	Ohio, Michigan, Indiana, Illinois	1984
Carlton Gary	Georgia	1970–1978
Kevin Haley and Reginald Haley	Southern California	1979–1984
Calvin Jackson	New York	1973–1974
Milton Johnson	Illinois	1983
Devernon LeGrand	New York	1968–1975
Michael Player ("Marcus Nisby")	Southern California	1986
Coral E. Watts	Michigan, Texas	1979–1983
Wayne Williams?	Georgia	?1979–1981?
Freeway Phantom?	Washington DC	1971–1972
Southside Slayer?	Southern California	1983–1987
Unsolved series?	Maryland, Washington, D.C.	1986–1987

have been subjected to this criticism (see Chapter 2). Given this caveat, it
should be emphasized that police in both the Washington and the Freeway Phantom cases consistently describe an African-American suspect
or suspects. Doubts may be raised about the exact number of African-
American offenders in this category, but there can be no doubt that such
killers do exist.

Coral Watts remains perhaps the most notorious of the African-
American serial killers, though he is anything but a household name.
Born in 1953, Watts's known record of sexual homicide began while he
was enrolled at Western Michigan University in 1974. After brief periods
of incarceration and mental treatment, he resumed his attacks against
women in 1979, first in the Detroit area, where he became known as the
Sunday Morning Slasher, and subsequently in Houston (Linedecker
1988). His career reached its height in Texas between 1980 and 1982, and
he confessed to ten murders in the Houston area. However, he has been
plausibly linked to over twenty killings (Newton 1990). This figure falls
short of the crimes linked to Bundy or Gacy, but it is in excess of the far-
better publicized cases of Jeffrey Dahmer, David Berkowitz, and Joseph
Kallinger.

Comparably obscure is Milton Johnson, believed to be responsible for
the Weekend Murders of some seventeen individuals in Joliet, Illinois,
during 1983. This case attracted intense local publicity, as it involved

several separate incidents of what has been described as "random wholesale slaughter" (Newton 1990:176–77). Four people died in one incident, five in another. Alton Coleman was an equally dangerous offender, a multiple sex offender, who launched a two-month crime spree through the Midwest in 1984, leaving some ten people dead (Linedecker 1988).

The question then arises of why blacks are so seldom depicted in the true-crime literature and still less in fiction that so few cases have earned popular notoriety. It appears that the celebrity of a particular case depends on neither the savagery of the attacks nor the absolute number of the victims. There are no in-depth true-crime studies of Alton Coleman, Milton Johnson, Calvin Jackson, Carlton Gary, or Coral Watts to compare with the proliferating genre that focuses on killers like Dahmer and Bundy (there are brief chapter-length studies of some black cases in collections like Linedecker 1988, 1990a; Crockett 1990, 1991). In terms of the number of victims, Coral Watts and Milton Johnson represented far graver social threats than the vast majority of the white individuals studied in the recent true-crime books (see Chapter 4). Hardly any thrillers, detective novels, or films depend on the investigation of crimes involving blacks as serial killers or even as victims.

One determining factor here is the attitude of publishers toward what constitutes newsworthy or salable material, and the assumption that cases of African-American offenders are less likely to appeal to a mass audience. Books of this sort are likely to relegated to the Black Studies sections of major stores, and even to be marketed only in urban centers. This was, for example, the case with Dettlinger and Prugh's excellent study of the Atlanta Child Murders, which was published by a small Atlanta concern. The few stores that stocked it elsewhere confined it to the Black Interest shelves, and it soon went out of print.

During midcentury, the absence of black offenders from popular culture representations of the serial murder phenomenon can partly be explained by the general neglect of blacks and black themes in most American media. African-Americans were not portrayed as serial killers in mainstream movies, but it could equally be argued that until very recently, they have but rarely received serious treatment in any role whatever. It is notable that blacks have not featured as villains in the slasher or psycho films of the last few years. Presumably, filmmakers do not wish to have their work categorized as exclusively of black interest, while they are also anxious to avoid being accused of depicting crude or controversial racial stereotypes.

This last element may also help to explain why criminal case studies have not included the stories of figures like Jarvis Catoe in the 1940s or Coral Watts in the 1980s. In the context of the midcentury, it might well have been thought inappropriate or tasteless to focus on the acts of black offenders. If unduly sensationalized, these events could have given ammunition to racists and segregationists anxious to justify their opinions about black violence and criminality. More recently, the presentation of serial killers as primitive atavistic monsters has drawn on ideas traditionally applied to blacks. If a modern book described a Coral Watts or Alton Coleman in similar jungle terminology, it would certainly be denounced as overtly racist. Whatever the reason, the consequence has been to limit the attention paid to African-American offenders, and thus to shape the stereotype of the multiple killer in a racially selective manner (Jenkins 1989, 1994).

The problem is neatly illustrated by two superficially similar (though unrelated) cases that occurred in Philadelphia during the mid-1980s. Gary Heidnik and Harrison "Marty" Graham both imprisoned and murdered a number of people in their respective houses in poor sections of the city, and the media widely reported the horrific scenes that were uncovered by police. In both cases, the killers tended to draw victims from a similar population, of street people and discharged mental patients, and on occasion the two operated within a few blocks of each other.

Heidnik became the center of national attention and is the subject of a book-length study (Englade 1988; compare Apsche 1993). In 1991, he was the subject of an interview on the network television show "60 Minutes." Part of Heidnik's story was popularized in the book and film versions of *The Silence of the Lambs*, where the fictional killer Buffalo Bill similarly imprisons young women in a basement. In contrast, Graham's case received little attention outside the Philadelphia area, although he was convicted of no less than seven murders, in contrast to Heidnik's three. There is no true-crime book on the affair, it has inspired no fictional work, and even in the Philadelphia media Graham received only a tiny portion of the coverage accorded to Heidnik (he is the subject of a chapter in Linedecker 1990a:1–24). There is no obvious reason for the disparity in treatment, though race provides a likely explanation. Heidnik is white and therefore fits accepted stereotypes of the multiple killer, while Graham is black and is thus far more difficult to characterize.

THE ROLE OF VICTIM CHOICE

Ethnic stereotyping may play an important role in shaping police investigations, to such an extent that it should be asked whether the cases we have record of are an accurate reflection of the total phenomenon. Many serial murder cases remain unknown to police, but it might be argued that cases involving black offenders and victims are especially likely to escape official attention. The racial element in the cultural construction of serial homicide may mean that the African-American component is seriously underrecognized.

This phenomenon can be explained in terms of the likelihood of a particular crime being recognized, first, as an act of homicide, and second, as part of a linked series of crimes. There are a number of factors at work here, but the victimological element is central. These victim-oriented factors are complex, but in general they tend to benefit criminals who operate in certain regions and disadvantage victims of particular racial and social groups (Jenkins, 1993).

For a number of reasons, law enforcement agencies are less likely to seek or find evidence of serial murder activity where the victims are African-American. Partly this may result from overt racism on the part of police agencies, and this has certainly been a factor in many periods of American history. Between about 1910 and 1935, one of the most prolific American serial killers was Albert Fish, a white man who chiefly preyed on black children in big cities like Washington, D.C., and New York (Schechter 1990; Jenkins 1989; see Chapter 2). Fish remained at large for a quarter of a century, which was remarkable in view of his flagrant record of perversion and child molestation. However, he made clear that he survived through a deliberate policy of victim choice. As he remarked in his final confession, the police simply did not care about "colored" children, and paid far less attention when they died mysteriously or disappeared suddenly. Fish's downfall came when he murdered the daughter of his white middle-class neighbors (Jenkins, 1989, 1994).

Discriminatory police attitudes go some way toward explaining the low priority attached to African-American murder victims, and this benefits any offender who chooses to pursue minority victims. As homicide is primarily an intraracial crime, this then means that African-American serial killers are far more likely to escape detection. Racial attitudes here are intimately linked to social stereotypes. It is not so much that blacks as such are assigned lower police priorities, but that poor people living in certain high-crime neighborhoods appear to inspire less concern when they die or vanish (Jenkins, 1993).

The case of Calvin Jackson is suggestive (Godwin 1978). When Jackson was arrested in 1974 for a murder committed in a New York apartment building, he confessed with little prompting to a series of other homicides committed in the same building over a six-month period. Before this confession, there had been no suggestion that any of the crimes were linked or indeed that most of the deaths were caused by anything other than natural causes. In retrospect, it seems that this lack of police concern was in large part a consequence of the nature of the victims and of the environment in which they died. The building in question was a single-occupancy hotel, where most of the guests were poor, isolated, and often elderly (see Chapter 6).

It was commonplace for police to be called to the hotel to deal with cases of sudden death or injury, often arising from problems associated with drugs, alcoholism, or old age. In the case of Jackson's victims, foul play was only recorded in cases where victims were killed with conspicuous signs of violence; and autopsies were rare. Deaths resulting from smothering were customarily dismissed as the result of natural causes. Where foul play was noted, the police saw no reason to suspect a serial killer and naturally viewed the crime as part of the interpersonal violence that was endemic in such a transient community. As there was no apparent evidence of grotesque sexual abuse, police saw no need to fit the crimes into the context of sex-killings, and thus linkages were ignored (Newton 1990).

In other words, police naturally approach a suspicious death with certain preconceptions that depend both on the nature of the victim and the social environment in which the incident occurs. In some contexts, a sudden death can be explained in many ways without the need to assume the existence of a random or repeat killer, and serial murder activity is thus less likely to be noted. This is particularly true of urban environments characterized by poverty, isolation, transience, and frequent violence. In Jackson's case, not all the victims were black; but the same factors apply with particular relevance to urban African-American communities.

Moreover, the police attitudes that allowed Jackson to continue unchecked for so long have not changed fundamentally since the mid-1970s. In fact, contemporary police agencies have even more preconceptions about the likely causes of sudden death in the inner cities, to the possible benefit of repeat killers. The deaths of young black city dwellers are all too likely to be attributed to factors such as gang conflict and disputes between rival drug traffickers, and it would not be farfetched to imagine a contemporary black serial killer with the intelligence to leave evidence at the site of his or her crimes to encourage such an interpretation. The deaths would probably be seen as falling into what is currently a well-known category of urban homicide, and serial murder would not be suspected. By such means, it would notionally be possible for such a murderer to continue to operate for years.

Serial murder activity by African-Americans does exist, it is certainly not a new phenomenon, and it is likely that even the records we have tend to understate the scale of the phenomenon. However, for a variety of reasons, the behavior is very likely to be underreported, and even when cases are acknowledged, they have made little impact on public consciousness. The omission of minority offenders from the popular stereotype of serial murder has permitted the growth of a factually misleading view about the racial composition of the phenomenon. This in turn allows the offense to be employed rhetorically as a glaring instance of racial bias and injustice.

Chapter 9

"A Homosexual Who Could Strike Again"

The eager lover aspires to the boy just as the wolf desires the tender lamb.
—Plato, *Phaedrus*

In the context of race and gender, the serial murder theme is employed rhetorically in a radical cause, to attack the position of the traditionally dominant social category of white males. It is suggested, however dubiously, that minorities and women are especially likely to fall victim to white male serial killers and that this represents a manifestation of general patterns of discrimination and abuse. However, the area of sexual orientation raises quite different questions, and the prevailing rhetoric tends to be extremely hostile to minority rights and interests. There certainly have been instances where gay rights activists have used serial murder occurrences to stigmatize homophobic sentiment, but instances of serial murder have commonly been used to stigmatize homosexuals, and thus to support conservative and actively homophobic conclusions. Such associations often emerge at times when gay rights issues are prominent in public debate.

Several common themes are thus used to discredit homosexuals as a category. First, there is a persistent failure to distinguish between homosexuality and pedophilia, so that sex-killers who target boys or young men are automatically described as homosexual killers. In addition, sexually motivated killers are often depicted in association with aspects of sexual inversion, such as transvestism or homosexual sadomasochism. Even when it is not directly stated that the offenders are actively homosexual, the implication is still that homosexuality is part of a spectrum of deviant behaviors that culminate in violence and multiple murder. The combined effect of such imagery is that homosexuality is powerfully mapped together with serial murder, especially the murder of children.

HOMOSEXUALITY AND SERIAL HOMICIDE

Such associations can often be seen in the American experience, inevitably perhaps when a large proportion of multiple sex-killers have chosen male targets. Apart from the celebrated cases of Dean Corll and John Wayne Gacy, there have in the last two decades been the murders associated with William Bonin, Patrick Kearney, Randy Kraft, Jeffrey Dahmer, and Ottis Toole.

The high number of victims in such "homosexual" murder cases merits explanation. During the late 1970s, there were no less than three major serial murder cases simultaneously in progress in California, each of which became one of the most prolific ever recorded in terms of the frequency of killings. These included the Trashbag Murders, which were attributed to Patrick Kearney and David Hill, and which claimed perhaps fifteen lives between 1973 and 1977; and the Freeway Killings carried out by a group led by William Bonin, which killed at least twenty victims between 1978 and 1980. In addition, Randy Kraft killed well over forty young men between about 1975 and 1983, operating chiefly in California but also claiming victims in different parts of the country (McDougal 1992). In the same years, Larry Eyler was implicated in twenty-three deaths in Illinois and Indiana (Kolarik and Klatt 1992). The numbers are very large and, unlike some other incidents, the totals are unlikely to be artificially inflated. At about the same time (1972–1978), John Wayne Gacy was killing about thirty-three boys and young men in the Chicago area; and these notorious incidents followed very shortly after the Corll and Corona cases of the early 1970s. Between them, these seven cases may have involved a total of two hundred victims. In England similarly, the "gay killings" of Dennis Nilsen represent the largest number of victims certainly attributed to a single individual in that nation's history (Lisners 1983; Masters 1985, 1991a).

 - The scale of these cases may well reflect the pattern of victim choice, in that most of these killers targeted young men and teenagers with few family or community ties, and who were thus unlikely to excite comment when they disappeared. They were exactly the sort of young people who were believed likely to disappear of their own volition, and who would not attract intense police attention even if a missing person report were ever filed. In addition, there were factors specific to the homosexual context of the killings, as the murderers were exploiting the tradition of casual and relatively impersonal sexual contacts that prevails in some homosexual subcultures. Most victims were thus drawn into intimate consensual contact and were prepared to go to isolated locations with a relative stranger. This created a highly vulnerable population of potential victims, many of whom could be killed before a pattern of serial homicide was recognized (compare the role of racial bias described in Chapter 8).

On the other hand, the apparent vulnerability of homosexuals to serial killers may owe at least as much to structural factors within law enforcement as to characteristics of homosexuality or the gay life-style. There is much evidence that the police often refuse to attach the same significance to homosexual murders as to others that occur in a "normal" social context. In 1990, for example, gay groups in Indianapolis protested to police that a killer had been preying on the homosexual community for a decade, but the crimes had not even been acknowledged as a series ("Cities Nationwide" 1990). In New York City, gay activists had urged the police to investigate an apparently related string of killings for over a year before a murder series was acknowledged. A gay activist complained, "You look at the pattern of crimes against the lesbian and gay community—the police largely don't take these reports seriously" (Osborne 1993). The cavalier attitude to the cases was suggested by terms used by investigators: for example, the trashbag killings were colloquially described by police as the "fag in a bag" murders (McDougal 1992).

CONSTRUCTING THE DAHMER CASE

This neglect may have resulted from an assumption that violence was endemic to the homosexual subculture or else a contempt for actual or potential victims. In the Dahmer case, racial bias was cited in the affair when the police returned a potential young victim to the killer's apartment (see Chapter 8). However, local gay activists expressed outrage over the same incident because the police had failed to intervene in an apparent instance of domestic violence between gay partners. This suggested that violence was regarded as normal in such a context, a "lover's quarrel" (Dvorchak and Holewa 1991:214). This idea was reinforced by police statements on an earlier Milwaukee dismemberment murder, which characterized it as "homosexual overkill" (p. 209). The National Gay and Lesbian Task Force responded predictably: "When, for example, has the term 'heterosexual overkill' ever been used to describe the serial killing of women by a male perpetrator?" (p. 213).

Multiple-murder cases involving homosexuals as either perpetrators or victims provide the opportunity for gay rights activists to attack official bias. A leader of Queer Nation/Milwaukee suggested, in terminology commonplace in black and feminist rhetoric, that if Dahmer's victims had been white daughters of middle class people, the police would have been doing a thorough state-wide search until they found out who was responsible. . . . The police make it clear that if you live the gay life-style, you deserve whatever you get. As long as they think it's a bunch of gay people hurting each other, it really doesn't deserve their attention. (pp. 208–9)

Another gay spokesman epitomized the common complaints when he remarked,

Gay men tend to be more vulnerable. If they disappear, they are not as likely to be reported missing. If they are reported as missing, they are not as likely to get the same type of police follow-up as a report of someone's daughter, husband or wife would get. (p. 208)

In the immediate aftermath of the Dahmer case, the National Gay and Lesbian Task Force denounced "anti-gay and racial bias on the part of Milwaukee police." They also sought to frame the murders as hate crimes:

[T]hese crimes were hate-motivated. By focussing on Dahmer's alleged homosexuality, [the media] has overlooked the fact that many of his victims were homosexual. Regardless of Dahmer's actual sexual identity, it is clear that he hates homosexuals enough to want to kill them. It is also apparent Dahmer's murders were racially motivated. Anti-gay and racial hatred are not innate characteristics. They are learned. Dahmer's behavior is the most extreme example of this type of hatred. (pp. 213–14)

Dahmer's savagery was thus mapped together with more ordinary acts of homophobia and prejudice, as "the ultimate in gay-bashing" (p. 212). The *Advocate* denounced the case as "murder by homophobia" (Dawidoff 1992).

GAY SERIAL KILLERS IN THE MEDIA

But the activists were struggling against powerful prejudices. As so often, media and law enforcement attitudes closely reflected one another, and the news reporting of gay cases left little doubt of the association that readers were intended to make between the sexual orientation of the offenders and their violence. Before the late 1970s, hostility could be both stark and quite overt, and both mass media and the professional literature shared a common assumption about the "particularly brutal crimes committed by homosexuals" (quoted in Katz 1992:187).

As late as 1974 one true-crime journalist wrote an account of "homicidal homosexuals" that would probably be regarded as quite unacceptable in print today (Lucas 1992:137). Discussing one repeat murder case,
he notes,

> Research has shown that homosexuals have an intensification of all the
> primitive destructive elements of sexuality which one sometime finds in
> heterosexual crimes. . . . All the more primitive attitudes, the passions of
> envy and jealousy, anger and revenge at rejection and refusal . . . are
> much more dangerous. . . . [T]the situation is complicated by the self-
> hatred of the homosexual, which is then projected or displaced onto an-
> other person, whom he then feels the need to harm (p. 141)

More recent authors are far more circumspect, but the linkage with
violence is still present. Newton (1992) writes of the tradition of "gay
killers," a curious juxtaposition of words.

In films also, there was a strong tradition associating multiple murder
with homosexuality or transvestism, an idea that had emerged strongly
in *Psycho*. Even the name Norman Bates refers to the sexual inversion of
the character, as he is "neither woman *nor man*" and practices *masturba-
tion*; he also *baits* his traps (Bloch 1993:229). The transvestite theme
reappeared in *No Way to Treat a Lady*, which was loosely based on the
Boston Strangler case, while a deranged homosexual killer claimed the
life of the (female) central figure in *Looking for Mr. Goodbar* (1977). It
might be argued that such films were merely depicting dangerous characters who happened to be homosexual, but the lack of more positive
homosexual images tended to suggest that any form of sexual "inversion" led to violent impulses (Tharp 1991; Russo 1981).

This identification survived into the present decade, and is suggested
for example by the depiction of Buffalo Bill in *The Silence of the Lambs*,
where the killer wishes to change his gender by constructing a "woman
suit" out of the skins of real women. Though the script specifies that
transsexuals normally tend to be relatively passive, the linkage was still
felt to be unacceptable, and the film was denounced as fundamentally
homophobic by writers in the *Village Voice* (March 12, 1991). Yet again in
1991, the remake of the classic *Cape Fear* presented a repeat sex killer as a
transvestite and homosexual.

The association between homosexuality and violence was naturally a
matter of great concern to political groups pressing for gay rights, and
the overtly hostile stereotyping of the 1970s coincided with a dramatic
expansion of gay militancy. This resulted in organized protests against
depictions of homosexual killers. In Europe, this focused on the 1973
film *Tenderness of the Wolves*, which ostentatiously described the grisly
crimes of Fritz Haarmann (Russo 1981:239). In the United States, the

greatest concern was expressed over the William Friedkin film *Cruising*, which was released in 1980. Though based on an earlier novel, the film was heavily influenced by two incidents in New York City, including the 1973 Gay Murders, and the series of mutilation Bag Murders within the gay community during 1977 and 1978, crimes that were later associated with Paul Bateson (Newton 1990:19).

Cruising was shot on location in the city, but filming was deeply controversial because the script focused almost entirely on conditions within the sadomasochistic gay subculture, and it was objected that this reinforced the gay/violence stereotype. In addition, the film implies that the central detective figure discovers his own homosexual tendencies, which are manifested in his carrying out the murder of a homosexual neighbor. Militant sentiments were aggravated by the timing of the film—the protests occurred about the time of major rioting in San Francisco following the reduced sentencing given a man who had assassinated the popular gay politician, Harvey Milk. Protest leaflets against the film argued that it would stimulate or justify "gay bashing" and homophobic attacks and claimed, "People will die because of this film." Russo's description of this campaign seems to accept the validity of this judgment; he notes, "In November 1980, outside the Ramrod Bar, the scene of the filming of *Cruising*, a minister's son emerged from a car with an Israeli submachine gun and killed two gay men" (1981:238). In 1992, similar protests were directed against the portrayal of the bisexual woman killer in the film *Basic Instinct* (Holub 1991).

Media accounts of gay cases have also been attacked because of the apparent tendency to blame victims, either the specific individuals killed or else homosexuals as a category. Russo's analysis of homosexual themes in American film emphasizes how frequently homosexual characters die violently, as if this were the natural consequence or due punishment for their condition. In news reporting, it is common to suggest that murders occur because the killers had themselves been assaulted by homosexuals, either through early child abuse, or else (more recently) through contracting AIDS. The revenge motif in such accounts often implies that attacks were understandable, even if not fully justified. Newton's discussion of Australian serial killer William McDonald typically claims, "Traumatized by a homosexual rape in his teens, the slayer was driven to seek revenge against gays selected at random" (1990:219). The account may be factually correct in explaining the motivation in this case, but it is reminiscent of the trend to blame mothers or wives for heterosexual killings, an idea so often denounced by feminists. When a number of London homosexuals were murdered during 1993, the British media soon suggested that the motivation was probably revenge for AIDS. The police stated that the offender might be "conducting a crusade," again a remarkably positive and sympathetic interpretation (Darnton 1993).

The consequence of such presentations is suggested by the responses to notorious cases. The Dahmer affair of 1991 resulted in a significant upsurge of gay bashing within Milwaukee, on the assumption that extreme violence was a homosexual characteristic. One gay newspaper received a letter declaring, "I don't care if you queers die of AIDS or dismemberment. Do us all a favor and hurry it up, okay? I hope Dahmer gets off on a technicality" (Dvorchak and Holewa 1991:205). Dismemberment and extreme violence were thus seen as perils of homosexual conduct quite as characteristic as AIDS.

PROTECTING THE CHILDREN?

Also controversial has been the linkage between homosexuality and pedophilia. Historically, there is an important case study of this phenomenon in the context of Germany in the 1920s, when there was intense debate over legislation concerning morality issues like divorce and abortion. Important pressure groups were demanding legal equality for homosexuals, but they received a decisive setback from the notorious serial murder case involving Fritz Haarmann of Hannover, who had a lengthy record of petty theft and indecency with children. However, he was protected from more serious legal difficulties by his close relationship with the police, for whom he was a valuable informant (Gaute and Odell 1989; Plant 1986:45–47). From 1918, he began to pick up runaway boys at the railway station, often pretending to be a police officer or detective, and he killed repeatedly. In 1924, the remains of many victims were found by a nearby river, and their belongings were found in Haarmann's possession. He confessed to some forty killings. The case achieved national celebrity, and "dominated the headlines for months" (Plant 1986:45). It stigmatized homosexuals as child molesters and violent sex criminals and thus set back attempts to liberalize the laws. Plant argues that this did much to encourage public support for the savage persecutions unleashed by the Nazi regime a few years later (pp. 45–48).

Similar arguments have recurred in modern times, with attempts to discredit homosexuals by associating them with sexual murder and pedophilia. In Great Britain, issues of gender and sexual orientation were central to political debate during the 1980s, with the predominantly Conservative press attempting to link the opposition Labour Party to the apparently extreme views espoused by radicals in the major cities. This may explain the repeated media emphasis on the homosexual aspect of some serial murder cases, like the attacks on small boys by the London "pedophile murder ring" exposed in the mid-1980s (Oliver and Smith 1993; Jenkins 1991, 1992a). Both in the media and in police statements, we repeatedly find statements such as "Police warn that the killer is a homosexual who could strike again." The implications of such a phrase are clear, especially when it was not similarly suggested that a contemporary murderer of young girls might be a heterosexual killer.

This linkage was a matter of great concern during the celebrated gay serial murder cases of the late 1970s. Individuals like Randy Kraft and William Bonin chose victims who ranged in age from pubescent teenagers to young men in their early twenties, but a large proportion of them were legally boys, in the sense of being below the age of sexual consent. Emphasizing that such individuals were gay serial killers therefore tended to confound homosexuals with pedophiles and to support contemporary claims that homosexuality represented a physical and moral threat to children.

The gay-killer connection is so frequent in the 1980s literature as to be overwhelming (Godwin 1978). Newton, for example, recounts the story of 1920s multiple killer Gordon Stewart Northcott, who murdered numerous teenage boys and children, some as young as ten or twelve. He is described as a "homosexual sadist in the mold of Dean Corll and John Gacy" (Newton 1990:252). Colin Wilson (1988) terms Gacy the "homosexual killer of at least thirty three boys," while Corll becomes the "homosexual mass murderer of Houston." In 1973, *True Detective* reported the Corll case in Houston under the title "Texas homosexual torture-murder horrors." In 1979, similarly, the Gacy case was headlined as the "Illinois homosexual homicide horror" (Crockett 1990:243).

In Atlanta, meanwhile, the "missing and murdered children" incidents of 1979–1981 led to a particular concern with the homosexual aspects of the case, that is, the apparent linkage to individual men and groups who sought sex with teenage boys. This was especially sensitive because of the possible stigma that could befall all homosexuals, and Mayor Andrew Young praised Police Chief Lee Brown "for publicly defusing any hint of homosexual connections with Atlanta's murders." However, investigator Chet Dettlinger has countered, "Since there obviously were homosexual connections, was it defusion [sic]—or a cover up? If so, for whom?" (Dettlinger and Prugh 1983:267–68). The connection was all the more potent following so swiftly on the Gacy case and the sensational trial.

The timing of such an unsavory linkage was particularly relevant in the late 1970s and early 1980s, as the pedophile theme was playing a pivotal role in contemporary gay rights referenda in Florida, California, and other states in 1977 and 1978, and in Texas a few years later (Greenberg 1988; Katz 1992). One notorious slogan suggested, "Homosexuals aren't born—they recruit." In the Dade County controversy, in which Anita Bryant became the chief activist, her anti–gay rights pressure group took the name Save Our Children, Inc. (D'Emilio and Freedman 1988:346–47). Apart from gay rights issues, the concern over pedophilia was also present in debates about censorship and sex education in schools. Pedophilia was central to antigay rhetoric until the mid-1980s, when it was largely replaced by the still more effective terror weapon of AIDS.

However, the issue has reemerged in recent attempts to weaken or abolish gay rights legislation, especially in the 1992 state and federal elections. The movement in Oregon was typical in the format of the legislation it sought: a proposed amendment to the state constitution, which would prohibit state or local governments from promoting or encouraging "homosexuality, pedophilia, sadism or masochism," suggesting a direct relationship between these various "deviations," and implicitly allying homosexuality to both offenses against children, and specifically to violent behaviors (Egan 1992a). Elsewhere, other proposed measures listed homosexuality alongside necrophilia and bestiality, in addition to pedophilia.

In this context, it is likely that the success of the campaign against serial murder from 1983 onwards owed much of its success to its use of similar stereotypical fears about homosexuals and pedophiles. It has already been remarked that much of the activism in this area focused on the alleged special vulnerability of children to serial killers, a danger stressed by John Walsh and Kenneth Wooden and repeatedly emphasized before the U.S. Senate's Subcommittee on *Juvenile* Justice (see Chapter 3). It should also be noted that the majority of cases cited involved not merely children but specifically boys and that the incidents most frequently mentioned involved the homosexual pedophiles Corll and Gacy. Also much stressed were the Atlanta killings, which were believed to have targeted children of both genders, though the alleged killer was the homosexual Wayne Williams. Much of the evidence about "children" disappearing at the hands of highly mobile killers actually draws on cases in which teenagers (rather than infants or toddlers) were killed by sexual sadists like the Freeway Killers.

It was suggested in Chapter 6 that the focus on child victims proved to be of great rhetorical value in the reassertion of conservative values in the early 1980s, and particularly benefited the moral New Right of the Reagan years. The stigmatization of homosexuality had the added advantage of discrediting a well-organized and substantially financed political group of strongly liberal inclination, while simultaneously consolidating support for "traditional" moral values against the hedonism that the gay community was believed to represent. The serial murder panic should thus be seen as at least in part a covert assault on the gay movement and gay political rights.

REDISCOVERING SEX PREDATORS

If homosexuals were really pedophiles, then pedophile killers in turn were characterized as homosexuals, and this assimilation of images contributed to a significant reshaping of perceptions of sexual deviance. In the late 1980s, there were a number of notorious cases of child killers, but none had the impact of Westley Alan Dodd, who was arrested in Washington state in 1990 for the murders of three boys, and executed in 1993. Dodd's frank and much televised interviews made him appear the epitome of the ruthless and unapologetic multiple killer, declaring at his sentencing hearing, "If I do escape, I promise you I will kill and rape again, and I will enjoy every minute of it" (see Chapter 3).

The Dodd case was often cited in political campaigns to pass stricter laws on sex offenders, together with the stories of other molesters including one who had assaulted a seven-year-old boy and mutilated his genitals. This represented a classic piece of domain expansion in problem construction, as the implication was that the sex offender problem was closely related to the issue of pedophilia, which was in turn exemplified by the multiple-child killer. The threatening image of Dodd thus justified draconian policies against offenders whose behaviors might in reality have been far less threatening and (generally) nonviolent, including voyeurs and exhibitionists (Alice Vachss 1993; Lanning 1987, 1989a). The campaign was so effective because it drew so extensively on the well-known rhetoric of threatened children; though all the cases cited involved pedophiles specifically accused of sexual violence against boys.

Some of the laws now passed were far harsher than had been considered acceptable for many years, and often represented a return to the indefinite sentences passed on "sex psychopaths" during the 1950s (Murphy 1992). Under the Washington State law that took effect in 1990, the state was empowered to detain a sex offense prisoner past his or her release date pending a hearing on civil commitment, while a finding of future dangerousness could lead to indefinite "treatment" in confinement (London 1991). The statute defined criteria under which an offender could be labeled a sexual predator and confined accordingly (Egan 1992b).

Ideologically, such a policy bore a close relationship to the hard-line law and order policies that prevailed during the Reagan years and that had led to profound skepticism about the possibility of rehabilitation. It also marked a sharpening of attitudes toward sexual deviance and a decisive shift in the typification of sexual deviation away from mental health perspectives and toward criminal justice interpretations. Though the movement was not initially perceived as directed against homosexuals as such, many references in the debate suggested an identification between gay killers and the supposed pedophile menace, and the broader category of sexual violence. Inevitably, the legal and political response to Dodd must be seen as part of the broader hostility toward homosexuals and their supposed predilection to molest and harm small boys.

The stigmatization of homosexuals as potential sex-killers represents in extreme form one of the commonest themes in the rhetorical exploitation of serial murder: the extrapolation of very uncommon behavior to denounce not merely a category of people, but their whole social and cultural system. And as in the case of racial and gender perspectives, this particular form of stereotyping is made possible only by the dissemination of inaccurate information about the prevalence of the offense and the composition of the offender population. In this case, the fundamental flaw is one of definition, and the failure to distinguish between homosexuals and pedophiles. However, the consequence of this misunderstanding is once more to influence the directions of legislation and law enforcement policy, in the interests of the political Right.

Chapter 10

"Darker Than We Imagine":
Cults and Conspiracies

Serial murder can be ascribed to various groups and social categories, but one of the most influential contemporary constructions of the phenomenon concerns crimes by hypothetical groups that may not even exist in reality. These are the *ritual* killers, either individuals or organized cults, who are accused of committing perhaps thousands of murders each year. This construction of multiple murder thus shades into familiar American traditions of political and religious conspiracy (Bennett 1990; Hofstadter 1979).

Police inability to resolve a lengthy series of linked murders is likely to be explained partly in terms of official malfeasance or incompetence, but even more sinister factors can be postulated. If a killer is evading such intense police attention, this might be explained in terms of his or her superior intelligence or organization, and this can lead to suggestions of elaborate conspiratorial structures. In addition, the savage violence and mutilation often characteristic of serial homicide invite suspicions that the crimes must have some ritualistic element. Such an interpretation is attractive because it offers a sort of rational explanation for acts that otherwise seem wholly outside human comprehension.

The exact group or organization to be blamed will depend on the ideological outlook of the particular claims-makers involved and the political expectations and fears of the community in question. Racial fears can lead to charges of involvement by political cults—white Ku Klux Klan or black Death Angels (see Chapter 8). During the 1980s, however, the dominance of the political Right and the power of religious fundamentalism favored interpretations of behavior that emphasized the presence of objective evil, and charges about sinister cults and conspiracies focused on movements that are generally occult or satanic in nature.

The concept of the satanic serial killer, or of multiple homicide as a form of human sacrifice, has come to be a potent weapon in the arsenal of anticult rhetoric, and it is widely used to denounce and stigmatize the perceived threat from occult and mystical fringe movements. The present chapter will trace the genesis and development of the idea in contemporary America, emphasizing once again the contribution of works that were originally intended as pure fiction or perhaps parody, yet supplied ideas that have come to be taken very seriously.

The transformation of fanciful stories into a purported problem coincided closely with the emergence of the serial murder issue. Both themes developed rapidly during 1980 and 1981, and there was intense cross-fertilization between the problems during the height of the murder panic of 1983–1985. By the end of the decade, the charges made by cult claims-makers were far more ambitious in scale than those advanced by even the most extreme adherents of a murder wave.

JACK THE RIPPER AS CULT KILLER

The idea of cult killings can be traced back to the original Jack the Ripper murders, which occurred in London during 1888, when the failure to locate a perpetrator gave rise to speculation about the powerful forces that might be at work (Abrahamsen 1992; Wilson and Odell 1987; Farson 1972; McCormick 1970; Odell 1965). Theories included the work of Indian *thuggee* or other Asian cults, either Hindu or Buddhist, and parallels were drawn with sects that were said to mutilate the genitals of their victims. Some argued that the dates of the murders reflected a particular ritualistic sacrificial calendar, oriented perhaps to the phases of the moon. The most harrowing view was that the culprit might be an Englishman who had encountered these groups in Asia and subsequently "gone native" or reverted to savagery (Rumbelow 1988:108–10: see Chapter 5). In some form, all these ideas have returned with great force in the contemporary United States.

One of the most potent and enduring theories of the Ripper murders involved anti-Semitic stereotypes. The crimes occurred against a local background of bitter religious and ethnic conflict, and it was suggested that the mutilations inflicted on the women victims reflected Jewish ritual practices (Holmes 1979). Rumors gained credence from a still controversial incident that occurred after one of the murders, when a senior police officer ordered the removal of a graffito claiming that "The Juwes [*sic*] are not the men that will be blamed for nothing" (Rumbelow 1988:122). In subsequent conspiracy theories, the removal of what might have been a significant clue has been interpreted as part of an official desire to conceal involvement by organized cultic elements, either Jewish or Masonic. The murders thus became a novel form of the ancient anti-Semitic blood-libel about the abduction and murder of Christian children; and this interpretation of the Ripper crimes survives today in circles of the British neo-Nazi Right.

Other views stressed the occult nature of the crimes and speculated on possible symbolism of the bizarre mutilations. One key theorist was the legendary occultist Aleister Crowley, whose writings on the case were accorded special significance by the many later theorists who viewed him as a uniquely sinister influence on the development of twentieth-century Satanism. In his widely read *Confessions*, he wrote:

> One theory of the motive of the murderer was that he was performing an Operation to obtain the Supreme Black Magical Power. The seven women had to be killed so that their seven bodies formed a "Calvary Cross of seven points" with its head to the west. The theory was that after killing the third or fourth, I forget which, the murderer acquired the power of invisibility, and this was confirmed by the fact that in one case a policeman heard the shrieks of the dying woman and reached her before life was extinct, yet she lay in a cul de sac with no possible exit save to the street; and the policeman saw no signs of the assassin, though he was patrolling outside, expressly on the lookout. (Crowley 1970:755)

The limited value of such assertions is perhaps indicated by the humorous tone with which Crowley would discuss the case and the associated media sensationalism. He recorded that later newspapers would associate him directly with the crimes, though he was only thirteen years old in 1888 (p. 364). In later years, he also remarked of the killer that "I didn't get on with him very well. He had no sense of humor." Despite such obvious levity, Crowley's remarks were believed to offer clear sanction for supernatural interpretations of the case (compare Harris 1987).

This theme recurs in the work of the popular fantasy-horror author Robert Bloch (see Chapter 4). In various stories during the 1940s and 1950s, he developed the idea of serial killers as demonically possessed (*Enoch*, [1946] 1977) or as cult devil worshipers (*Sweet Sixteen*, [1960] 1990). These ritual themes may well have been influenced by the cult speculations surrounding the Cleveland and Philadelphia murder series in 1938 and 1939 (see Chapter 2). One of his most popular and widely anthologized stories remains "Yours Truly, Jack the Ripper" ([1943] 1977), which supposes that the original Ripper carried out his murders in order to secure eternal life and youth, and that the same individual was in fact responsible for countless murders in successive decades:

The trail is there, the pattern. Unsolved crimes. Slashed throats of women.
With the peculiar disfigurations and removals. Yes, I've followed a trail of
blood. . . . eighty-seven such murders—and to the trained criminologist,
all bear the stigma of the Ripper's handiwork. Recently, there were the so-
called Cleveland torso slayings. (p. 5)

"Yours Truly, Jack the Ripper" was dramatized on U.S. television in
the early 1960s, and shortly afterwards it was updated to form the theme
of a "Star Trek" episode, "Wolf in the Fold," in which the same eternal
Red Jack is continuing his career of murder into the twenty-third century. In 1967, Harlan Ellison wrote of the original story, "The number of
times it has been reprinted, anthologized, translated into radio and TV
scripts, and most of all plagiarized, is staggering" (1974:Vol.1, p. 181).
Both Bloch and Ellison wrote sequels in which Jack is portrayed in a
superhuman time-traveling context. Essentially the same ideas recurred
in the more "literary" setting of Peter Ackroyd's 1985 novel *Hawksmoor*.

Other cult speculations about the Ripper murders entered the realms
of serious scholarship. In the early 1970s, attention focused not on the
occult aspects of the crimes but rather on their alleged Masonic and
political nature. A series of largely spurious stories suggested that the
crimes had been committed in order to conceal the potentially scan-
dalous secret marriage between the Duke of Clarence, a member of the
royal family, and a commoner of the Catholic religion (Knight 1976;
Harrison 1972). In this view, highly placed royal associates had murdered women with knowledge of the case, and had used the mutilations
described in Masonic rituals, where the Juwes (not Jews) are characters.
For example, bodies had been found in specific symbolic locations outside the gates of the City of London, and the disembowelment of the
victims corresponded neatly to the grisly threats pledged in Masonic
oaths. The "Clarence theory" in its various guises was popular in the
1970s and 1980s, and the Masonic aspects were popularized in the film
Murder by Decree (1979), as well as in numerous fictional accounts.

CHARLES MANSON AND JIM JONES: 1969–1979

The Ripper speculations did much to create the hypothetical linkage
between multiple homicide and cult activity, a bond that was greatly
strengthened after 1969 by the investigation of the "Manson family"
murders in California. These crimes coincided with an upsurge of occult
and satanic interests, especially among young people associated with
the alternative hippie culture of the time, and it was hypothesized that
other killer cults might emerge from this milieu. In 1970, another mass

killing in California drew attention to the use of occult and Tarot card imagery by the offender, John Linley Frazier, and other apparently occult-linked multiple homicides followed in subsequent years (Lunde 1976). This was also the time of the Zodiac murders in northern California, killings ostensibly undertaken by a lone individual with strong occult and astrological beliefs. As in the case of Jack the Ripper, there are theories that the original Zodiac continued his activities many years after people believed the crimes had ceased (Graysmith 1987).

Interest in other murderous cults stemmed from the investigation of the milieu of the Manson family, and in 1971 Ed Sanders's book *The Family* made statements that became widely influential. He placed Manson firmly in the context of the numerous occult and mystical movements then flourishing in northern California, such as the Kirke cult (Sanders [1971] 1972:125). One much-quoted story linked Manson to a group of British origin known as the Church of the Process (or simply the Process), a connection that the group bitterly disputed in the courts (Bainbridge 1978; Sanders's suggestion is supported by Bugliosi and Gentry 1976). *The Family* "alludes to the existence of a sort of modern Thuggee or Satanic underground, in which he claims The Process to have been a central organizing factor" (Parfrey 1990:159; see also Bainbridge 1991).

Sanders also reported stories of a murder cult supposedly known as the Four Pi movement under its leader, the Grand Chingon, which among other rituals sacrificed and skinned large dogs. The theme often occurs in the movements described by Sanders ([1971] 1972; see, for example, pp. 187–91). In the late 1970s, reported discoveries of skinned and mutilated dogs in the New York City area led to allegations of cult murder activity there (Terry 1987:162). Four Pi, described by Terry as a "Process splinter group" (p. 179) was said to be linked to a number of serial murder cases, including that of California cannibal killer Stanley Dean Baker, while cultists were associated with the making of "snuff" movies. These charges have been cited as factual by a number of authors on cults and multiple homicide, including Terry (1987:172–81), Kahaner (1988:83), Raschke (1990:111–16), and Newton (1990). Linedecker asserts that the West Coast *thuggee* is not merely a metaphorical term, but actually is carried out by literal worshipers of Kali (Linedecker 1990a:272).

It is often difficult to assess the factual value of Sanders' work. The book undoubtedly reflects the rumors and tales common in the California posthippie underground and indicates that accounts of ritual murder were developing, though with what foundation it is difficult to tell. Moreover, the tone of these stories makes them difficult to assess, and Sanders often indulges in considerable irony in order to parody the sensationalistic press exposés of the Manson clan. For example, his work concludes with the portentous words, "And only when all these evil affairs are known and exposed can the curse of ritual sacrifice, Helter Skelter and satanism be removed from the coasts and mountains and deserts of California" ([1971] 1972:348). Whatever the intent, the ideas presented in *The Family* found a growing audience. In Britain, for example, one newspaper reported in late 1971 that "police are trying to stamp out an evil new cult which is sweeping America." The alleged national cult was "Satan's Satanic Servants—groups who hero-worship hippie murderer Charles Manson and his Satan's Slaves," and the movement was said to be involved in numerous ritual homicides (Sampson 1971).

Ritual murder theories developed a following among fundamentalist Christian groups, initially on the extreme fringes, but increasingly among more orthodox groups. Apart from the usual sources, these accounts drew heavily on confessions from the numerous alleged defectors from occult movements, who were anxious to portray the movement's satanic records in as sinister a light as possible in order to highlight the wonders of their conversion experience (Warnke 1972). The emerging mythology is illustrated by *The Broken Cross*, a 1974 comic book published by the California fundamentalist group headed by Jack Chick and allegedly based on the expert advice of a former "Druid high priest."

Broken Cross depicts a small town satanic cult, which carries out at least eight human sacrifices each year. Victims are normally drawn from abducted hitchhikers, often young teenage girls, and the group maintains its immunity because cult members include all the powerful local citizens: the sheriff, mayor, pastor, librarian, and so on. Affiliated with the cult are itinerant multiple killers, and one scene reproduces closely the 1970 arrest of Stanley Dean Baker, who when found with human remains had declared, "I have a problem. I'm a cannibal" (Newton 1990:16). Normally, Chick publications have only a tiny minority appeal, but the images presented here as early as 1974 offer in remarkably well-developed form the ideas about ritual murder that became so common during the 1980s.

The spread of such ideas into the social mainstream was assisted by their growing influence in the anticult movement (Richardson et al. 1991; Hicks 1991). During the mid-1970s, there was widespread concern about religious cults such as "Jesus People" and "Moonies," and organized groups developed to combat their influence. The liveliest issue at this stage concerned the brainwashing techniques cults were said to use in order to control their members, and the legal and ethical bases of the "deprogramming" required to reverse this. However, fears about violence, physical threats, and even murder gangs gradually developed on the fringes of the anticult movement, where there was substantial overlap with evangelical and fundamentalist Christian ideas.

Concern about violence intensified following the mass suicides of the People's Temple followers in Jonestown, Guyana. This incident drew attention to the extreme and irrational violence apparently associated with fringe religious groups and the sexual and physical abuse said to be inflicted on children. And as in the case of the Manson murders, the Jonestown affair excited the interest of police officers and journalists who later became important writers on cult activities: police officers like Sandi Gallant of San Francisco or Pat Metoyer of Los Angeles. Metoyer's first contact with cults developed in 1970, when he was assigned to protect a witness testifying against the Manson group, and over the next few years he became interested in brainwashing by nonoccult cult groups. After the Jonestown case, his attention turned to cult violence and abuse.

THE IDEAS COALESCE: 1980–1981

Another key activist was Kenneth Wooden, whose book *The Children of Jonestown* (1981) offers an influential analysis of the Jonestown incident (for Wooden as an influential claims-maker in the area of serial murder, see Chapters 3 and 6). It can also be seen as the pioneering text in inventing the notion of cults ritualistically abusing young people and perhaps engaging in the murder of small children. He argues, "Babies, born into cults, their births unregistered, are reported to have died of unnatural causes and to have been buried in secrecy, like pets" (p. 205). Wooden was especially important in disseminating the concept of cult abuses because of his role as a television reporter and producer. It was also about this time that the book *Michelle Remembers* (Smith and Pazder 1980) drew attention to the developing idea of ritualized child abuse, explicitly suggesting that the violent cults involved in the exploitation of children were satanic in nature (see also Victor 1993; Jenkins and Maier-Katkin 1991, 1992; Hicks 1991; for earlier parallels, see Tallant 1946).

Meanwhile, charges of bizarre ritualistic behavior by cults were encouraged by speculations surrounding alleged animal mutilations reported from many western states (Goode 1992:303–43; Kahaner 1988:145–49). These incidents, which were also attributed to extraterrestrial activity, are now widely regarded as a classic example of the spread of rumor and popular delusion, but at the time they were often linked to cults of various kinds.

By the end of the 1970s, several ongoing investigations were in various ways focusing attention on the violent or criminal activities of real or supposed cults, which were increasingly likely to be perceived as satanic. In the fall of 1980 the San Francisco police department issued a circular warning of itinerant satanic groups involved in "animal mutilations and ritualistic homicides of human beings wherein internal organs are removed from the victims and used in church baptisms and rituals" (Kahaner 1988:16–17). Also in late 1980, the Kansas City, Missouri, police department was gathering intelligence on what was claimed to be a powerful local satanic cult (Rivera 1988).

It was at this time (1979–1980) that Maury Terry's journalistic investigation of the Son of Sam killings in New York City was studying the activities of alleged satanic conspiracies. Terry suggests, inter alia, that the 1976–1977 murders were not—as they appeared—the unassisted work of the convicted offender David Berkowitz. In this view, Berkowitz was only part of a much larger satanic cult, possibly thousands strong. The network might have national ramifications, tied to the Church of the Process and possibly to the O.T.O., the *Ordo Templi Orientis*, based on the teachings of Aleister Crowley (Terry 1987:172–81, 386–88). Terry mentions in passing the Atlanta Child Murders, where during April 1981 it was alleged that the deaths were sacrificial murders by "a cult involved with drugs, pornography and Satanism," which marked its ritual sites with inverted crosses (Dettlinger and Prugh 1983:95–98; Newton 1990:9).

Meanwhile, Ted Gunderson was beginning the investigations that would make him a leading advocate of the concept of satanic murder gangs. Gunderson was a former head of the FBI's regional office in Los Angeles, a prestigious post that gave considerable weight to his assertions. He had become interested in the case of Jeffrey MacDonald, an army Green Beret whose family had been murdered in 1970 (Terry 1987:452–62). MacDonald was convicted of the killings himself, but always maintained that the crimes had in fact been perpetrated by a group of young people, who had chanted hippie slogans such as "Acid is groovy! Kill the pigs." The crimes thus appeared analogous to the then-recent Manson murders.

Macdonald's claims met widespread skepticism, but Gunderson claimed to have located members of the actual cult, and he became convinced of the existence of national networks of ritualistically motivated murder gangs. A breakthrough occurred in October 1980, when Gunderson and another officer obtained a signed confession from a woman who had allegedly participated in the killings, "who stated that she and members of her satanic cult" carried out the crimes "in connection with her initiation into the group" (Peterson 1988:1).

By 1981, apparently isolated charges of violent cult activity were beginning to appear with increased frequency, and—more important— local investigators and theorists were beginning to form links and exchange ideas. This made it more likely that an investigation into one type of occult activity would actively seek other symptoms of the problem, so that (for example) an instance of animal mutilation would be mapped together with allegations from nearby areas concerning ritual murder, cult recruitment, or child abuse. Connections would thus be drawn, to create a systematic picture of what was believed to be a vast menace.

CREATING A RITUAL MURDER PROBLEM: 1982–1990

The growing interest in satanism and cult crime coincided exactly with new perceptions of the scale and severity of the serial murder problem. There emerged an increasingly vocal group of theorists who argued that ritual and cult murders were a common phenomenon in contemporary America and that many serial murders should be seen as a subset of the generalized cult threat. Estimates about the numbers of victims of this modern *thuggee* varied greatly, but one commonly cited figure suggested that some fifty thousand ritualistic sacrifices occurred each year. In 1988, for example, *The American Focus on Satanic Crime* (a work especially targeted at law-enforcement professionals) suggested that satanists are connected with

> the murders of unbaptized infants, child sexual abuse in day-care, rape, ritual abuse of children, drug trafficking, arson, pornography, kidnapping, vandalism, church desecration, corpse theft, sexual trafficking of children and the heinous mutilation, dismemberment and sacrifices of humans and animals. [They are] responsible for the deaths of more than 60,000 Americans each year, including missing and runaway youth. (Peterson 1988: foreword)

Gunderson contributed to this work, and stated:

> I have been told it is a common occurrence for these groups to kidnap their victims (usually infants and young children) from hospitals, orphanages, shopping centers and off the streets. . . . A Boise, ID police officer believes that fifty thousand to sixty thousand Americans disappear each year and are victims of human sacrifices of satanic cults. . . . Most of the victims are cremated, thus there is no body and no evidence. I know of an occult supply store in Los Angeles, California that sells portable crematories.

These ideas were closely related to the more general 1983–1985 panic over serial murder and concurrent fears about perceived threats to

American children (see Chapter 3). It was also in these years that there emerged the idea of a cult threat to the young, the suggestion that the supposed thousands of missing children were being kidnapped for the evil purposes of satanic organizations, which indulged in mass human sacrifice.

Support for such charges was drawn from the statistics commonly cited in the construction of the serial murder problem. One Christian fundamentalist denouncing ritualized and satanic child abuse claimed that such cult activities were a massive threat:

> In every state of the nation, there are reports and investigations of satanic crimes. More than two million American children, each year, are reported missing, many of them too young to be runaways. In addition, more than five thousand unidentifiable bodies of children are found, annually, in the United States. (Peterson 1988:7)

Kenneth Wooden claimed in 1988, "Twenty-five percent of all unsolved murders are ritualistic in nature and the victims are children and women" (quoted in Victor 1993:125).

The idea of satanic or ritualistic child abuse emerged about 1980, but such charges achieved national notoriety from late 1983, with events that coincided exactly with the height of the murder panic. The most important cases involved charges of mass child abuse at the McMartin play school, in Manhattan Beach, California, and in the town of Jordan, Minnesota. In both instances, large numbers of adults were allegedly abusing numerous children, in a context that involved ritualistic-seeming elements like robes, candles, and the mutilation or sacrifice of animals (*America's Best Kept Secret* 1988; Eberle and Eberle 1986).

Child abuse was now contextualized together with large-scale child pornography and satanic or ritual elements, a heady mixture that often recurred in numerous ritual abuse trials over the next decade (Spencer 1989; Stratford 1988; Eberle and Eberle 1986). And while the whole concept of ritual abuse has been bitterly attacked, there remain in the 1990s many experts who believe in the reality of the problem, including the notion of mass child sacrifice. Such views have been expressed in publications as widely read as *MS.* and *Vanity Fair*, and the theories have acquired strong support among radical feminists (Rose 1993; Bennetts 1993; "Silent Suffering" 1992; Sakheim and Devine 1992). For attacks on the concepts, see Wright (1993), Victor (1993), Jenkins (1992a), Lanning (1989b, 1992), Hicks (1991), Jenkins and Maier-Katkin (1991, 1992). MacLean (1993) discusses the related issues of adult recall and memory on which so many of the claims hinge. As in the Jonestown era, belief in possible atrocities by fringe religious groups was fostered by renewed cult scandals like the 1993 Waco massacre: "Consensus on ritual abuse seems remote despite reminders like Waco that the fabric of society is darker than we imagine" (Bennetts 1993:60).

In late 1984, the Jordan investigations turned their attention to charges of occult rituals and human sacrifice, rumors that were never substantiated; but the charges themselves were widely publicized, and over the next year, there were frequent journalistic investigations into the homicidal operations of imagined rings or cults. The ABC television news program "20/20" played a critical role in publicizing allegations, and Kenneth Wooden served as a leading spokesman. In May, 1985, a "20/20" segment entitled "The Devil Worshipers" stated that satanic cults were widely active in child ritual abuse and human sacrifice. The following month, national publicity was given to an Ohio sheriff who attempted to dig the alleged site of satanic rituals where dozens of sacrificial murder victims were believed to be buried. The charges proved wholly spurious, and the Lucas County affair was a fiasco; but the concept of ritual murder cults was not laid to rest (Jenkins and Maier-Katkin 1992; Jenkins 1992c; Kahaner 1988:167–79). Growing police interest in occult topics is suggested by the number of related stories in the professional press from middecade, as well as the proliferation of training seminars (Hicks 1991; Bates 1990; Clark 1988).

It was against this background that attention turned once more to the idea of a ripper as occultist or devil-worshipper, a concept made plausible by the arrest in August 1985 of the Night Stalker, Richard Ramirez, a serial killer who boasted of satanic loyalties and displayed a pentagram symbol on his hand. Also in southern California, a false confession caused speculations that the Southside Slayings were satanic-related. (Perhaps significantly, the story broke on Halloween 1987; "Youth Accused" 1987.) An occult context was also suggested for Randy Kraft's multiple killings (McDougal 1992:276). The notion now began to penetrate the sensationalistic true-crime literature (compare Larson 1989:24–27). In 1985, *True Detective* offered what would be the first of many such case studies under the title "Six Lovely Girls for Satan's Flesh-Eaters," while the following year *Official Detective* presented "The Weird Case of the Satan-Loving Night Stalker."

Henry Lee Lucas himself claimed among many other things that he had carried out murders for a cult organization active throughout the American South and Southwest, known as the Hand of Death: "The cult killed by contract and performed ritual cremations and crucifixions of animals and humans to promote a reincarnation of the devil" (quoted in Hicks 1991:50). According to his confessions recorded in 1983 and 1984, the group had been involved in ritual murder, child abduction, drug dealing, and snuff films, and its rituals involved a satanic bible and a

cannibalistic black mass [Norris (1992:86–128); Cox (1991) virtually ig-
nores these charges]. Eager as ever to assist investigators, Lucas spoke
freely on these matters to antisatanic theorist Pat Pulling, with whom he
is photographed in her book, *The Devil's Web: Who is Stalking Your Children for Satan?* (1989:54–55).

The materials were clearly present for attempts to synthesize these
various elements into a grand threat or conspiracy menace, and these
works began to appear in middecade (compare Larson 1989; Johnston
1989; Schwartz and Empey 1988). One influential contribution to the
genre came from Maury Terry, who depicted a national conspiracy in a
book with the appropriately ambitious title, *The Ultimate Evil* (1987).
Apart from his claims about the Process and the O.T.O., Terry suggested
that other homicidal cults were still operational, including the "Chingon
cult" (Terry 1987:510). The Process often featured in such conspiracy
speculations, including the Lucas County farrago, but no plausible linkage has ever been proven.

Terry's major sources included Ed Sanders and Ted Gunderson, and
Gunderson in particular became a visible figure in promoting charges
about cults. Many of the most sweeping charges were presented in
America's Best-Kept Secret, which stated that serial murder was often sa-
tanically motivated. For example, Richard [*sic*] Berkowitz and Henry Lee
Lucas "have both confessed to being part of satanic cults involving blood
sacrifice" (Peterson 1988:11), while this activity explained the crimes of
Stanley Dean Baker, Charles Manson, and Richard Ramirez, and the
Cannibal Murders, which occurred in Illinois in 1981 and 1982 (pp. 59–
61: see below for the Illinois case). Such a serial killer was *"an evil, drug-
lubricated butchering machine* who justifies his behavior by exalting Satan"
(p. 62, emphasis in original).

EXPOSING SATAN'S UNDERGROUND: 1988

Terry, Gunderson, and Wooden often appeared as experts on cult-
killers on talk shows and television news programs, including the controversial Geraldo Rivera special, "Devil Worship: Exposing Satan's
Underground," which was shown shortly before Halloween 1988. This
program provided the ritual murder charges with unprecedented national visibility. It included a substantial segment on occult-influenced
serial killers such as Charles Manson and Leonard Lake, and noted that
"Berkowitz, Lucas, Ramirez, and Manson are the all-stars in the halls of
infamy but the vast majority of these ritual murders are not the work of
the celebrated psychopaths—there are literally hundreds of cases most

of us have never heard of." The suggestion is that there is a vast number of such crimes, but in the face of this danger, police agencies and prosecutors are uninformed or naive, and fail to follow leads that would lead them to the conspiratorial networks behind certain outrageous crimes, including human sacrifice and cattle mutilations. Rivera even speculated about "a network of these satanic murderers in this country."

The tone of the program is indicated by its extensive coverage of the case of serial killer Robert Berdella, which had occurred in Kansas City, Missouri. He had been arrested the preceding April after an incident in which he imprisoned and tortured a young man. On searching his house, the police found numerous photographs of captive young men, many showing signs of torture and abuse, and human bone fragments were found in his yard. Berdella was jailed for life on one count of murder in the first degree and he pleaded guilty to four other counts of second degree murder. Authorities let it be known that he was suspected in a total of at least eight deaths.

So much is generally agreed, but there is much controversy about the interpretation of the case, especially since Berdella owned many curious items including "a pair of human skulls, occult literature, and a Satanic ritual robe" (Newton 1990). The Geraldo Rivera program presented Berdella as final proof of the charge that "many satanic crimes are not recognized as such. . . . These ritualistic crimes are everywhere, and yet in most communities they are either overlooked or underreported." After describing the crimes, Rivera asserted, "The police and prosecutor in this town seem either unable or unwilling to draw the obvious connection between what happened here and Satanism." Berdella's involvement with devil worship was "easily apparent," and the surviving victim had been "ritualistically tortured" (though in a ritual sufficiently in tune with the modern world to involve electric shocks).

Berdella was portrayed as a highly placed member of a large satanic cult, members of which had participated in the crimes but had escaped punishment. Proof of the cult's existence was taken from the testimony of alleged survivors or defectors, and also from the 1980 Kansas City intelligence report (discussed above). The program suggested that police and prosecutors were willfully blind to cult charges, either through simple ignorance or else through more sinister motives, and that further investigation would produce much new evidence on the local problem of "missing *children* and missing young adults" (my emphasis).

The young were said to be especially at risk from satanic violence, and the program recounted the stories of several teenage boys who had committed murders, allegedly under the influence of local satanic movements. These cases were frequently discussed in accounts of the alleged danger of satanism to the young, and teenaged serial killer Sean Sellers was much quoted in books and television programs (Sellers 1990; Holmes 1989; Dawkins and Higgins 1989; St. Clair 1987).

The Rivera special was widely condemned as "trash television", but it gave national publicity to the most outrageous allegations of cult involvement in violent crime and serial homicide. Also in 1988 similar allegations were compiled in Larry Kahaner's book *Cults That Kill*, which indicated the proliferation of police officers and therapists who had become convinced of the dangers from organized satanic murder gangs. Drawing on the statements of numerous "cult cops" and other experts from across the United States, Kahaner claimed to present a consistent and menacing picture of a widespread danger from ritualistic murderers. He suggested that this danger was coming to be recognized as one of the greatest evils facing society: "This is new territory, just as drug crimes were in the 1960s, computer crimes in the 1970s, terrorism in the 1980s" (1988:viii).

CROSSING THE BORDER: MATAMOROS

Such extravagant claims gained credence from the exposure in April 1989 of the ritualistic drug cult active in and around Matamoros, Mexico. This had been involved in at least fifteen murders, including that of student Mark Kilroy, "American, White, someone's son," who was kidnapped and tortured (Provost 1989:13; compare Humes 1991; Green 1991; Hicks 1991:72–84; Linedecker 1990b; Kilroy and Stewart 1990; Schutze 1989; and see Chapter 5). The Matamoros affair was cited by anticult theorists as ample vindication of their allegations, while Henry Lee Lucas stated that the cult was part of the very organization for which he had earlier carried out killings (Provost 1989:176–77, 187, 196).

Fundamental to the cult interpretation of Matamoros was that the religious rituals involved were diabolical and could thus be legitimately contextualized together with satanism. This is in itself questionable, as the cult was ostensibly linked with traditional Afro-Caribbean religions (Burnett 1989). In addition, the actual religious trappings of the affair were largely artificial and syncretistic, derived in part from the scholarly anthropological readings of leader Adolfo Constanzo's girlfriend Sara Aldrete, coupled with her interest in the 1987 Martin Sheen film, *The Believers* (Garcia 1989). However, occult and devil-worship language pervaded reports of the incident, and commentators like Geraldo Rivera presented the story alongside alleged satanic atrocities by WASP teenagers (see, for example, the special report on the affair on "Geraldo," November 13, 1990). *Newsweek* simply headlined "Ritual Murder in Mexico" (April 24, 1989).

The Matamoros affair gave immense publicity to ritual murder accusations, and the extraordinary impact of the case requires explanation. The association of cult activity with drug abuse was an especially potent symbolic linkage at a time when the drug war was nearing its height. In September that year President Bush declared, "All of us agree that the gravest domestic threat facing our nation today is drugs. [O]ur most serious problem today is cocaine and in particular crack" ("Text of President's Speech" 1989). The 1990 *Geraldo* program on Matamoros suggested that "in more and more drug arrests, satanic paraphernalia has been found. . . . Drug use and satanism are starting to go hand in hand." Ted Gunderson concurred, suggesting that drugs and satanism "go hand in glove" (Provost 1989:197). "It is a partnership formed in Hell" (Linedecker 1990b:274). The two deviant activities were therefore joined in a classic amplification spiral.

The threat potential of this incident was aggravated by its geographical and ethnic context, as it recalled all the controversies and tensions that had prevailed along the U.S.-Mexican border over the previous decade, issues such as drugs, illegal immigration, and possible political subversion (Bennett 1990). American conservatives had long been troubled by the apparently exposed nature of this border, and in the mid-1980s, President Reagan had emphasized the military threat of the leftist government of Nicaragua by pointing out that nation's proximity to Harlingen, Texas, which was close to Matamoros. Linedecker's discussion of the context of the Matamoros case includes all these conflicts in a chapter entitled "A Border War" (Linedecker 1990b:41–58; compare Green 1991). At the end of 1989, the linkage between drugs, subversion, and "Hispanic witchcraft" was reinforced by the overthrow of Panamanian leader Manuel Noriega, who was said to possess a "cauldron of blood and animal entrails" among other "ritual" objects (Linedecker 1990b:273).

Moreover, these ethnic tensions were influential far beyond south Texas, and several Sunbelt states and cities used the cult aspects of the case to support legislation restricting or abolishing different forms of Afro-Caribbean religion. Bills were introduced in the Texas legislature prohibiting the religious practice of cannibalism or blood-drinking; while Hialeah, Florida, and Los Angeles attempted to abolish ritual animal sacrifice. As a symbol, Matamoros effectively focused widespread preexisting ethnic anxiety and religious fears.

The impact of Matamoros is apparent in the flood of anticult works that appeared in 1989 and 1990 (see, for example, Larson 1989; Johnston 1989; Pulling 1989). For academic Carl A. Raschke, the case "was to our understanding of the satanic cult and crime problem in this part of the world as the gruesome findings at Dachau and Auschwitz was to our understanding of Nazi Germany, what they were really up to" (interview on "Geraldo" November 13, 1990). His 1990 book *Painted Black* was subtitled *From Drug Killings to Heavy Metal—How Satanism is Besieging Our Culture and Our Communities* and included chapters like "The Epidemic of Satanic Crime in America," "The Occult Underworld," and "The Age of Satan." It also included photographs of Manson, Ramirez, and the defendants in the McMartin child abuse trial. Lyndon LaRouche's *Executive Intelligence Review* purported to expose the "dreadful hoax" that denied the obvious satanic connections between Matamoros, Charles Manson, and the Atlanta child murders ("Manson Revisited" 1989).

By the end of the decade, therefore, the concept of ritualistic serial murder ("killer cults") was firmly established in the public consciousness. When in 1993 three young boys were murdered in a small Arkansas town, the three teenagers who had allegedly killed them soon confessed to being members of a cult that (among other things) sacrificed dogs. These allegations achieved immediate national notoriety, and national news media headlined the story with phrases such as "satanic murders" ("NBC Nightly News," June 7, 1993). Occult and satanic aspects have also been attributed to so many other serial murder cases that there is now a substantial anthology of true-crime accounts published under the title *Cult Killers* (Mandelsberg 1991; compare Newton 1993a; Scammell 1992; Dunning 1989).

ASSESSING CLAIMS

Obviously, such far-reaching charges did not go without challenge, and the concept of ritualistic murder has not gained credence among major law enforcement agencies. The FBI, in particular, has systematically criticized the claims, and BSU expert Kenneth Lanning has written extensively on the problems of evidence and definition that beset the debate. Lanning (1989b) draws a critical distinction between the primary motivation of a murder and the symbolic or ritualistic trappings which may be associated with it. In recent writing on serial homicide, it is common to note the importance of ritualistic behavior by offenders, and such manifestations are much used by federal agencies in profiling; but *ritualistic* here has a specific and technical meaning.

We might imagine a man who killed several women and in each case left the body naked except for one glove. Such a compulsive and repetitive behavior might well be described as sexual ritualism, though there is no implication of any religious or supernatural motive, nor had the body been employed in any form of ceremony. Nor is there any necessary suggestion of group activity (Holmes and DeBurger 1988; Jenkins 1988a). FBI experts often use this kind of terminology, exemplified by John Douglas's remark, "You look to see if there is some type of ritual . . . placing the victim in a certain position, something that goes beyond just the murder" (Squitieri 1990). Question 134 on the VICAP form asks if there is evidence that "a deliberate or unusual ritual/act/thing had been performed on, with or near the victim, such as an orderly formation of rocks, burnt candles, dead animals, defecation, etc."

But let us suppose that there is, in fact, hard evidence for such a ceremony and that an individual or group performed a religious ritual that either intentionally or by accident resulted in death. We might even imagine that the perpetrators explicitly claimed that the crime had the purpose of placating supernatural forces and that it was intended as a sacrifice to the devil. Many would accept that this could legitimately be described as a ritual crime; but it is questionable if even such a case can properly be linked to satanism or the occult.

It is quite common for acts of extreme violence to have as their goal some imagined religious motive, such as a response to a divine commandment. Receiving orders from supernatural forces is a common manifestation of paranoid schizophrenia, a condition believed to be present in a number of multiple homicide cases (see the typology in Holmes and DeBurger 1988:72–80). In the 1970s, for example, California multiple killers Herbert Mullin and John Linley Frazier were both "visionary" killers who committed their crimes in response to divine commands, and Frazier was one of many who found special significance in the biblical book of Revelation (Lunde 1976). The appeal of Revelation among fringe cults and religious eccentrics is suggested by the case of Waco's messianic leader David Koresh, and the sacrificial killings attributed to heretical Mormon "prophet" Jeffrey Lundgren (Earley 1993; Sassé and Widder 1992). Among serial killers, the orders often take the form of an injunction to carry out a special mission: This might involve the killing of immoral and sinful women, as in the English case of the Yorkshire Ripper Peter, Sutcliffe.

In all these cases, the offenders received orders from what they perceived to be the Christian God, and this is the norm in the vast majority of such delusions. We have no precise figures, but the number of murders attributed by an offender to divine command is certainly many times greater than those blamed on Satan. On the other hand, it would surely be unacceptable to describe such actions as "Christian ritual killings" or "biblical sacrifices." These were disturbed individuals whose psychiatric conditions happened to be expressed in the language and rhetoric of a belief system widespread in their particular social background.

A disturbed individual might well claim to be acting in the name of Satan with no more plausibility than another might kill in the cause of Christ or Allah. This is especially important when considering the widely publicized cases of teenage murderers like Sean Sellers and Pete Roland, both of whom attributed their actions to satanic worship and belief. But we may well believe that if Sean Sellers had never heard of satanism, he would still have been sufficiently disturbed to commit essentially similar crimes, though attributed to whatever other ideological baggage lay to hand (Sellers 1990). In the case of Pete Roland, psychiatric testimony suggested the role of drug-induced psychosis (Rodgers-Melnick 1989).

For Lanning, therefore, a ritual murder has to fulfill quite stringent criteria. It should be defined as an act "committed by two or more individuals who rationally plan the crime and whose *primary* motivation is to fulfill a prescribed satanic ritual calling for the murder By this definition, [I have been] unable to identify even one documented satanic murder in the United States" (Lanning 1989b:82). Naturally enough, Lanning's definition has been angrily denounced by cult theorists like Larry Jones, who see it as part of a concerted federal attempt to play down the scale of the problem.

IN SEARCH OF RITUAL MURDER

The importance of the definition is seen when applied to cases that even many skeptical observers would admit to be ritualistic in nature, such as the Matamoros cult killings. Lanning, however, stresses that the *primary* motivation of these offenders derived from the extremely sadistic personalities of the group's leaders, especially Adolfo Constanzo, who took sexual pleasure in the torture and mutilation of young men. The incident would not therefore differ in substance from the cases of secular killers like Corll and Gacy. A similar analysis applies to the Berdella case, which subsequent investigations have explained purely in terms of the classic sexual sadism of one individual (Clark and Morley 1993:252–99). Rivera's account of Berdella has been described as "incorrect information sandwiched between Rivera's impassioned rhetoric," and no corroboration was found of any of the extravagant cult charges (Jackman and Cole 1992:226–33).

These cases resemble that of San Francisco murderer Clifford St. Joseph, who at first sight appears to be a plausible example of a true ritual murderer and was presented as such in Geraldo Rivera's television special (compare Kahaner 1988). A victim was killed in the context of an apparent satanic meeting, and ritual symbols were carved on his body. However, once again it should be asked whether St. Joseph's group differed in substance from other group serial homicides of the last two decades, where a number of men abducted, tortured, and killed young victims, usually male. These crimes (several of which have occurred in northern California) are normally categorized as gay serial killings, and these events would probably not have been substantially different if the paraphernalia of devil-worship had been lacking (see Chapter 9). It is interesting that one of the symptoms commonly cited by investigators as a symptom of ritual practice is the presence of candles and melted wax, which was indeed found on the victim in this case; yet hot candle wax is one of the tools most frequently employed to inflict pain in sado-masochistic sessions, almost always consensual in nature.

The problem of definition is also demonstrated by a Chicago case that occurred in 1982, when a group of four young men were implicated in what was initially known as the work of Jack the Ripper, but which subsequently attracted the name the Cannibal Murders. Up to fifteen women were murdered (Linedecker 1990a; Newton 1990). In every case, victims were subjected to extreme mutilation, which often included the removal of breasts, and the circumstances involved rituals such as canni-balism and the drinking of blood. Inevitably, perhaps, the room where such events occurred was dubbed a "satanic chapel" by police and me-dia, and *True Detective* termed the group "Satan's Flesh Eaters." This is perhaps the most convincing instance that can be cited of a cult that killed, but even here there was no evidence that victims were killed to fulfill the demands of a particular religious system, and (for example) the dates of murders follow no known satanic calendar. Moreover, the crimes bear many parallels to the work of many other extreme sexual sadists recorded in recent history, some of whom similarly worked in pairs or groups. Even here, therefore, the evidence of cult murder is difficult to substantiate.

THE APPEAL OF THE STORIES

It is extremely difficult to find an authentic instance of ritual murder in contemporary America, and all but impossible to find a genuine cult, satanic or otherwise, that practices the kind of modern *thuggee* sug-gested by many writers. But if this is the case, it is important to explain the torrent of claims and assertions to the contrary made during the last decade. Several major elements may be suggested, above all the sensa-tionalistic appeal of the allegations. The alleged wrongdoings of satanic gangs offered rich pickings to the increasingly sensationalistic media of the 1980s, while the stories had strong potential for excitement or shock value.

They also had the attraction of any exposé journalism, in that the investigators could present themselves as courageous seekers after truth, pursuing genuinely dangerous enemies, and thus proving the diligence and courage of that particular news source. At a more practical level, pursuing imaginary cults is far safer and more profitable than investigating authentic criminal or deviant activities, as nonexistent cult satanists cannot take legal action to protect themselves, and their activities can be presented with whatever degree of hyperbole seems desirable. In contrast, authentic organizations like the Process and the O.T.O. tend to sue critics and, on occasion, to win.

The cult stories can also be expected to appeal because the images they present fit so well with known popular stereotypes of the absolute Other, who has so frequently been depicted as a homicidal cannibal (see Chapter 5). In fact, there is evidence that there was an American market for such stories long before there were even allegations that this sort of behavior was possible in the contemporary world. In 1969, one American paperback offered numerous gruesome accounts of *The Blood Cults*:

> the shocking secret societies whose gory tentacles transcend the law, who exist by torture, death and destruction, and whose members may include that nice boy next door, or the head of your PTA. . . . grotesque erotic rituals and brutal vows of violence. (Lefebure 1969)

This work ranged broadly for examples sufficiently sinister, including the Kenyan *Mau Mau*, West African Leopard Cults, the Italian *Carbonari*, and the medieval German *Vehm*; but could find no recent or contemporary American examples, except for the curious but nonhomicidal *Penitentes* of the southwest. The book appeared shortly before the exposure of the Manson case, which would surely have been included if known. The suggestion is that there was a latent interest in such events even without a contemporary American tag, but that this appeal would be immeasurably enhanced if the threat could be presented as a menace to present-day America.

THE APPEAL OF THE CLAIMS

However, the invention of the satanic killer can also be seen as the outcome of interest group politics, and the stories offered rewards to a variety of activists, who were given frequent platforms by the media. There were, for example, the cult cops and occult experts, who sought to validate their expertise by demonstrating the authenticity and seriousness of the menace they sought to denounce. In addition, religious and anticult groups made great play of the ritual killers as the logical culmination of other abuses they wished to expose, which would normally appear harmless or merely consensual victimless offenses. Serial murder thus offered the rhetorical opportunity to condemn other behaviors through a form of guilt by association, or—in Hall's (1978) terms— raising the danger threshold of those lesser activities.

Raschke was typical in seeing ritual murder as the culmination of spectrum of activities that also included occult and New Age interests, heavy metal rock and roll music, and perhaps drug trafficking. Other theorists also included fantasy role-playing games such as *Dungeons and Dragons*, and violent horror films or slasher movies. If these appeared innocuous, then the theorist could respond that drugs and heavy metal music appeared to have incited the crimes of Richard Ramirez, Sean Sellers, and Pete Roland; while the ideas of Aleister Crowley were associated with the Process and thus, indirectly, with the Manson murders. In this view, occult crimes were not only a palpable menace, they fell only little short of active participation in multiple murder.

In ideological terms, the emphasis on the satanic danger contributed to the theological assumptions of the fundamentalist and evangelical groups who were so well represented among the cult theorists; and this may explain why ideas about cult satanism and ritual murder developed so rapidly around 1980, at a time when the fundamentalists were approaching the zenith of their political power (see Chapter 1). During the 1970s, there had been an increasing polarization within Protestant Christian groups: between conservative evangelicals and fundamentalists on the one hand, and more liberal mainstream churches on the other. While the liberals favored socially oriented religious work, the conservatives emphasized personal holiness and traditional doctrines like sin, redemption, and the power of evil.

In quantitative terms, the evangelicals were clearly winning by about 1980, and conservative groups like the Southern Baptists and Assemblies of God experienced impressive increases in membership, while liberal denominations like the Episcopalians, Methodists, and United Church of Christ declined at a quite precipitous rate during the 1970s and 1980s. Evangelical growth was reflected in the emergence of networks of bookstores, radio stations, and television programs, all of which gave the conservative churches a far-flung audience for their views and a chance to disseminate opinions on issues like occult crime and ritual murder. In terms of social problem construction, this gave the churches considerable resources to invest in the developing issue, from which they hoped to win such lavish rewards.

Central to fundamentalist rhetoric is the real power of the devil in the world as the source of all evil, a key belief that differentiated them from liberal or secularized churches. If it was accepted that satanic followers did indeed represent a powerful alternative religion in America, then this was yet another argument that religious liberalism had failed and the churches must come to a more basic acceptance of the reality of the force of evil. An upsurge of diabolism was believed to support the fundamentalist belief in the imminence of the Second Coming of Christ, which would be preceded by the triumph of Antichrist. A belief in satanism, and of the most active and sinister hue, was thus intimately linked to the fundamentalist diagnosis of both the secular and spiritual ills of society. The religious groups did not initiate the ritual murder idea—that distinction probably belongs to fantasy authors like Robert Bloch—but they were among the greatest beneficiaries of the emerging mythology.

Chapter 11

_____

Conclusion: Making and Establishing Claims

During the 1980s, the issue of serial murder was established as a major social problem, and the stereotypical serial killer became one of the best-known and most widely feared social enemies. For research in problem construction, the process raises three fundamental questions: Why did the problem arise at the time it did? Why did it take the particular form that it acquired in these years? And why did the diverse claims enjoy such outstanding and quite rapid success?

In each case, particular attention should be directed toward the identification of claims-makers, those individuals and groups who attempt to present an issue in a particular way. The study of such claims-makers is central to the constructionist approach to social problems, in which "the theoretical task is to study how members define, lodge and press claims; how they publicize their concerns, redefine the issue in question in the face of political obstacles, indifference or opposition; how they enter into alliances with other claims-makers" (Kitsuse and Schneider 1989:xii–xiii). This chapter will describe the development of the claims that shaped public perceptions of the serial murder problem, and the means by which claims came to be established as authoritative. It will be suggested that such an exploration has important implications both for the framing of social problems, and for the study of the mass media.

Our first question is one of chronology: Why did the problem arise when it did? The answer may seem obvious, in that from the mid-1970s onwards, there appeared to be a significant increase in both the number of sensational cases and the scale of victimization in the separate incidents. This marked a genuine departure from conditions in the 1950s and 1960s. Every few years brought a case that broke previous records for the total number of known victims, while several of the major instances lasted for months or years before arrests were made, permitting far-reaching speculation by pressure groups and the media. It was therefore likely that concern would peak by about 1980–1981 and that some

211

endeavor would be made to provide a context that incorporated the diverse cases in a general social problem.

On the other hand, there have been many other years in American history when there was a similar concatenation of nationally publicized multiple-murder cases. To take only the most spectacular periods, this was true of the mid-1870s, the years between 1910 and 1915, the mid-1920s, and the late 1930s (see Chapter 2). Yet neither in 1915, 1928, nor 1939 was there a national murder panic on anything like the model observed in 1983.

Equally, it is by no means inevitable that a multiple homicide problem would be constructed in the particular way that has recently occurred in the United States. In midcentury, it was the psychiatric and therapeutic experts who had exercised ownership of an earlier manifestation of the problem, when it had been understood as part of the general issue of sex crime and mental illness. It was not then typified as a criminal justice issue, and the political context determining the appropriate responses was generally liberal. The experience of offenders like Charles Whitman, Richard Speck, or Lee Harvey Oswald could be cited to support more enlightened policies of child rearing and community mental health, or extending the scope of psychiatric detection and intervention (see, for example, Menninger 1968). Moreover, such individual-oriented and psychodynamic theories might have led to multiple murder continuing to be viewed through the medium of discrete case studies, rather than in terms of a general problem.

By 1980–1981, moreover, there were several other competing groups of claims-makers, each with its distinctive interpretation of the murder issue: black groups who viewed it as part of systematic racial exploitation; feminists who saw the offense as serial femicide, a component of the larger problem of violence against women; children's rights activists concerned with missing and exploited children; as well as religious and other advocates of a ritual murder threat. That such activism could promote an alternative construction is suggested by the experience of contemporary England, in which the Yorkshire Ripper case of the late 1970s secured the dominance of an essentially feminist analysis of serial murder. This gave the femicide theory an authoritative position, which profoundly influenced the mass media and academic criminology and also shaped law enforcement practice (Jenkins 1992a). Moreover, this occurred in a conservative political environment quite reminiscent of Reagan's America.

THE ROLE OF FEDERAL LAW ENFORCEMENT

In any event, the interpretation that prevailed in the 1980s defined the new problem in terms of interjurisdictional cooperation, intelligence gathering, and overcoming linkage blindness—in short, as a problem of law enforcement and federal power rather than one of mental health or social dysfunction. This construction does much to illuminate the composition of the groups most active in developing or pressing claims, as well as their motives and interests. The serial murder problem was defined according to the specifications of the U.S. Justice Department, and above all the FBI's behavioral science experts at Quantico. This recognition goes far toward explaining why the problem was defined in the manner it was, while the timing should be seen as at least in part a response to the bureaucratic needs of an expanding agency.

The dominance of the FBI's experts can be observed throughout the process of construction. They successfully presented themselves as the best (or only) authorities on the topic, and they assisted journalists and writers who reciprocated with favorable depictions of the agency. It was the FBI that originated and popularized the high statistics about the scale of the crime, and once disseminated, these figures shaped the public perception that serial murder represented a grave social threat. The same group at Quantico also guided the debate in other ways, above all in drawing attention to the "roaming" killers who operated in several states.

In terms of their underlying interests in making these claims, the federal officials stood to gain substantially in terms of their bureaucratic position because establishing the reality of a problem provided added justification for the BSU, a new and rather unorthodox agency seeking to validate its skills in areas such as profiling and crime scene analysis. In terms of the agency as a whole, focusing on a social menace of this sort was likely to erode public opposition to the enhancement of FBI powers and resources, at a time when such a development was politically opportune. The successful creation of the serial murder problem marked a critical expansion of what both public and legislators felt to be the appropriate scope of federal police powers.

Moreover, this could easily be seen as the thin end of the wedge: Once it was established that the FBI could and should have jurisdiction over this type of crime, it was not difficult to seek similar involvement in other offenses that could plausibly be mapped together with serial homicide. In 1986, it was proposed that the NCAVC might soon expand its powers over other serial crimes, including "rape, child molestation, arson and bombing" (Jenkins 1988a). This represents an ingenious form of verbal sleight-of-hand, by which the simple adjective *serial* has come to mean much more than merely *repeated*, and implies sinister characteristics such as irrationality, compulsiveness, extreme violence, highly transient offenders, and so on. Serial offenses of any kind are thus framed as ipso facto both federal in nature, and the peculiar responsibility of the mind-hunters.

In terms of the FBI's broad interests in defining the problem, it is necessary to see this incident as part of a long bureaucratic tradition. Historically, federal law enforcement was virtually non-existent in the United States before the present century, and agencies only established themselves gradually during the Progressive era and afterwards. In the case of the FBI, the agency was founded in 1908, but made virtually no impact before the early 1930s, when it was regarded as the essential antidote to a perceived wave of kidnapping (Powers 1983). The *New York Times* described this as "a rising menace to the nation" (quoted in Schechter 1990:101). The media presented the offense as the work of ruthless and itinerant predators assaulting American children in their homes, and the official response was to declare the action a federal crime (Alix 1978). The law was to be enforced by an enhanced FBI under its director J. Edgar Hoover, who presented himself as the head of a national super–police agency leading a "war on crime" (Powers 1983, 1987; Summers 1993).

This was only the first of several successive panics through which the unit developed immense prestige and widespread jurisdiction (Kessler 1993). Respectively, these supposed public enemies included gangsters and bank robbers like John Dillinger, Nazi fifth columnists, and Communist spies. The bureau suggested that each problem in turn was a severe public threat and was moreover interjurisdictional in nature, so that on both counts federal action was required. The FBI was presented as the appropriate agency because of its superior professionalism and forensic skills, exactly the sort of technocratic arguments that were employed in the 1980s demands for federal war against serial killers (Ungar 1976). These ideas were often portrayed in the mass media, for example, in the 1959 James Stewart film *The FBI Story*, which was made under the close supervision of the bureau. Federal law enforcement thus had a long record of benefiting from public panics about itinerant predatory criminals, especially where children were said to be involved.

The FBI also had vast resources in making its claims, and were par excellence insider claims-makers with an unchallenged right to present their views before legislative and policymaking bodies. They had much to offer journalists or investigators that might encourage them to accept their view of an emerging problem. J. Edgar Hoover had cultivated the closest possible links with the media, and there was thus a long tradition of regarding the FBI as an authoritative source on law enforcement matters. In the specific instance of serial murder, the agency benefited from being literally the only group offering a systematic overview of the phenomenon, an unchallenged position suggested by the absence of skepticism about its early quantitative claims, either from law enforcement agencies or academics.

On a personal basis, BSU agents could also claim immense authority due to their extensive personal contacts with the imprisoned killers, who were an unparalleled resource. Agents like Robert Ressler and John Douglas were articulate speakers who could be relied on to provide interesting and lively accounts of the crimes they had investigated, and their views were substantiated by their wide and somewhat perilous experiences in border crossing—attempting to enter the minds of heinous offenders. This offered the potential for vicarious excitement for a news audience, while the empirical nature of their research confirmed the prima facie likelihood that these officials were, in fact, the best qualified experts in the field. Since they could draw freely on the language of both practical investigation and personal observation on the one hand, and theoretical psychology and criminology on the other, they could be viewed neither as "just cops" nor as ivory-tower intellectuals. The image presented was both attractive and convincing.

The opinions of the BSU experts thus appeared to be of great value, even when they were addressing quantitative or political issues in which their expertise was far more dubious. Once this perception of authority was established, the FBI had much discretion in the access it provided to these valuable resources. It could permit or deny the interviews that would be essential for any writer seeking to investigate serial murder, either with federal experts like Ressler, Heck, Hazelwood, or Douglas or (to some extent) with the killers themselves. Obviously, these favors were more likely to be granted to those journalists or academics likely to show themselves sympathetic to the interests of the organization. Meanwhile, anyone with access to the information and opinion controlled by the BSU had the potential for frequent stories and features that were almost guaranteed to be newsworthy. Certainly in 1983 and 1984, the FBI made shrewd use of the information it was acquiring in the area of serial murder, developing a reciprocal relationship with the journalists, academics, and filmmakers who obtained access to the agency.

Ressler has written with refreshing candor about the development of the serial murder problem:

> There was somewhat of a media feeding frenzy, if not a panic, over this issue in the mid-1980s and we at the FBI and other people involved in urging the formation of VICAP did add to the general impression that there was a big problem and that something need to be done about it. We didn't exactly go out seeking publicity, but when a reporter called, and we had a choice whether or not to cooperate on a story about violent crime, we gave the reporter good copy. In feeding the frenzy, we were using an old tactic in Washington, playing up the problem as a way of getting Congress and the higher-ups in the executive branch to pay attention to it.

The difficulty was that some people in the bureaucracy went too far in their quest for attention. (Ressler and Schachtman 1992:203)

Ressler describes how his hospitable treatment of a reporter resulted in a flattering 1980 article in the *Chicago Tribune*, which in turn "led to a flood of other articles, including important ones in *The New York Times*, *People* and *Psychology Today*, just to name a few, as well as invitations for me to appear on various radio and television programs" (p. 232). He also stresses the importance of the unit's outreach to academic psychology and criminology, and, of course, to the popular media. He advised authors like Thomas Harris and Mary Higgins Clark, and in 1987 he addressed the annual meeting of the Mystery Writers of America. And he obviously knew the sort of pithy phrases that the news media would delight in quoting ("Serial killing—I think it's at epidemic proportions"; "America is going to turn into *A Clockwork Orange*"; see Chapter 3). The BSU experts were from an early stage quite familiar with the necessity to cultivate the media and the means of so doing.

This assistance might pay very rich dividends indeed, though it is difficult to imagine anyone in the agency foreseeing that the aid accorded to Thomas Harris would reap quite such splendid rewards (see Chapter 4). At the end of the decade, the decision to permit location shooting at Quantico for *The Silence of the Lambs* was brilliantly effective in reinforcing the linkage between the real-life behavioral sciences experts and Harris's fictional heroes, while the ensuing publicity more than negated the disastrous consequences of the recent *Iowa* investigation.

Also valuable as a resource was the FBI's ability to present plausible statistical evidence, which was of special value in the early 1980s. As has been noted, there then existed several interest groups seeking to present their interpretation of a serial murder problem, but both the media and the diverse activist groups all had a common vested interest in emphasizing certain aspects of the murder problem, above all its very large scale. Whether pressure groups wished to stigmatize child abductions, sexual violence, or satanist conspiracies, they all shared a desire to see very high statistics presented for the numbers of serial killings. The FBI helped to secure its ownership of the issue by being the first and indeed only group to offer such a quantitative foundation, one that seemed sufficiently high to satisfy the various claims-makers. It established the critical frame around which other groups could embellish; so that the simple four or five thousand serial murder victims swiftly became five thousand women and children, or five thousand victims of ritual murder.

In addition, there were many points of underlying agreement between FBI experts like Hazelwood and the feminist theorists, both of whom emphasized the sexual content of the violence and the role of pornography in the etiology of serial homicide. It is remarkable to note the respectful attention often paid to Justice Department claims by feminists like Jane Caputi, who rarely makes positive remarks about law enforcement agencies (Downs 1989). This tactical alliance assured that federal claims were less likely to be assailed from liberal critics in Congress, the news media, or the academic world. Intentionally or otherwise, the FBI's sympathy for the sexual violence construction did much to create a consensus for its interpretations.

Since the early 1980s, it has been unthinkable to present either a news story or a fictional account of serial murder without due acknowledgment of the assistance granted by BSU experts, who in more or less fictionalized form often appear as the heroes of the novels and films. This has had a cyclical effect in that these media depictions reinforce the stereotype of the experts as well-informed and heroic, and ensures that future accounts will continue to rely on these unquestioned authorities. In consequence, the media have still returned to the FBI personnel for comments and quotes even after they have been shown to be fallible or even wrong about key issues. And in the cases where the FBI authorities were not quoted directly, their views and theories still permeate the literature through the use of terminology like *organized* and *disorganized* offenders, *unsubs*, and *blitz* attacks, and the emphasis on the offender's acting out of violent fantasies. The language and theory of serial murder study were created at Quantico.

In terms of social problem construction, there are few examples where a federal agency has so decisively acquired ownership of a topic: the all-but-unchallenged right to interpret the issue according to its assumptions and interests. The media came to rely for information and opinion upon on a very small body of accredited experts, in this case the FBI investigators and some of their associates in the academic or law enforcement worlds. This reliance meant that the views of each individual claims-maker acquired disproportionate significance, while such a highly focused approach created a high likelihood that errors or misstatements would remain uncorrected, or that views hostile to these initial claims-makers were unlikely to be expressed. The point is illustrated by what we might call the *negative* claims-making activity of another BSU agent, Kenneth Lanning, who resisted considerable pressure to grant the FBI's imprimatur to satanic murder and ritual abuse claims. This individual decision was of critical importance in ensuring that these ideas remained firmly on the intellectual fringe and never developed into the full-fledged panic that often seemed imminent in the late 1980s.

Nor was this influence confined to the United States, as the new construction of serial murder had by the late 1980s caused a general reevaluation of multiple homicide in several industrialized countries. In Great Britain, serial murder has been a recognized phenomenon at least since the time of Jack the Ripper in 1888, but the media of the 1980s affected to discover it as something new, startling, and specifically American. During a wave of such cases during 1986, it was the prestigious *Sunday Times* that claimed, "With thousands of police in the hunt for the Stockwell Strangler and the Railway Killer in London, the specter of the serial murderer, now common in America, has been established in Britain" (Deer 1986). There was "growing alarm . . . that Britain could be seeing the growth of what their American counterparts are calling recreational murder, where there is no apparent motive" (*Sunday Times*, July 27, 1986).

The responses were predictable, with the emergence of a centralized HOLMES data bank to collect information on serious crimes (Jenkins 1991, 1992a). Quantico profilers were also invited to assist in several investigations from 1981 onwards. In 1986, it was announced that "Scotland Yard and the American FBI have launched an unparalleled joint campaign to give Britain the benefit of the FBI's experience of serial murders, where the same killers strike again and again" (*Sunday Times*, July 27, 1986). Serial murder and the mind-hunter image were the subject of two major television programs in the early 1990s, both of which made great use of American experts like Robert Ressler (Clark and Morley 1993). Britain now has a specialized True Crime publishing imprint specializing in serial murder stories, with a heavy emphasis on Quantico-style profiling (see, for example, Berry-Dee and Odell 1992, 1993; Wilson and Seaman 1992).

In Australia and Canada, similarly, a serial murder problem was noted during the 1980s, and the exemplars cited were almost entirely American cases, supplemented by one or two domestic offenders (Mann 1989; Andrew Rule 1988). The new problem provided a media tag for coverage of local incidents, as in 1989 when the Australian press reported a Sydney serial murder case. Many articles contextualized the case with reference to the United States, where "up to five thousand people a year" were victims of such crimes, and "up to 350 [*sic*] serial killers are thought to be on the loose" (Robinson 1989). In response, Australian criminal justice experts called for a national homicide register, to provide some of the information available to the American NCAVC.

American true-crime case studies were widely available in translation throughout Western Europe, and France even published accounts of American cases that were not available in the country of origin. Florida serial killer Gerard Schaefer has become a well-known figure in France through a memoir and a television documentary, though he remains little known in the United States (Bézard 1992:44, 90–94). Even the phrase *serial killer* has entered French parlance, untranslated. It seems that American criminals and investigators have come to define the expected international norms for this problem.

Federal law enforcement agencies such as the FBI have a long history of employing the mass media to promote their own interests, while suppressing or discouraging rival views; and it must be asked how far a deliberate policy of manipulation explains the successful imposition of the Justice Department view of serial murder. Ressler (see above) portrays the BSU as opportunistic rather than manipulative, but it would be disingenuous to ignore the immense weight carried by statements from such a specialized FBI unit. It is—to say the least—surprising that the authorities who issued the terrifyingly high statistics about the prevalence of the offense were unaware of the serious methodological flaws in these data or that they did not foresee the enormous public impact that these figures would have.

Constraints and Opportunities

On the other hand, it would be simply unacceptable to attribute the emergence of the serial murder problem to any sort of conscious or conspiratorial abuse of evidence. The facts and figures offered by the BSU became significant only when they were accepted as a fair and accurate analysis of circumstances, a process that implies the agency was in a sense telling the public what they wished and expected to hear. The statistics were important because they achieved instant credibility with the politicians and interest groups involved in the successive congressional hearings, suggesting that such a threatening picture must have responded to political or rhetorical needs. The prominence of the many news stories on this subject can only be understood if in fact the FBI's interpretations of the problem were closely attuned to media perceptions of popular needs and fears, and if the images presented matched substantially with underlying expectations. Furthermore, it is more difficult to trace a Justice Department role in the second panic during the early 1990s, which achieved an intensity little inferior to that of 1983–1985.

In other words, the success of the Justice Department model was shaped by a number of constraints and opportunities in the general social and political environment. Especially significant were prevailing ideological conditions, above all the New Right perspective then at its zenith. While not absolutely determining the interpretations that were be likely to be successful for the new problem, the political environment did impose constraints, by discouraging any view that partook of the "failed liberalism" of the previous two decades. This effectively made it impossible to resuscitate the therapeutic model of earlier years, while implicitly favoring a justice-oriented scheme that emphasized the extreme predatory violence of the offenders.

It is equally important to consider the lateral dimension to any given problem: that is, to take account of other problems and panics that were under way more or less simultaneously and that helped form popular thinking on criminal violence and related menaces. Problem construction is a cumulative or incremental process, in which each issue is to some extent is built upon its predecessors, in the context of a steadily developing fund of socially available knowledge. The nature of these other issues provides the intellectual environment for the formu la-tion of the new problem, and again provides both constraints and opportunities.

It is difficult to understand the serial murder panic of 1983–1985 without tracing its relationship to other originally separate scares of earlier years, especially the concern over missing and exploited children, and organized pedophilia, as well as ill-defined concerns about the prevalence of homosexuality. These issues acted as essential precursors, though they originally had little obvious or necessary relevance to multiple homicide. None of these incidents should be seen in isolation from the others: The later panics would not have had the force they did if they had not built upon earlier memories and preconceptions, especially about threats to children.

THE MAKING OF NEWS

Perhaps the most important opportunities were those provided by the news media themselves, and for both print and electronic media, the claims presented by the FBI from the early 1980s were both timely and valuable. For several years, there had been numerous stories about multiple homicide, and these met obvious public interest. Now, however, claims about an emerging murder problem gave the theme several new elements that made it appear all the more frightening or exciting.

Multiple homicide has long occupied a high position in media perceptions of what constitutes a newsworthy story, as suggested by numerous incidents from the Ripper murders of 1888 through the New York child murders of 1915, the Son of Sam case of the 1970s, and the more recent affairs of Jeffrey Dahmer and Joel Rifkin. This attraction is not difficult to comprehend. Different newspapers and television programs have different values about what constitutes worthwhile news, but there are some common criteria, and serial murder fulfills most of them. Like great drama, a newsworthy story should evoke an emotional response such as fear, outrage, or pity, which is why innocent victims like children or animals feature so regularly. The story should also suggest a phenomenon that appears to be a real threat, that affects or could affect a large number of the readers or viewers of that particular item. It might offer excitement or shock value in the form of unusual sexual activity or violence, and often concerns well-known people in whom there is a good deal of established public interest. Ideally, the story should also offer a platform for social action ("something must be done"), perhaps indicated by the demands of politicians, police, or bureaucrats.

All these criteria are illustrated by a typical serial murder story. It offers drama in the confrontation of good and evil; excitement in the pursuit of the villain; and fear in the likelihood of potential violence befalling members of the news audience. The themes of the coverage are epitomized by the formulaic devices that occur in the television news programs on such cases, which almost invariably include interviews with the family of a victim or victims. Such encounters serve to emphasize the ordinariness and decency of the bereaved parents as individuals and clearly invite identification. This is intended to attract sympathy and to heighten the contrast with the wanton brutality of the offender. Parental interviews also stress the very common nature of the danger, which may exist in apparently safe environments, and thus the universality of the murder threat is reinforced. This is confirmed by the interviews with the perpetrator's neighbors or colleagues, who generally declare that he appeared harmless and innocent, thus indicating once more the random danger from a "stranger next door."

In a sense, serial murder represents for the media the perfect social problem, in that there is no need to resort to any of the rhetorical devices that are normally required to package an issue to make it palatable or interesting for the audience. In the case of an issue like AIDS, child abuse, or homelessness, a story will normally need an opening "grabber," some dramatic story or incident to secure the reader's attention, and some effort has to be expended ensuring that the reader will realize that this issue causes genuine harm or damage. In addition, a story has to be personalized in such a way as to provide reader or viewer identification, as illustrated by the effect on AIDS coverage of sensational cases like those of Rock Hudson and Kimberly Bergalis.

In contrast, serial murder stories usually have such elements built in. The crime may well be discovered in a particularly gruesome way, with the finding of a mass graveyard or a body in a car, and the press has an automatic grabber in its accounts of this extremely aberrant behavior.

There may also be a powerful visual image, which can encapsulate public fears and concerns: John Wayne Gacy's crawl space, Jeffrey Dahmer's apartment, Joel Rifkin's pickup truck. Furthermore, any arrested offender immediately acquires celebrity status, so that coverage is inevitably personalized. Nor is there any doubt that such behavior involves authentic harm, especially when the crimes so often involve archetypally evil activities such as cannibalism, necrophilia, or human butchery.

It is not difficult to understand why the cases of the late 1970s were all so attractive to newspapers and television, and all were treated as headline-making stories. However, the FBI's presentation of a wave of serial murder presented the chance to contextualize individual cases as part of a highly newsworthy national phenomenon. This greatly amplified the potential threat of the behavior by bringing the danger home to every community and household across the nation, and moreover the new construction emphasized the danger to children and the young. It was an ideal news story at several distinct levels, offering as it did the opportunity to indulge in political advocacy, demands for the reform of legislation and policing, as well as wide-ranging social analysis. The value was all the greater when it offered such rich rhetorical opportunities to many different interest groups. The FBI earned the credit for bringing the issue to public attention, and also appeared to be the only group with a serious practical agenda to combat the new menace.

The potency of the new problem is illustrated by its longevity. As Best has noted,

> Claims makers must compete for attention. Social problems drop from view when they no longer seem fresh or interesting. New waves of claims-making may depend on the claims-makers' ability to redefine an issue, to focus on a new form of an old threat (e.g., crack or heavy metal music) or to find other wrinkles. (Best 1989:140)

In the case of serial murder, the panic of 1983–1985 was followed by several years of simmering interest, and then a dramatic growth of renewed concern from 1990 onwards, while there is no reason to doubt that there will be an indefinite number of future revivals.

The resilience of the topic owes much to its pervasive presence in popular fiction, especially from the end of the 1980s, and the novels, films, and true-crime books vastly increased the fund of socially available knowledge. This reinforced public expectations about the severity of the threat and provided numerous tags that could be employed for further media coverage of the story. Apart from its inherent qualities, the serial murder theme also fit well with the changing news priorities of

the 1980s and the growth of sensationalistic "trash television" epitomized by successive Geraldo Rivera specials (and Rivera made this type
of homicide one of his favorite topics).

Nor is it difficult to speculate about the next manifestations of the
issue, as there are already potentially newsworthy developments merely
awaiting a sensational case or discovery to provide a focus for concern.
For instance, we know that the VICAP system is already indicating
apparent links between murders that would not hitherto have been
connected. The resulting upsurge in alleged murder series will almost
certainly be taken as proof of a rise in the behavior itself, rather than a
simple change in investigative technology. In addition, demographic
changes make it likely that future fears will be directed toward multiple
killers who prey on the elderly, sick, and institutionalized. There always
have been such offenders, who are the subjects of several books and
other studies, but they are likely to be the subject of much sharper
concern in a rapidly aging population. It is also possible that a quite
unforeseen circumstance might reawaken dormant fears about cult or
racial conspiracies underlying serial homicide.

Shaping the Image

The serial murder problem illustrates the complex relationship between three apparently independent forces: the law enforcement bureaucracy, the news media, and popular culture. Once the original
theme was established, innovative interpretations of the problem ("other wrinkles") could originate in any of the three areas, before spreading
rapidly to gain acceptance in both the other components of the triangle.
This process serves not only to keep alive an interest in serial murder,
but also to define ever more sharply the image of the killer in the monster stereotype formulated during the 1980s, to the exclusion of other
possible interpretations.

During 1991, this interaction was well illustrated by the complex relationship between reality and fiction in the construction of both villains
(Hannibal Lecter and Jeffrey Dahmer) and heroes (Jack Crawford, his
BSU prototypes, and his countless fictional imitators). The Justice Department formulates the image, which is transformed and publicized in
fiction, which in turn shapes public attitudes and expectations; while the
news media present stories that respond to these images and stereotypes. In turn, the investigative priorities of bureaucratic agencies are
formed by public and legislative expectations, which are derived from
popular culture and the news media. Media images can also frame the
expectations and behavior of individual agents and administrators:

"New applicants to the BSU are taking Jodie Foster's character as a role model: they too want to be supersleuths" (Ressler and Schachtman 1992:242).

In this process, the killers themselves often play a claims-making role that is important, if sparsely explored. In any discussion of serial homicide, particular weight is attached to the remarks of incarcerated offenders, which are felt to provide the best validation for particular theories about the etiology of violence or the development of the homicidal personality. In documentaries of the 1980s, there were frequent appearances by killers like Ted Bundy, Henry Lee Lucas, and Edmund Kemper, while more recently interviews with Westley Alan Dodd have often been aired and cited. Published confessions by notorious killers are the most popular of true-crime books, as is illustrated by the great popularity of Ted Bundy's published interviews (Michaud and Aynesworth 1983, 1989). There has even appeared a *Diary* controversially ascribed to the original Jack the Ripper (Harrison 1993).

It is widely assumed that these statements enjoy a peculiar authority as firsthand autobiography and self-analysis, but this view is open to question. There is a well-known sociological process by which offenders come to be labeled, to accept not only the deviant status that is imputed to them by agents of control, but also to accept the interpretations of this evil that are proffered to them. Serial killers are influenced by the media as well as by academic psychology, and many make a specific study of earlier offenders. Peter Kürten was one of many to have found a role model in the original Jack the Ripper, while recent killers like Joel Rifkin possess substantial libraries about true-life murder cases.

This influence may go far to explaining why killers in different eras tend to reproduce explanations of their offense that closely mimic the prevailing ideological perspective of the day or even of the particular investigator to whom they are confessing. Thus the psychodynamic confessions of an earlier day have given way to common assertions that the criminal in question had been the victim of extreme sexual abuse during childhood. Others aggressively affect the monster image, as when Westley Dodd declared, "At that point, I became a hunter and a killer, and that's all that I was" (interview on CBS's "48 Hours," May 8, 1991).

There are also legal considerations, in that a killer may wish to present himself or herself in such a way as to promote a particular judicial outcome, above all an insanity defense. In contrast, Westley Dodd apparently tried to present himself as a ruthless monster with the explicit goal of preventing obstacles being placed in the path of his much desired execution. Other individuals have certainly confessed to crimes far beyond those they actually committed. By definition, this is neither a rational nor a conventional population, so much caution should be exercised in accepting its statements at face value.

In addition, the psychopathic personality type so frequently represented among serial killers often manifests itself in a desire to please and manipulate, to tell whatever story will win the sympathy of the listener, and this may explain why the final confessions of Ted Bundy to an evangelical writer laid so much emphasis on the sinister influence of pornography. Moreover, the successive confessions of a given killer over the years are likely to contain numerous contradictions, so that a particular claims-maker can choose whatever quotation may seem opportune for his or her cause. Medical murderer Donald Harvey has asserted the influence on his conduct of early childhood sex abuse with quite the confidence with which he had earlier denied the same interpretation.

Whatever the explanation, the serial killers add an important element to the complex feedback relationship between investigators, media, and popular culture. Though they often do little more than reflect the commonplaces of the culture and the academic environment, the offenders do this with such apparent authority that their remarks are likely to be taken as the ultimate warrant for any desired view or explanation.

STUDYING SOCIAL PROBLEMS

The sweeping success of the serial murder problem may be difficult to reproduce in future, as few other issues have anything like this instant newsworthiness or appeal. However, much can still be learned from this incident that can be applied to the construction of other contemporary problems. One of the most important lessons concerns the fundamental controversy between those who espouse *objectivist* and *constructionist* approaches to a given issue or problem (Holstein and Miller 1993; Miller and Holstein 1993; Best 1989; Spector and Kitsuse 1987; Schneider and Kitsuse 1984). An objectivist scholar accepts that a particular phenomenon exists and constitutes a problem by virtue of causing harm or disturbance to a significant section of the society. The role of the social scientist might be to quantify that problem, to explore its origins, and perhaps to suggest possible solutions.

A constructionist may or may not accept that the phenomenon exists, or if it does, whether it is indeed harmful; but such questions are subsidiary to the more fundamental issue of how and why the condition or event comes to be viewed as a problem. Within the constructionist endeavor, there is a further division between *strict* and *contextual* approaches. For a strict constructionist, it is unnecessary and perhaps impossible to know the objective reality behind a problem: "The strict constructionist is not interested in assessing or judging the truth, accuracy, credibility, or reasonableness of what members say and do" (Kitsuse and Schneider 1989:xii–xiii). A contextual constructionist holds a more moderate position and seeks first to examine the plausibility and factual basis of the claims made in order to support the reality of a problem.

In the case of serial murder, an objectivist might accept the general thesis that serial murder represented a real threat, which would mean accepting wildly inflated statistics; or else he or she would deduce from the quantitative evidence that the phenomenon was so insignificant that it did not merit study. This latter approach would be equally dubious intellectually, in that it would fail to address the question of how and why the problem came to occupy so central a place in contemporary culture. The constructionist approach therefore seems far better suited to this kind of research.

Moreover, a contextual constructionist approach appears more rewarding in that it permits the observer to assess the accuracy of the statements by the various activists. Of course, it is not claimed that we can ever form a perfect or comprehensive picture of the "objective nature" of serial murder, but we can state with some certainty what that phenomenon is not. We can ascertain the rough statistical limits of that reality and what can be said about its historical development. To forgo such research would be to sacrifice an invaluable tool for academic analysis: how far claims-makers were in fact expressing "the truth, accuracy, credibility, or reasonableness" of the issue, and whether they knew they were departing from reality as they understood it.

Nowhere is the role of contextual analysis more critical than in the historical dimension of problem construction. In a sense, the reality and significance of virtually every problem is justified in historical terms, in that the terminology employed will usually involve a contrast between past and present conditions. Any given phenomenon is a source of concern because it is "more" or "worse," it involves a "growing menace" or a "rising tide of violence." Virtually never are such remarks substantiated by critical historical or quantitative analysis, to compare current and bygone conditions. When such claims are examined, they very often show that the issues in question demonstrate a striking continuity over time. This has been suggested for issues like drug abuse, child sex abuse, immoral popular music, or violent crime, and it is assuredly true of serial homicide (Jenkins 1992a; Best 1989). However, even those studies that criticize current claims about serial murder rarely offer the detailed historical study that is so essential to provide a context. Nor is this research a complicated project, as even a brief survey of readily available newspaper archives produces quite enough material to contradict most of the basic assertions about the "growing menace." All too often, the most basic claims used to validate a putative social problem rely on the historical amnesia of the assumed audience.

Historical analysis must also pay due attention to the broader political context, while fully recognizing the danger of drawing facile linkages that verge on conspiracy theory. It has been argued here that the serial murder panic was to some extent a reflection of contemporary conservative ideologies, which is not to argue that officials or legislators cynically concocted a menace in order to promote their bureaucratic goals. However, studying the construction of this problem reveals at every point the significance of events during 1980 and 1981, a time of impressive creativity by claims-makers ranging from feminists and black activists to Justice Department experts and ritual crime theorists. Inevitably, all these groups were to some extent influenced by prevailing political currents, whether or not they regarded these trends as beneficial. It is quite legitimate to draw analogies between the rhetoric of a particular social problem and the political commonplaces of the same era, even if these latter appear to concern quite unrelated matters of foreign or economic policy. The prolific new problems of the early 1980s were defined against an intellectual background of the same rhetoric of decadence and the same quest for enemies that also shaped attitudes in more mainstream political controversy. The study of social problems is, or should be, as integral to the academic domain of political science as of sociology or criminology.

The serial murder instance is also an important reminder of the imperative need to place claims-making in the broadest cultural context. It would be impossible to understand the framing of this problem without due reference throughout to popular culture: to slasher films, true-crime books, thriller novels, and above all to the work of Thomas Harris and Robert Bloch. There is a pressing need not only to identify and study the works in question, but to acknowledge their commercial context, for example, the changing censorship standards of the 1970s and the ever younger demographics of the cinema audience in the next decade.

It is or should be unthinkable to study the formulation of social problems without due reference to this vast and influential section of the mass media. In the specific case of satanism and the ritual crime problem, it is only ignorance of its pulp fiction roots that permits the continued serious discussion of the issue by competent scholars. The potential value of such material for problem analysis is well illustrated by Best's (1990) discussion of the threatened child theme in horror and detective fiction, or in Clover's (1992) examination of the culture of slasher films. The study of social problems is one of the academic areas that has most to gain from the insights and methodologies of the burgeoning field of cultural studies.

This represents an area of some difficulty for the academic researcher, who now has access to a bewildering range of databases and search facilities that allow him or her to access quite obscure material in learned journals or official documents. However, there is little comparable to permit a thematic search of "trashy novels," still less of violent "B-films," television movies, "real-life" police shows, or episodes of television series. To take a specific example from this study, there is currently no thematic search facility that would allow one to find the science fiction novel that was the source of the rumor that the Atlanta Child Murders were a clandestine medical experiment, nor would this important reference be discovered by the most thorough examination of serial murder fiction (see Chapter 8). Research in popular culture must therefore depend on a considerable element of serendipity and sheer chance.

Finally, the serial murder issue indicates the necessity to approach contemporary problems with the insights of a broad range of methodologies, including anthropology and social psychology, both of which have made such an impact in contemporary cultural studies. The need for these approaches is indicated by the extremely ambiguous attitudes that are suggested toward scientific and rationalistic assumptions in recent public discourse concerning social problems. On the surface, serial murder was discussed in ways that employed the language and thought of contemporary social and behavioral science. The seriousness of the issue was asserted in quantitative terms, and what statistics were available (four thousand victims) were regarded as definitive proof of the severity of the threat, being quoted in virtually every media story in middecade. On the other hand, the figures were permitted to flourish unchecked despite their counterintuitive nature and obvious contradictions. Even after the original figures had been discredited, the media continued to give great prominence to serial murder stories, though it was openly acknowledged that the offense represented such a tiny proportion of all homicides, still more of all serious criminality. The issue thus seems immune to invalidation.

Similarly, the solutions advocated were to be found in state-of-the-art information technology and behavioral science: Was not the *Behavioral Science* Unit the most quoted source on every aspect of the putative crisis? However, the experts who gained the widest acceptance did so not because of their academic credentials, but because of their personal narratives of traveling to the heart of darkness that is the mind of the "monster among us." This is the language of shamanism rather than psychology.

Once the problem was accepted as genuine, even the superficially scientific rhetoric of the claims-makers was soon lost among a welter of remarkably primitive language and concepts, ancient fears about the limits and definition of "real" humanity, the reversion to savagery, the pollution of cannibalism, and above all the threat of monsters. That such images can still have such apparent force is a striking and instructive lesson for claims-makers themselves, who will apparently succeed to the degree to which they can plausibly make their particular issues respond to these visceral fears. For social scientists, this is a sobering warning about the limits of any attempt to derail an incipient panic by pointing out the contradictions in the evidence used to support it. For all the science and quantification used to substantiate a new problem, its true momentum will be located in its appeal to deep-rooted anxieties that respond poorly to rational inquiry, still less rebuttal.

References

Abrahamsen, David (1944). *Crime and the Human Mind*. New York: Columbia University Press.

_____ (1960). *The Psychology of Crime*. New York: Columbia University Press.

_____ (1973). *The Murdering Mind*. New York: Harper and Row.

_____ (1983). "Confessions of Son of Sam." *Penthouse* (November).

_____ (1985). *Confessions of Son of Sam*. New York: Columbia University Press.

_____ (1992). *Murder and Madness: The Secret Life of Jack the Ripper*. London: Robson.

Achenbach, Joel (1991). "Serial Killers: Shattering the Myth," *Washington Post* (April 14).

Ackroyd, Peter (1985). *Hawksmoor*. New York: Harper and Row.

Adelman, R. H. (1970). *The Bloody Benders*. New York: Stein and Day.

Alix, Ernest K. (1978). *Ransom Kidnapping in America 1874–1974: The Creation of a Capital Crime*. Carbondale: Southern Illinois University Press.

Allen, William (1976). *Starkweather: The Story of a Mass Murderer*. Boston: Houghton Mifflin.

Altick, Richard (1973). *Victorian Studies in Scarlet*. London: Dent.

Altimore, Michael (1991). "The Social Construction of a Scientific Myth: Pornography and Violence." *Journal of Communication Inquiry* 15(1).

Altman, Jack and Marvin Ziporyn (1967). *Born to Raise Hell*. New York: Grove.

"Ambitious Federal Plan for Violence Research Runs Up Against Fears of Its Misuse" (1992). *Chronicle of Higher Education* November 4.

Ambroise-Rendu, Marc (1987). "The Granny Murders." *Guardian Weekly/Le Monde* December 20.

America's Best Kept Secret (1988). Video produced by *Passport Magazine*, West Covina, CA.

Anderson, Chris and Sharon McGehee (1992). *Bodies of Evidence*. New York: St. Martin's.

Anderson, Paul (1984). "U.S. Crime Unit Will Coordinate Police Searches". *Philadelphia Inquirer* July 11.

Apsche, Jack (1993). *Probing the Mind of a Serial Killer*. Morrisville, PA: International Information Associates.

Arens, William (1979). *The Man-Eating Myth*. Oxford University Press.

Askill, John and Martyn Sharpe (1993). *Angel of Death*. London: Michael O'Mara.

Athens, Lonnie H. (1992). *The Creation of Dangerous Violent Criminals*. Champaign: University of Illinois Press.

Ault, Richard L. and James T. Reese (1980). "A Psychological Assessment of Crime Profiling." *FBI Law Enforcement Bulletin* (March).

Bainbridge, William Sims (1978). *Satan's Power: A Deviant Psychotherapy Cult*. Berkeley: University of California Press.

Bakos, Susan Crain (1989). *Appointment for Murder*. New York: Pinnacle.

Baldwin, James (1985). *The Evidence of Things Not Seen*. New York: Holt, Rinehart and Winston.

Banay, Ralph S. (1956). "Psychology of a Mass Murderer." *Journal of Forensic Psychology* 1:1.

Barfield, Velma (1985). *Woman on Death Row*. Minneapolis, MN: Worldwide.

Barker, Martin (1984). *A Haunt of Fears: The Strange Case of the British Horror Comics Campaign*. London: Routledge.

Bart, Pauline B. and Eileen Geil Moran, eds. (1993). *Violence Against Women*. Newbury Park, CA: Sage.

Bates, Warren (1990). "Edward Bennett." *Police* (January).

Baumann, Ed (1991). *Step into My Parlor*. Chicago: Bonus Books.

Baumann, Ed and John O'Brien (1993). *Murder Next Door*. New York: Diamond.

Bayer, O. W., ed. (1947). *Cleveland Murders*. New York: Duell, Sloan and Pearce.

Beattie, John (1981). *The Yorkshire Ripper Story*. London: Quartet.

Beaver, Ninette, B. K. Ripley, and Patrick Trese (1974). *Caril*. Philadelphia: Lippincott.

Ben-Yehuda, Nachman (1990). *The Politics and Morality of Deviance: Moral Panics, Drug Abuse, Deviant Science, and Reversed Stigmatization*. Albany: SUNY Press.

Bennett, David H. (1990). *The Party of Fear*. New York: Vintage.

Bennetts, Leslie (1993). "Nightmares on Main Street." *Vanity Fair* (June).

Berger, Joseph (1984). "Traits Shared by Mass Killers Remain Unknown to Experts." *New York Times* (August 27).

Berry-Dee, Christopher and Robin Odell (1992). *A Question of Evidence*. London: Virgin True Crime.

———— (1993). *Lady Killer*. London: Virgin True Crime.

Best, Joel, ed. (1989). *Images of Issues*. Hawthorne, NY: Aldine de Gruyter.

———— (1990). *Threatened Children: Rhetoric and Concern about Child Victims*. Chicago: University of Chicago Press.

Bézard, Isabelle (1992). "Images of the Serial Killer 1980–1992," *Memoire de Maitrise*, University of Paris, Institut d'Anglais Charles V.

Bigelow, Bruce V. (1986). "A Killer Continues in L.A. as Police Struggle for Clues." *Philadelphia Inquirer* August 10.

Biondi, Ray and Walt Hecox (1988). *All His Father's Sins: Inside the Gerald Gallego Sex-Slave Murders*. Rocklin, CA: Prima.

———— (1992). *The Dracula Killer*. New York: Pocket Books.

Birkerts, Sven, et al. (1991). "Editorial Judgment or Censorship?" *Writer* (May):20–23.

Black, Joel (1991). *The Aesthetics of Murder: A Study in Romantic Literature and Contemporary Culture*. Baltimore: Johns Hopkins University Press.

Blackburn, Daniel J. (1990). *Human Harvest: The Sacramento Murder Story*. New York: Knightsbridge.

Blair, Danya (1993). "The Science of Serial Murder." *American Journal of Criminal Law* 20(2).

Blake, Sterling (1993). *Chiller*. New York: Bantam.

Bland, Lucy (1992). "The Case of the Yorkshire Ripper." Pp. 233–52 in *Femicide*, edited by Jill Radford and Diana E. H. Russell. New York: Twayne.

Bloch, Robert ([1943] 1977). "Yours Truly, Jack the Ripper." Pp. 1–20 in *The Best of Robert Bloch*. New York: Ballantine/Del Rey.

——— ([1946] 1977). "Enoch." Pp. 21–38 in *The Best of Robert Bloch*. New York: Ballantine/Del Rey.

——— (1947). *The Scarf*. New York: Dial.

——— ([1960] 1990). *Sweet Sixteen*. Pp. 13–34 in *Devil Worshippers*, edited by Martin H. Greenberg and Charles G. Waugh. New York: DAW.

——— (1977a). *The Best of Robert Bloch*. New York: Ballantine/Del Rey.

——— (1977b). *The King of Terrors*. New York: Mysterious Press.

——— (1993). *Once Around the Bloch*. New York: Tor.

Block, Carolyn R., (1987). *Homicide in Chicago*. Chicago: Loyola University of Chicago, Center for Urban Policy.

Boles, Jacqueline and Philip Davis (1988). "Defending Atlanta: Press Reactions to a Movie on the Missing and Murdered Children." *Journal of American Culture* 11:61–66.

Bradbury, Ray (1957). *Dandelion Wine*. Garden City: Doubleday.

Branigan, Augustine (1986). "Mystification of the Innocents." *Criminal Justice History* 7:111–44.

Brearley, H. C. (1932). *Homicide in the United States*. Chapel Hill: University of North Carolina Press.

Breo, Dennis L. and William J. Martin (1993). *The Crime of the Century*. New York: Bantam.

Brian, Denis (1986). *Murderers Die*. New York: St. Martins.

Broeske, Pat H. (1992). "Serial Killers Claim Movies as Their Prey." *New York Times* (December 13).

Bromberg, Walter (1948). *Crime and the Mind: An Outline of Psychiatric Criminology*. Philadelphia: J. B. Lippincott.

Brooks, Pierce R., Michael J. Devine, Terence J. Green, Barbara L. Hart, and Merlyn D. Moore (1987). "Serial Murder: A Criminal Justice Response." *Police Chief* 54:37–45.

Brown, James S. (1991a). "The Psychopathology of Serial Sexual Homicide: A Review of the Possibilities." *American Journal of Forensic Psychiatry* 12(1):13–22.

——— (1991b). "The Historical Similarity of Twentieth Century Serial Sexual Homicide to Pre-Twentieth Century Occurrences of Vampirism." *American Journal of Forensic Psychiatry* 12(2).

Brownmiller, Susan (1975). *Against Our Will*. London: Secker and Warburg.

Brunvand, Jan Harold (1981). *The Vanishing Hitchhiker*. New York: Norton.

_____ (1984). *The Choking Doberman*. New York: Norton.

Bugliosi, Vincent and Curt Gentry (1976). *Helter Skelter*. New York: Norton.

Burn, Gordon (1984). *Somebody's Husband, Somebody's Son*. London: Heinemann.

Burnett, John (1989). "Magic and Murder in Matamoros." *Christian Century* (September 13).

Burnham, David (1984). "FBI May Test Computer Index for White Collar Crime Inquiries." *New York Times* (October 25).

Cahill, Tim (1986). *Buried Dreams*. New York: Bantam.

Cameron, Deborah (1992). "That's Entertainment?" Pp. 184–88 in *Femicide*, edited by Jill Radford and Diana E. H. Russell. New York: Twayne.

Cameron, Deborah and Elizabeth Frazer (1987). *The Lust to Kill*. London: Polity.

Campbell, Ramsey ([1979] 1985). *The Face That Must Die*. New York: Tor.

Capote, Truman (1965). *In Cold Blood*. New York: Random House.

Caputi, Jane (1987). *The Age of Sex Crime*. London: Women's Press.

_____ (1989). "The Sexual Politics of Murder." *Gender and Society* 3(4).

_____ (1990a). "The New Founding Fathers: The Lore and Lure of the Serial Killer in Contemporary Culture." *Journal of American Culture* 13:1.

_____ (1990b). "Femicide: Speaking the Unspeakable." *MS.* (September).

_____ (1992). "Advertizing Femicide." Pp. 203–21 in *Femicide*, edited by Jill Radford and Diana E. H. Russell. New York: Twayne.

Caputi, Jane and Diana E. H. Russell (1992). "Femicide." Pp. 13–24 in *Femicide*, edited by Jill Radford and Diana E. H. Russell. New York: Twayne.

Cartwright, Gary (1992). "Free to Kill." *Texas Monthly* (August).

Casey, Kathryn (1992). "The Devil Inside." *Ladies Home Journal* (June).

Casey, Lee, ed. (1946). *Denver Murders*. New York: Duell, Sloan and Pearce.

Cauffiel, Lowell (1993). *Forever and Five Days*. New York: Zebra.

Caunitz, William J. ([1991] 1992). *Exceptional Clearance*. New York: Bantam.

Chapman, Ivan (1982). *Private Eddie Leonski: The Brownout Strangler*. Sydney, Australia: Hale and Iremonger.

Chappell, Duncan (1989). "Sexual Criminal Violence." Pp. 68–108 in *Pathways to Criminal Violence*, edited by Neil Alan Weiner and Marvin Wolfgang. Newbury Park, CA: Sage.

Cheney, Margaret (1976). *The Co-Ed Killer*. New York: Walker.

Chesler, Phyllis (1992a). "A Double Standard for Murder?" *New York Times* (January 8).

_____ (1992b). "Sex, Death and the Double Standard." *On the Issues* (Summer).

_____ (1993). "A Woman's Right to Self-Defense." *St. John's Law Review* 66(4).

"Cities Nationwide Ask: Serial Killer At Work?" (1990). *Law Enforcement News* (October 31).

Clark, James W. (1988). "Occult Cops." *Law Enforcement News* (November 15).

Clark, Mark ([1987] 1989). *Ripper*. New York: Berkley.

Clark, Mary Higgins (1992). *Loves Music, Loves to Dance*. New York: Pocket Books.

Clark, Steve and Mike Morley (1993). *Murder in Mind: Mindhunting the Serial Killers*. London: Boxtree.

Clover, Carol J. (1992). *Men, Women, and Chainsaws*. Princeton, NJ: Princeton University Press.

Cohen, Fred (1980). *The Law of Deprivation of Liberty*. St. Paul, MN: West.

Cohen, Stan (1972). *Folk Devils and Moral Panics: The Creation of the Mods and Rockers*. Oxford: Blackwell.

Cohen, Stan and Jock Young, eds. (1973). *The Manufacture of News: Social Problems, Deviance and the Mass Media*. London: Constable.

Cohn, Norman (1975). *Europe's Inner Demons*. New York: Basic Books.

Collins, Gail (1991). "Wages and Sin." *Working Woman* (March).

Collins, T., ed. (1944). *New York Murders*. New York: Duell, Sloan and Pearce.

"Condemned Killer Says He Can't Get a Fair Deal" (1986). *New York Times* (May 30).

Conover, Pamela Johnston and Virginia Gray (1983). *Feminism and the New Right*. New York: Praeger.

Conradi, Peter (1992). *The Red Ripper*. New York: Dell.

Conway, Flo and Jim Siegelman (1982). *Holy Terror*. New York: Doubleday.

Cook, Thomas H. (1992). *Early Graves*. New York: Dutton.

Coram, Robert ([1992] 1993). *Running Dead*. New York: Signet.

Cornwell, Patricia D. ([1990] 1991). *Post-Mortem*. New York: Avon.

———— ([1992] 1993). *All That Remains*. New York: Avon.

———— (1993). *Cruel and Unusual*. New York: Scribners.

Coston, John (1992). *To Kill and Kill Again*. New York: Onyx.

Cox, Mike (1991). *The Confessions of Henry Lee Lucas*. New York: Pocket Star Books.

Craft, Nicki (1992). "Inspiring Protest." Pp. 325–45 in *Femicide*, edited by Jill Radford and Diana E. H. Russell. New York: Twayne.

Craig, Kit (1992). *Gone*. Boston: Little Brown.

Crewdson, John (1988). *By Silence Betrayed: Sexual Abuse of Children in America*. New York: Little Brown.

Critchley, T. A. and P. D. James (1971). *The Maul and the Pear Tree*. London: Constable.

Crockett, Art, ed. (1990). *Serial Murderers*. New York: Pinnacle.

————, ed. (1991). *Spree Killers*. New York: Pinnacle.

Cross, Roger (1981). *The Yorkshire Ripper*. New York: Dell.

Crowley, Aleister (1970). *The Confessions of Aleister Crowley*, edited by John Symonds and Kenneth Grant. New York: Hill and Wang.

Cullen, Robert (1993). *The Killer Department*. New York: Pantheon.

"The Curse of Violent Crime" (1981). *Time* (March 23).

D'Emilio, John and Estelle B. Freedman (1988). *Intimate Matters: A History of Sexuality in America*. New York: Harper and Row.

Dalrymple, James (1991). "Slaughter of the Lambs." *Sunday Times* (London), June 23).

Daly, Martin and Margo Wilson (1988). *Homicide*. Hawthorne, NY: Aldine de Gruyter.

Damio, Ward (1974). *Urge to Kill*. New York: Pinnacle.

Damore, Leo (1990). *In His Garden*. New York: Dell.

Daniels, Les (1974). *Comix: A History of Comic Books in America*. London: Granada.

Darnton, John (1993). "Serial Killer Is Stalking London Homosexuals." *New York Times* (June 18).

Darrach, Brad and Joel Norris (1984). "An American Tragedy." *Life* (August).

Davies, Nick (1993). *Murder on Ward Four*. London: Chatto and Windus.

Davis, David Brion (1957). *Homicide in American Fiction 1798–1860*. Ithaca, NY: Cornell University Press.

Davis, Don (1991). *The Milwaukee Murders*. New York: St. Martin's.

Dawidoff, Robert (1992). "Murder by Homophobia." *Advocate* (July 30).

Dawkins, Vickie L. and Mina Downey Higgins (1989). *Devil Child*. New York: St. Martin's.

De La Torre, L. (1955). *The Truth About Belle Gunness*. New York: Gold Medal.

De Noux, O'Neil (1992). *Crescent City Kills*. New York: Zebra.

DeFord, Miriam Allen (1965). *Murderers Sane and Mad*. New York: Abelard Schuman.

Derleth, August (1968). *Wisconsin Murders*. Sauk City, WI: Mycroft and Moran.

Dettlinger, Chet and Jeff Prugh (1983). *The List*. Atlanta, GA: Philmay Enterprises.

Dietz, Park E., Bruce Harry, and Robert R. Hazelwood (1986). "Detective Magazines: Pornography for the Sexual Sadist?" *Journal of Forensic Sciences* 31:197–211.

Domingo, Chris (1992). "What the White Man Won't Tell Us." Pp. 195–202 in *Femicide*, edited by Jill Radford and Diana E. H. Russell. New York: Twayne.

Doney, Richard H. (1990). "The Aftermath of the Yorkshire Ripper," Pp. 95–112 in *Serial Murder*, edited by Steven A. Egger. New York: Praeger.

Dorner, Marjorie ([1990] 1992). *Freeze Frame*. New York: Zebra.

Douglas, Adam (1993). *The Beast Within*. New York: Chapman's/Trafalgar Square.

Douthwaite, L. C. (1929). *Mass Murder*. New York: Henry Holt.

Downs, Donald A. (1989). *The New Politics of Pornography*. Chicago: University of Chicago Press.

Drukteinis, Albert M. (1992). "Serial Murder: The Heart of Darkness." *Psychiatric Annals* 22(10):532.

Dubner, Stephen J. (1992). "Portrait of a Serial Killer." *New York* (October 19).

Du Clos, Bernard (1993). *Fair Game*. New York: St. Martin's.

Duncan, Robert L. ([1989] 1990). *The Serpent's Mark*. New York: St. Martin's.

Dunning, John (1989). *Mystical Murders*. London: Arrow.

Dürrenmatt, Friedrich (1959). *The Pledge*. New York: Knopf.

Dvorchak, Robert J. and Lisa Holewa (1991). *Milwaukee Massacre*. New York: Dell.

Earley, Pete (1993). *Prophet of Death*. New York: Avon.

Eberle, Paul and Shirley Eberle (1986). *The Politics of Child Abuse*. Secaucus, NJ: Lyle Stuart.

Eckert, Allan W. ([1985] 1986). *The Scarlet Mansion*. New York: Bantam.

Edmiston, Susan (1991). "The First Woman Serial Killer?" *Glamour* (September):302–22.

Eftimiades, Maria (1993). *Garden of Graves*. New York: St. Martin's.

Egan, Timothy (1992a). "Oregon Measure Asks State to Repress Homosexuality." *New York Times* (August 16).

——— (1992b). "Child-Killer, Awaiting Noose, May Have Slain Illusions Too." *New York Times* (December 29).

_____ (1993). "13 Unsolved Deaths Feed Indian Mistrust of FBI." *New York Times* (April 18).

Egger, Steven A. (1984). "A Working Definition of Serial Murder." *Journal of Police Science and Administration* 12(3):348–57.

_____ (1985). *An Analysis of the Serial Murder Phenomenon and the Law Enforcement Response*. Ph.D. thesis, Sam Houston State University, Huntsville, TX.

Egger, Steven A., ed. (1990). *Serial Murder: An Elusive Phenomenon*. New York: Praeger.

Egginton, Joyce (1990). *From Cradle to Grave*. New York: Jove.

Eilberg-Schwartz, Howard (1990). *The Savage in Judaism*. Bloomington: Indiana University Press.

Elkind, Peter (1989). *The Death Shift*. New York: Viking.

Ellis, Bret Easton (1991). *American Psycho*. New York: Vintage.

Ellison, Harlan, ed. (1974). *Dangerous Visions*. London: Sphere.

Ellroy, James, (1986). *Silent Terror*. New York: Avon.

Emmons, Nuel (1987). *Manson in His Own Words*. New York: Grove.

Englade, Ken (1988). *Cellar of Horror*. New York: St. Martin's.

Erikson, Kai (1966). *Wayward Puritans*. New York: Free Press.

"Experts Say Mass Murderers Are Rare But on the Rise" (1988). *New York Times* (January 3).

Farr, Louise (1992). *The Sunset Murders*. New York: Pocket Books.

Farson, Daniel (1972). *Jack the Ripper*. London: Michael Joseph.

Fawkes, Sandy (1978). *Killing Time*. London: Hamlyn.

"FBI Launches Frontal Attack on Serial Killers" (1984). State College, PA, *Centre Daily Times* (July 11).

Fischer, Mary A. (1991). "Was Wayne Williams Framed?" *GQ* (April):228ff.

Flagg, Gordon (1991). "Fired Librarian Blames *American Psycho* Purchase." *American Libraries* November.

Flowers, Anna (1993). *Blind Fury*. New York: Pinnacle.

Frank, Gerold (1967). *The Boston Strangler*. London: Jonathan Cape.

Freeman, Lucy, (1955). *"Before I Kill More . . ."* New York: Crown.

Fuller, R. C. and R. D. Myers (1941). "The Natural History of a Social Problem." *American Sociological Review* 6.

Furneaux, Rupert (1957). *The Medical Murderer*. New York: Abelard Schumann.

Gaddis, Thomas E. and James O. Long (1970). *Killer: A Journal of Murder*. New York: Macmillan.

Galvin, James A. V. and John M. MacDonald (1959). "Psychiatric Study of a Mass Murderer." *American Journal of Psychiatry* 115:1057.

Gammage, Jeff (1991). "Serial Murders Are on the Rise, Say Experts." *Philadelphia Inquirer* (September 8).

Ganey, Terry (1989). *St. Joseph's Children: A True Story of Terror and Justice*. New York: Lyle Stuart/Carol.

Garcia, Guy (1989). "The Believers." *Rolling Stone* (June 29).

Gardiner, Muriel (1976). *The Deadly Innocents*. New York: Basic.

Gaute, J. H. H. and Robin Odell (1989). *The Murderers' Who's Who*. London: Harrap.

Gelb, Barbara (1975). *On the Track of Murder*. New York: William Morrow.

Gibney, Bruce (1990). *The Beauty Queen Killer*. New York: Pinnacle.

Gilmour, Walter and Leland E. Hale (1991). *Butcher Baker*. New York: Onyx.

Ginsburg, Philip E. (1993). *Shadow of Death: The Hunt for a Serial Killer*. New York: Scribners.

Ginzburg, Carlo (1991). *Ecstasies: Deciphering the Witches' Sabbath*. New York: Pantheon.

Girard, James Preston (1993). *The Late Man*. New York: Atheneum.

Godwin, John (1978). *Murder USA*. New York: Ballantine.

Goffman, Erving (1974). *Frame Analysis: An Essay on the Organization of Experience*. New York: Harper and Row.

Goldberg, Leonard S. ([1991] 1992). *Deadly Medicine*. New York: Signet.

Goleman, Daniel (1991). "Child's Love of Cruelty May Hint at the Future Killer." *New York Times* (August 7).

Gollmar, Robert H. (1989). *Edward Gein: America's Most Bizarre Murderer*. New York: Pinnacle.

Gonzalez, David and Donatello Lorch (1991). "Intricate Trail to Bronx Murder Charges." *New York Times* (July 13).

Goode, Erich (1989). "The American Drug Panic of the 1980s." *Violence-Aggression-Terrorism* 3(4):327–48.

——— (1992). *Collective Behavior*. New York: Harcourt Brace Jovanovich.

——— (1993). *Drugs in American Society*, 4th ed. New York: McGraw Hill.

Goodman, Mark (1991). "Cops, Killers and Cannibals." *People Weekly* (April 1):62–70.

Gorman, Ed. and Martin H. Greenberg, eds. (1993). *Predators*. New York: Roc Books.

Gould, Stephen Jay (1981). *The Mismeasure of Man*. New York: Norton.

Gove, W. R., M. Hughes, and M. Geerken (1985). "Are Uniform Crime Reports a Valid Indicator of the Index Crimes?" *Criminology* 23:451–501.

Grant, Jaime (1992). "Who's Killing Us?" Pp. 145–60 in *Femicide*, edited by Jill Radford and Diana E. H. Russell. New York: Twayne.

Graysmith, Robert (1987). *Zodiac*. New York: Berkley.

——— ([1981] 1990). *The Sleeping Lady*. New York: Dutton.

Green, Martin and John Swan (1993). *The Triumph of Pierrot*. University Park, PA: Pennsylvania State University Press.

Green, Thomas A. (1991). "Accusations of Satanism and Racial Tensions in the Matamoros Cult Murders." Pp. 237–48 in *Satanism Scare*, edited by James F. Richardson, Joel Best, and David Bromley. Hawthorne, NY: Aldine de Gruyter.

Greenberg, David F. (1988). *The Construction of Homosexuality*. Chicago: University of Chicago Press.

Grossberg, Lawrence, Cary Nelson, and Paula A. Treichler, eds. (1992). *Cultural Studies*. London: Routledge.

Gurwell, John K. (1974). *Mass Murder in Houston*. Houston: Cordovan.

Gusfield, Joseph (1981). *The Culture of Public Problems*. Chicago: University of Chicago Press.

Gutierrez, Cris (1993). "Aileen Wuornos, Hothead Paisan, and Me." *Frighten the Horses* 11(Winter).

Halberstam, Judith (1991). "Skin-Flick." *Camera Obscura* (September).

Hall, Stuart, with Chas Critcher, Tony Jefferson, John Clarke, and Brian Roberts (1978). *Policing the Crisis: Mugging, the State, and Law and Order*. London: MacMillan.

Halleck, Seymour (1965). "American Psychiatry and the Criminal: A Historical Review." *American Journal of Psychiatry* 121(9, supplement):i–xxi.

Hamer, A. C., ed. (1948). *Detroit Murders*. New York: Duell, Sloan and Pearce.

Harris, Melvin (1987). *Jack the Ripper: The Bloody Truth*. London: Columbus.

Harris, Ruth (1989). *Murders and Madness: Medicine, Law and Society in the Fin de Siècle*. Oxford: Clarendon.

Harris, Thomas ([1988] 1989). *The Silence of the Lambs*. New York: St. Martin's.

———— ([1981] 1990). *Red Dragon*. New York: Dell.

Harrison, Barbara Grizzuti (1991). "*American Psycho*—Bestseller from Hell." *Mademoiselle* (May):148–50.

Harrison, Michael (1972). *Clarence*. London: W. H. Allen.

Harrison, Shirley (1993). *The Diary of Jack the Ripper*. New York: Hyperion.

Harrison, Tom (1986). *Brady and Hindley*. London: Ashgrove.

Harvey, James Neal ([1989] 1990). *By Reason of Insanity*. New York: St. Martin's.

———— ([1991] 1992). *Painted Ladies*. New York: St. Martin's.

Hawkins, Darnell (1986). *Homicide Among Black Americans*. Boston: University Press of America.

Hawkins, Harriet (1993). "Maidens and Monsters in Modern Popular Culture." *Textual Practice* 7(2).

Hazelwood, Robert R. and Ann W. Burgess (1987). *Practical Aspects of Rape Investigation*. New York: Elsevier.

Hazelwood, Robert R. and John E. Douglas (1980). "The Lust Murderer." *FBI Law Enforcement Bulletin* 49(4):18–22.

Hazelwood, Robert R. and Janet Warren (1989). "The Serial Rapist." *FBI Law Enforcement Bulletin* 58(1–2).

Headley, Bernard D. (1986). "Ideological Constructions of Race and the Atlanta Tragedy." *Contemporary Crises* 10:181–200.

Heffernan, William (1993). *Scarred*. New York: Signet.

Heimer, Mel (1971). *The Cannibal*. New York: Lyle Stuart.

Hickey, Eric W. (1991). *Serial Murderers and Their Victims*. Monterey, CA: Brooks-Cole/Wadsworth.

Hicks, Robert D. (1991). *In Pursuit of Satan: The Police and the Occult*. New York: Prometheus.

Hilberry, Conrad (1987). *Luke Karamazov*. Detroit: Wayne State University Press.

Hill, Carol DeChellis (1993). *Henry James' Midnight Song*. New York: Poseidon.

Hoffman, F. (1925). *The Homicide Problem*. San Francisco: Prudential.

Hofstadter, Richard (1979). *The Paranoid Style in American Politics*. Chicago: University of Chicago Press.

Holloway, Wendy (1984). "'I Just Wanted to Kill a Woman.' Why? The Ripper and Male Sexuality." Pp. 26–46 in *Sweeping Statements: Writings from the Women's Liberation Movement 1981–1983*, edited by Hannah Kanter et al. London: Women's Press.

Holmes, Colin (1979). *Anti-Semitism in British Society 1876–1939*. London: Edward Arnold.

Holmes, Ronald M. (1989). "Youths in the Occult." *Criminal Justice in the Americas* October.

Holmes, Ronald M. and James DeBurger (1985). "Profiles in Terror," *Federal Probation*.

——— (1988). *Serial Murder*. Beverly Hills, CA: Sage.

Holmes, Ronald M. and Stephen T. Holmes (1993). *Murder in America*. Newbury Park, CA: Sage.

Holstein, James A. and Gale Miller, eds. (1993). *Reconsidering Social Constructionism*. Hawthorne, NY: Aldine de Gruyter.

Holub, Kathy (1991). "Ballistic Instinct." *Premiere Magazine* (August 1).

Howard, Clark (1980). *Zebra*. New York: Berkley.

Hsia, R. Po-chia (1988). *The Myth of Ritual Murder*. New Haven, CT: Yale University Press.

——— (1992). *Trent 1475*. New Haven, CT: Yale University Press.

Huebner, Frederick D (1994). *Methods of Evaluation*. New York: Simon and Schuster.

Humes, Edward (1991). *Buried Secrets: A True Story of Serial Murder, Black Magic and Drug-Running on the U.S. Border*. New York: Dutton.

Hunter, Jessie Prichard (1993). *Blood Music*. New York: Turtle Bay.

Iannone, Carol (1991). "PC and the Ellis Affair." *Commentary* (July):52–54.

"In the Land of the Rising Gun" (1989). *Economist* (August 26).

Izzi, Eugene (1988). *The Eighth Victim*. New York: St. Martin's.

Jackman, Tom and Troy Cole (1992). *Rites of Burial*. New York: Pinnacle.

James, Caryn (1991). "Now Starring, Killers for the Chiller Nineties." *New York Times* (March 10).

James, Earl W. K. (1991). *Catching Serial Killers*. Lansing, MI: International Forensic Services.

James, P.D. ([1988] 1989). *Devices and Desires*. New York: Warner.

James, P. D. and T. A. Critchley (1987). *The Maul and the Pear Tree*. New York: Mysterious Press.

Jeffers, H. Paul (1992). *Who Killed Precious?* New York: St. Martin's.

Jeffreys, Sheila (1979). "Rape." *Leveller* 25.

——— (1990). *Anticlimax: A Feminist Perspective on the Sexual Revolution*. London: Women's Press.

Jenkins, Philip (1984). *Crime and Justice: Issues and Ideas*. Monterey, CA: Brooks-Cole/Wadsworth.

——— (1988a). "Myth and Murder: The Serial Murder Panic of 1983–1985." *Criminal Justice Research Bulletin* 3(11)1–7.

——— (1988b). "Serial Murder in England 1940–1985." *Journal of Criminal Justice* 16(1):1–15.

——— (1989). "Serial Murder in the United States 1900–1940: A Historical Perspective." *Journal of Criminal Justice* 17(5):377–92.

——— (1990). "Sharing Murder: Understanding Group Serial Homicide." *Journal of Crime and Justice* 13(2):125–47.

——— (1991). "Changing Perceptions of Serial Murder in Contemporary England." *Journal of Contemporary Criminal Justice* 7(4):210–31.

———— (1992a). *Intimate Enemies: Moral Panics in Contemporary Great Britain*. Hawthorne, NY: Aldine de Gruyter.

———— (1992b). "A Murder Wave? Serial Murder in the United States 1940–1990." *Criminal Justice Review* 17(1):1–19.

———— (1992c). "Investigating Occult and Ritual Crime: A Case for Caution". *Police Forum* 2(1):1–7.

———— (1993). "Chance or Choice." Pp. 461–78 in *Homicide: The Victim-Offender Connection*, edited by Anna Victoria Wilson. Cincinnati: Anderson.

———— (1994). "African-Americans and Serial Homicide." *American Journal of Criminal Justice (forthcoming)*.

———— (forthcoming). "A Historical Perspective on Serial Murder: England, Germany, & the USA 1900–1940." In *Serial and Mass Murder: Theory, Research, Policy*, edited by Thomas O'Reilly-Fleming and Steven Egger. Toronto: University of Toronto Press.

Jenkins, Philip and Daniel Maier-Katkin (1991). "Occult Survivors: The Making of a Myth" Pp. 127–44 in *The Satanism Scare* edited by Richardson, James F., Joel Best, and David Bromley. Hawthorne, NY: Aldine de Gruyter.

———— (1992). "Satanism: Myth and Reality in a Contemporary Moral Panic." *Crime, Law and Social Change* 17:53–75.

Johnson, Steve (1991). "Microscope on Monsters at Serial Murder Seminar." *Chicago Tribune* (August 1).

Johnston, Jerry (1989). *The Edge of Evil: The Rise of Satanism in North America*. Dallas, TX: Word.

Jones, Valarie and Peggy Collier (1993). *True Crime: Serial Killers and Mass Murderers*. Forestville, CA: Eclipse Books.

Joyce, Fay S. (1983). "Two Suspects' Stories of Killings Culled." *New York Times* (November 4).

Junod, Tom (1993). "Deadly Medicine." *GQ* (June).

Kagan, Dan (1984). "Serial Murderers." *Omni* (June).

Kahaner, Larry (1988). *Cults That Kill*. New York: Warner.

Kane, Larry (1991). *Naked Prey*. New York: Zebra.

Karpman, Benjamin (1947–1948). *Case-Studies in the Psychopathology of Crime*. Washington DC: Medical Science Press.

———— (1954). *The Sexual Offender and His Offenses*. New York: Julian.

Katz, Jonathan Ned (1992). *Gay American History*, rev. ed. New York: Meridian.

Kellerman, Jonathan (1987). *Over the Edge*. New York: Atheneum.

———— ([1988] 1989). *The Butcher's Theater*. New York: Bantam.

Kendall, Elizabeth (1981). *The Phantom Prince*. Seattle: Madrona.

Kennedy, Dolores (1992). *On a Killing Day*. Chicago: Bonus Books.

Kennedy, Foster, Harry R. Hoffman, and William H. Haines (1947). "A Study of William Heirens." *American Journal of Psychiatry* 104:113.

Keppel, Robert (1989). *Serial Murder*. Cincinnati: Anderson.

Keppel, Robert and Joseph G. Weis (1993). "Improving the Investigation of Violent Crime." *National Institute of Justice: Research in Brief* August.

Kernan, Bill (1993). "The Original Cambodian." *New Internationalist* (April).

Kerr, Philip ([1992] 1993). *A Philosophical Investigation*. New York: Farrar Straus Giroux.

Kessler, Ronald (1993). *The FBI*. New York: Pocket Books.

Keyes, Daniel (1986). *Unveiling Claudia*. New York: Bantam.

Keyes, Edward (1977). *The Michigan Murders*. London: New English Library.

Kidder, Tracy, (1974). *The Road to Yuba City*. New York: Doubleday.

Kienzle, William ([1979] 1989). *The Rosary Murders*. New York: Ballantine.

Kilroy, James and Bob Stewart (1990). *Sacrifice*. Dallas, TX: Word.

Kimball, Stephen (1993). *Red Days*. New York: Signet.

King, Charles ([1992] 1993). *Mama's Boy*. New York: Pocket Books.

King, Gary C. (1992). *Blood Lust: Portrait of a Serial Sex Killer*. New York: Onyx.

———— (1993). *Driven To Kill*. New York: Pinnacle.

King, Stephen (1987). *Misery*. New York: Signet.

Kitsuse, John I. and Joseph W. Schneider (1989). "Preface." Pp. xi–xiii in *Images of Issues*, edited by Joel Best. Hawthorne, NY: Aldine de Gruyter.

Kittrie, Nicholas N. (1971). *The Right to Be Different*. Baltimore: Johns Hopkins University Press.

Klausner, Lawrence D. (1981). *Son of Sam*. New York: McGraw Hill.

Klein, Lloyd (1992). "The Milwaukee Chainsaw Massacre: Serial Murder as Deviant Social Behavior." Paper presented to the Academy of Criminal Justice Sciences, Pittsburgh, PA, March.

Knight, Stephen (1976). *Jack the Ripper: the Final Solution*. London: Harrap.

Kolarik, Gera-Lind, with Wayne Klatt (1992). *Freed to Kill: The True Story of Serial Murderer Larry Eyler*. New York: Avon.

Kolata, Gina (1991). "Critic of Genetic Fingerprinting Tests Tells of Pressure to Withdraw Paper." *New York Times* (December 20).

Koontz, Dean (1993). *Dragon Tears*. New York: Berkley.

Krafft-Ebing, R. von ([1886] 1978). *Psychopathia Sexualis*. New York: Scarborough.

Krivich, Mikhail and Ol'gert Ol'gin (1993). *Comrade Chikatilo*. Fort Lee, NJ: Barricade.

Kuhn, Philip A. (1990). *Soul Stealers: The Chinese Sorcery Scare of 1768*. Cambridge, MA: Harvard University Press.

Kuncl, Tom and Paul Einstein (1985). *Ladies Who Kill*. New York: Pinnacle.

Kunen, James (1990). "A Killer on the Campus." *People Weekly* (September 17).

Lacy, Suzanne (1992). "In Mourning and in Rage." Pp. 317–24 in *Femicide*, edited by Jill Radford and Diana E. H. Russell. New York: Twayne.

Lane, Brian (1991). *Murder Update*. New York: Carroll and Graf.

Langlois, Janet L. (1985). *Belle Gunness: The Lady Bluebeard*. Bloomington: Indiana University Press.

Lanning, Kenneth V. (1987). *Child Molesters: A Behavioral Analysis*. Washington, DC: National Center for Missing and Exploited Children.

———— (1989a). *Child Sex Rings: A Behavioral Analysis*. Washington, DC: National Center for Missing and Exploited Children.

———— (1989b). "Satanic, Occult and Ritualistic Crime: A Law Enforcement Perspective." *Police Chief* (October):62–85.

———— (1992). *Investigator's Guide to Allegations of "Ritual" Child Abuse*. Quantico, VA: National Center for the Analysis of Violent Crime, NCAVC. FBI Academy.

LaPlante, Lynda ([1991] 1993). *Prime Suspect*. New York: Dell.

———— (1993). *Prime Suspect 2*. New York: Dell.

Larsen, Richard (1980). *Bundy: The Deliberate Stranger*. Englewood Cliffs, NJ: Prentice Hall.

Larson, Bob (1989). *Satanism: The Seduction of America's Youth*. Nashville: Thomas Nelson.

Laymon, Richard (1989). "Mess Hall." Pp. 21–41 in *Book of the Dead*, edited by John Skipp and Craig R. Spector. New York: Bantam.

Lefebure, Charles (1969). *The Blood Cults*. New York: Ace.

Leith, Ron (1991). *The Torso Killer*. New York: Pinnacle.

Leo, John (1990). "Marketing Cynicism and Vulgarity." *U.S. News and World Report* (December 3).

Leps, Marie-Christine (1992). *Apprehending the Criminal: The Production of Deviance in Nineteenth Century Discourse*. Durham, NC: Duke University Press.

Lesser, Wendy (1993). *Pictures at an Execution: An Inquiry into the Subject of Murder*. Cambridge, MA: Harvard University Press.

Levin, Jack and James A. Fox (1985). *Mass Murder: America's Growing Menace*. New York: Plenum.

Leyton, Elliott (1986). *Compulsive Killers*. New York: New York University Press.

Leyton, Elliott, William O'Grady, and James Overton (1992). *Violence and Public Anxiety*. St. Johns, Newfoundland: Memorial University of Newfoundland, Institute of Social and Economic Research.

Lieberman, Herbert ([1989] 1990). *Shadow Dancers*. New York: St. Martin's.

Lindesmith, A. and Y. Levin (1937). "The Lombrosian Myth in Criminology." *American Journal of Sociology* 42:653–71.

Lindsay, Paul (1992). *Witness to the Truth*. Thorndike, ME: Thorndike.

Lindsay, Philip (1958). *The Mainspring of Murder*. London: John Long.

Lindsey, David L. ([1990] 1991). *Mercy*. New York: Bantam.

———— (1993). *Body of Truth*. New York: Bantam.

Lindsey, Robert (1984a). "Officials Cite a Rise in Killers Who Roam U.S. for Victims." *New York Times* (January 22).

———— (1984b). "Stopping Them Before They Kill Again and Again and Again." *New York Times* (April 22).

Linedecker, Clifford (1980). *The Man Who Killed Boys*. New York: St. Martin's.

———— (1988). *Thrill Killers*. Toronto: Paper Jacks.

———— (1990a). *Serial Thrill Killers*. New York: Knightsbridge.

———— (1990b). *Hell Ranch*. New York: Tor.

———— (1991). *Night Stalker*. New York: St. Martin's.

Linedecker, Clifford and William A. Burt (1990). *Nurses Who Kill*. New York: Windsor/Pinnacle.

Lisners, J. (1983). *House of Horrors*. London: Corgi.

London, Robb (1991). "Strategy on Sex Crimes Is Prison, Then Prison." *New York Times* (February 8).

Lopez, Barry Holstun (1978). *Of Wolves and Men*. New York: Scribners.

Lourie, Richard (1993). *Hunting the Devil*. New York: Harper Collins.

Love, Robert (1991). "Psycho Analysis." *Rolling Stone* (April 4):45–51.

Lucas, Norman (1992). *The Sex Killers*. London: Virgin True Crime.

Lunde, D. T. (1976). *Murder and Madness.* New York: Norton.

Lunde, D. T. and Jefferson Morgan (1980). *The Die Song.* New York: Norton.

Lynch, Michael J. and E. Britt Patterson, eds. (1992). *Race and Criminal Justice.* Fairfax, VA: Harrow and Heston.

MacAloon, John J., ed. (1984). *Rite, Drama, Festival, Spectacle: Rehearsals Toward a Theory of Cultural Performance.* Philadelphia: Institute for the Study of Human Issues.

MacDonald, John Marshall (1961). *The Murderer and His Victim.* Springfield, IL: Charles Thomas.

———— (1968). *Homicidal Threats.* Springfield, IL: Charles Thomas.

———— (1976). *Psychiatry and the Criminal.* Springfield, IL: Charles Thomas.

Mackenzie, Doris Layton, Phyllis Jo Baunach, and Roy Roberg, eds. (1990). *Measuring Crime: Large Scale, Long Range Efforts.* Albany: SUNY Press.

MacLean, Harry N. (1993). *Once Upon a Time: A True Story of Memory, Murder and the Law.* New York: Harper Collins.

MacNamara, Mark (1991). "Kiss and Kill." *Vanity Fair* (September).

MacPherson, Malcolm (1991). "Let's Make a Deal." *Premiere Magazine* (December).

Mailer, Norman (1991). "Children of the Pied Piper." *Vanity Fair* (March).

Mallowe, Michael (1990). "The Nobody Murders." *Philadelphia Magazine* (August):168–70, 235–39.

Mandelsberg, Rose G., ed. (1991). *Cult Killers.* New York: Pinnacle.

———— (1992). *Medical Murderers.* New York: Pinnacle.

Manguel, Alberto (1991). "Designer Porn." *Saturday Night* (July):46–48.

Mann, Paul (1989). "The Net Tightens on 'Family' Killers." *New Idea* (Australia) (September 23).

"Manson Revisited: The Story Behind Matamoros" (1989). *Executive Intelligence Review* (May 12).

Marder, Dianna (1992). "A New Generation of Killers, Feeling No Blame and No Shame." *Philadelphia Inquirer* (December 6).

Margolin, Phillip (1993). *Gone But Not Forgotten.* New York: Doubleday.

Markman, Ronald and Dominick Bosco (1989). *Alone with the Devil.* New York: Doubleday.

Martin, David (1991). *Lie To Me.* New York: Pocket Star.

Martini, Steve (1993). *Prime Witness.* New York: Putnam.

Masters, Brian (1985). *Killing for Company.* New York: Stein and Day.

———— (1991a). "The Devil in Us All." *Evening Standard* March 7.

———— (1991b). "Inferno." *Vanity Fair* (November).

McAllister, Casey ([1992] 1993). *Catch Me If You Can.* New York: Avon.

McBain, Ed ([1984] 1985). *Lightning.* New York: Avon.

McCarty, John (1986). *Psychos.* New York: St. Martin's Press.

McClaren, Angus (1993). *A Prescription for Murder: The Victorian Serial Killings of Dr. Thomas Neill Cream.* Chicago: University of Chicago Press.

McCormick, Donald (1970). *The Identity of Jack the Ripper.* London: Arrow.

McDonnell, Owen F. (1939a). "Witchcraft in Philadelphia Revealed by Bolber in Own Story of His Life." *Philadelphia Inquirer* (August 3).

———— (1939b). "Bolber Tells of Cures He Effected in Philadelphia with His Witchcraft." *Philadelphia Inquirer* (August 7).

—— (1939c). "Bolber Says Petrillo Lost $1000 By Trying to Be a Witch Doctor." *Philadelphia Inquirer* (August 8).

McDougal, Dennis (1992). *Angel of Darkness*. Warner.

McGuire, Christine (1993). *Until Proven Guilty*. New York: Pocket Books.

McIntyre, Tommy (1988). *Wolf in Sheep's Clothing*. Detroit: Wayne State University.

McKinley, James C. (1990). "Police Hunt Common Thread in Five Dumped by Bronx Roads." *New York Times* (October 26).

Menninger, Karl (1968). *The Crime of Punishment*. New York: Viking.

Meyer, Gerald (1974). *The Memphis Murders*. New York: Seabury.

Michaud, Stephen G. (1986). "The FBI's New Psyche Squad." *New York Times Magazine* (October 26).

—— (1987). "Identifying Argentina's Disappeared." *New York Times Magazine* (December 27).

Michaud, Stephen G. (1988). "DNA Detectives." *New York Times Magazine* (November 6).

Michaud, Stephen G. and Hugh Aynesworth (1983). *The Only Living Witness*. New York: Simon and Schuster.

—— (1989). *Ted Bundy: Conversations with a Killer*. New York: New American Library.

Miller, Gale and James A. Holstein, eds. (1993). *Constructionist Controversies*. Hawthorne, NY: Aldine de Gruyter.

Miller, Tom (1993). *The Copeland Killings*. New York: Pinnacle.

Modleski, Tania (1988). *The Woman Who Knew Too Much: Hitchcock and Feminist Theory*. New York: Methuen.

Molloy, Pat (1988). *Not the Moors Murders*. Llandyssul, Wales: Gomer.

Monninger, Joe ([1991] 1993). *Razor's Song*. New York: Avon.

Montecino, Marcel ([1988] 1989). *The Cross-Killer*. New York: Pocket Books.

Moore, Kelly and Dan Reed (1988). *Deadly Medicine*. New York: St. Martin's.

Moser, Don and Jerry Cohen (1967). *The Pied Piper of Tucson*. New York: New American Library.

Mulgrew, Ian (1991). *Final Payoff*. Toronto: Seal.

Murphy, Sean P. (1992). "Nation Getting Tougher with Its Sex Offenders." *Boston Globe* (June 16).

Musto, David F. (1987). *The American Disease*, expanded ed. New York: Oxford University Press.

Mydans, Seth (1990). "Criticism of San Diego Police Rises as Prostitutes' Killings Go Unsolved." *New York Times* (September 22).

Nash, Jay Robert (1980). *Murder America*. New York: Simon and Schuster.

—— (1981). *Look for the Woman*. New York: M. Evans.

—— (1990). *Encyclopaedia of World Crime*. Wilmette, IL.: Crime Books.

"The National Center for the Analysis of Violent Crime" (1986). Quantico, VA: Behavioral Sciences Services, FBI Academy.

Neufeld, Peter and Neville Colman (1990). "When Science Takes the Witness Stand." *Scientific American* (May):46–53.

Neustatter, Walter (1957). *The Mind of the Murderer*. New York: Philosophical Library.

Newman, Graeme (1979). *Understanding Violence*. New York: Lippincott.

Newton, Michael (1988). *Mass Murder: An Annotated Bibliography*. New York: Garland Reference Library of Social Science.

———— (1990). *Hunting Humans*. Port Washington, WA: Loompanics.

———— (1992). *Serial Slaughter*. Port Washington, WA: Loompanics.

———— (1993a). *Raising Hell: An Encyclopedia of Devil Worship and Satanic Crime*. New York: Avon.

———— (1993b). *Bad Girls Do It!: An Encyclopedia of Female Murderers*. Port Washington, WA: Loompanics.

Nickel, Steven (1989). *Torso*. Winston-Salem, NC: John F. Blair.

Norris, Joel (1988). *Serial Killers*. New York: Dolphin.

———— (1991). *Henry Lee Lucas*. New York: Zebra Books.

———— (1992a). *Arthur Shawcross: The Genesee River Killer*. New York: Pinnacle.

———— (1992b). *Jeffrey Dahmer*. New York: Windsor.

Oates, Caroline (1988). "The Trial of a Teenage Werewolf: Bordeaux 1603." *Criminal Justice History* 9:1–29.

O'Brien, Darcy (1987). *Two of a Kind*. New York: New American Library.

O'Brien, Maureen (1990). "The Book from Hell." *Village Voice* (December 18).

Odell, Robin (1965). *Jack the Ripper in Fact and Fiction*. London: Harrap.

Oliver, Ted and Ramsay Smith (1993). *Lambs to the Slaughter*. London: Warner.

Olsen, Jack (1974). *The Man with the Candy*. New York: Simon and Schuster.

———— (1993). *The Misbegotten Son: A Serial Killer and His Victims*. New York: Delacorte.

Osborne, Duncan (1993). "Too Little, Too Late." *Advocate* (September 21):28–29.

Osterburg, James W. and Richard H. Ward (1992). *Criminal Investigation*. Cincinnati: Anderson.

O'Reilly-Fleming, Thomas and Steven Egger, eds. (forthcoming). *Serial and Mass Murder: Theory, Research, Policy*. Toronto: University of Toronto Press.

Papazoglou, Orania ([1992] 1993). *Charisma*. New York: Zebra.

Papke, David Ray (1987). *Framing the Criminal*. Hamden, CT: Archon.

Paretsky, Sara (1991). "Soft Spot for Serial Murder." *New York Times* (April 28).

Parfrey, Adam, ed. (1990). *Apocalypse Culture*, rev. ed. Los Angeles: Feral House.

Parker, Robert P (1988). *Crimson Joy*. New York: Delacorte.

Parker, T. Jefferson (1993). *Summer of Fear*. New York: St. Martin's.

Patterson, James (1993). *Along Came a Spider*. Boston: Little Brown.

Patti, Paul (1992). *Death Mate*. New York: St. Martin's.

Pearson, E. (1924). *Studies in Murder*. New York: Macmillan.

———— (1928). *Five Murders*. New York: Doubleday Doran.

Pearson, Ridley ([1988] 1989). *Undercurrents*. New York: St. Martin's.

———— [1990] 1991). *Probable Cause*. New York: St. Martin's.

———— [1992] 1993). *The Angel Maker*. New York: Delacorte.

Pederson, Rena (1992). "Rising Violence Against Women Must Stop." *Dallas Morning News*. Reprinted in State College, PA, *Centre Daily Times* (May 18).

Perry, Michael R. (1992). *The Stranger Returns*. New York: Pocket Star.

Peterson, Alan H., ed. (1988). *The American Focus on Satanic Crime*, Vol. 1. South Orange, NJ: American Focus.

_____ (1990). *The American Focus on Satanic Crime*, Vol. 2. South Orange, NJ: American Focus.

Plant, Richard (1986). *The Pink Triangle: The Nazi War Against Homosexuals*. New York: Holt.

Porter, Bruce (1983). "Mind Hunters." *Psychology Today* (April).

Powers, Richard Gid (1983). *G-Men: Hoover's FBI in American Popular Culture*. Carbondale: Southern Illinois University Press.

_____ (1987). *Secrecy and Power: The Secret Life of J. Edgar Hoover*. New York: Free Press.

Protzman, Ferdinand (1991). "Vienna Nurses' Aides Guilty of Killing 42 Patients." *New York Times* (March 31).

Provost, Gary (1989). *Across the Border: The True Story of the Satanic Cult Killings in Matamoros, Mexico*. New York: Pocket Books.

Pulling, Pat (1989). *The Devil's Web: Who Is Stalking Your Children for Satan?* Lafayette, LA: Huntington House.

Quindlen, Anna (1993). "Gynocide." *New York Times* (March 10).

Quinney, Richard (1970). *The Social Reality of Crime*. Boston: Little, Brown.

_____ (1979). *Criminology*, 2nd ed. Boston: Little, Brown.

Radford, Jill (1992). "Introduction." Pp. 3–12 in *Femicide*, edited by Jill Radford and Diana E. H. Russell. New York: Twayne.

Radford, Jill and Diana E. H. Russell, eds. (1992). *Femicide*. New York: Twayne.

Randall, Willard S. (1992). "Tom Quick's Revenge." *MHQ: The Quarterly Journal of Military History* 4(4).

Rapping, Elayne (1991). "The Uses of Violence." *Progressive* (August):36–38.

Raschke, Carl A. (1990). *Painted Black: From Drug Killings to Heavy Metal—How Satanism Is Besieging Our Culture and Our Communities*. San Francisco: Harper and Row.

Read, Piers Paul (1979). *Alive*. New York: Avon.

Rebello, Stephen (1991). *Alfred Hitchcock and the Making of Psycho*. New York: Harper Perennial.

Reinarman, Craig and Harry G. Levine (1989). "The Crack Attack: Politics and Media in America's Latest Drug Scare." Pp. 115–37 in *Images of Issues*, edited by Joel Best. Hawthorne, NY: Aldine de Gruyter.

Reinhardt, James M. (1960). *The Murderous Trail of Charlie Starkweather*. Springfield, IL: Charles Thomas.

_____ (1962). *The Psychology of Strange Killers*. Springfield, IL: Charles Thomas.

Rennie, Ysabel (1978). *The Search for Criminal Man*. Lexington, MA: Lexington Books.

Renseberger, Boyce (1992). "The Nakedly Aggressive Ape." *Guardian Weekly* (April 5).

Ressler, Robert K., Ann W. Burgess, and John E. Douglas (1988). *Sexual Homicide: Patterns and Motives*. Lexington, MA: Lexington-Heath.

Ressler, Robert K. and Tom Schachtman (1992). *Whoever Fights Monsters*. New York: St. Martin's.

Reynolds, Michael (1991). "The Terror in Gainesville." *Playboy* (February).

_____ (1992). *Dead-Ends*. New York: Warner.

Richardson, James F., Joel Best, and David Bromley, eds. (1991). *The Satanism Scare*. Hawthorne, NY: Aldine de Gruyter.

Richter, David (1989). "Murder in Jest: Serial Killing in the Post-Modern Detective Story." *Journal of Narrative Technique* 19(1):106–17

Riedel, Marc and Margaret Zahn (1985). *The Nature and Patterns of American Homicide*. Washington: Justice Department, NIJ.

Ritchie, Jean (1988). *Myra Hindley: Inside the Mind of a Murderess*. London: Angus and Robertson.

Rivera, Geraldo (1988). *Devil Worship: Exposing Satan's Underground*. NBC television documentary, October 25.

Robinson, Jane (1989). "On the Trail of the Serial Killers." *Queensland (Australia) Northern Star* (December 13).

Rodgers-Melnick, Ann (1989). "Rumors from Hell." *Pittsburgh Press* (September 3, 5, 6).

Rose, Elizabeth S. (1993). "Surviving the Unbelievable: Cult Ritual Abuse Exists." *MS.* (January–February):40–47.

Rose, Harold M. and Paula D McClain (1990). *Race, Place and Risk: Black Homicide in Urban America*. SUNY Press.

Rosenbaum, Ron (1991). "The Evil Movies Do." *Mademoiselle* (February): 72–74.

———— (1993a). "The FBI's Agent Provocateur." *Vanity Fair* (April).

———— (1993b). "The Devil in Long Island." *New York Times Magazine* (August 22).

Rosenblatt, Roger (1990). "Snuff this Book." *New York Times Book Review* (December 16).

Rothman, William (1982). *Hitchcock: The Murderous Gaze*. Cambridge, MA: Harvard University Press.

Rule, Andrew (1988). *Cuckoo*. Melbourne, Australia: Floradale Press.

Rule, Ann (1980). *The Stranger Beside Me*. New York: New American Library.

———— (1983a). *Lust Killer*. New York: Signet. [Written under the pseudonym Andy Stack.]

———— (1983b). *Want-Ad Killer*. New York: Signet. [Written under the pseudonym Andy Stack.]

———— ([1983] 1984). *Possession*. New York: Signet.

———— (1984). *The I-5 Killer*. New York: Signet. [Written under the pseudonym Andy Stack.]

———— (1988). *Small Sacrifices*. New York: Signet.

———— (1989). "Final Attraction" *Red Book* (February).

———— (1993). *A Rose for her Grave*. New York: Pocket Books.

Rumbelow, Donald (1988). *Jack the Ripper: The Complete Casebook*, Chicago: Contemporary Books.

Russell, C. (1978). "The Social Biology of Werewolves." In *Animals in Folklore*. Cambridge University Press.

Russell, Diana (1992). "Slavery and Femicide." Pp. 167–69 in *Femicide*, edited by Jill Radford and Diana E. H. Russell. New York: Twayne.

Russell, Diane E. H. and Ellis, Candida (1992). "Annihilation by Murder and by the Media." Pp. 161–62 in *Femicide*, edited by Jill Radford and Diana E. H. Russell. New York: Twayne.

Russell, Sue (1992). *Damsel of Death*. London: Virgin.

Russo, Vito (1981). *The Celluloid Closet*. New York: Harper and Row.

St. George, Donna (1991). "A Troubled Woman and a Trail of Dead Men." *Philadelphia Inquirer* (August 4).

St. George, Donna (1993). "The Tuskegee Study's Legacy." *Philadelphia Inquirer* (August 15).

St. Clair, David (1987). *Say You Love Satan*. New York: Dell.

Sakheim, David K. and Susan E. Devine (1992). *Out of Darkness: Exploring Satanism and Ritual Abuse*. New York: Lexington Books.

Sammon, Paul R., ed. (1990). *Splatterpunks*. New York: St. Martin's.

Sampson, John (1971). "Satan's Servants Accused of Torture Murder." *London Sun* (November 8).

Sanders, Ed (1972). *The Family*. London: Panther.

Sanders, Lawrence ([1972] 1980). *The First Deadly Sin*. New York: Berkley.

—————— [1981] 1982). *The Third Deadly Sin*. New York: Berkley.

Sandford, John ([1989] 1990). *Rules of Prey*. New York: Berkley.

—————— ([1990] 1991). *Shadow Prey*. New York: Berkley.

—————— ([1991] 1992). *Eyes of Prey*. New York: Berkley.

—————— ([1992] 1993). *Silent Prey*. New York: Berkley.

—————— (1993). *Winter Prey*. New York: Putnam.

Sanginiti, Terri (1990). "Woman Found Dead in Her Frankford Apartment." *NorthEast Times* (Philadelphia, September 11).

Sassé, Cynthia Stalter and Peggy Murphy Widder (1992). *The Kirtland Massacre*. New York: Zebra.

Scammell, Henry (1992). *Mortal Remains: A True Story of Ritual Murder*, New York: Harper paperbacks.

Schechter, Harold (1990). *Deranged*. New York: Pocket.

—————— (1991). *Deviant*. New York: Pocket.

Schmalz, Jeffrey (1989). "Deaths of Nineteen Prostitutes Pose a Mystery in Miami." *New York Times* (June 4).

Schneider, Joseph and John Kitsuse, (1984). *Studies in the Sociology of Social Problems*. Norwood, NJ: Ablex.

Schneider, Karen S. (1991). "Bloody Claims." *People Weekly* September 30.

Schutz, Benjamin (1986). *Embrace the Wolf*. New York: Bantam.

Schutze, Jim (1989). *Cauldron of Blood: the Matamoros Cult Killings*. New York: Avon.

Schwartz, Anne E. (1992). *The Man Who Could Not Kill Enough*. Secaucus, NJ: Carol.

Schwartz, Ted (1982). *The Hillside Strangler*. New York: Doubleday.

Schwartz, Ted and Kelli Boyd (1981). "Kenneth Bianchi." *Hustler* (August).

Schwartz, Ted and Duane Empey (1988). *Satanism: Is Your Family Safe?* Grand Rapids, MI: Zondervan.

Scott, Jay (1991). "*Psycho* is A Walk on the Vile Side." *Chatelaine* (June).

Sears, Donald J (1991). *To Kill Again: The Motivation and Development of Serial Murder*. Wilmington DE: Scholarly Resources.

"Secrets of a Serial Killer" (1992). *Newsweek* (February 3).

Segrave, Kerry (1992). *Women Serial and Mass Murderers: A Worldwide Reference, 1580 through 1990*. Jefferson, NC: McFarland.

Sellers, Sean (1990). *Web of Darkness*. Tulsa, OK: Victory House.

Sharrett, Christopher (1991). "New Movie Monsters." *USA Today* (September).

Sikes, Gini (1992). "Such a Nice Young Man." *Mirabella* (April): 68–72.

"Silent Suffering" (1992). *MacLean's* (June 1).

Simenon, Georges (1979). *Maigret Sets a Trap*. New York: Harvest/Harcourt Brace Jovanovich.

Simpson, A. W. B. (1984). *Cannibalism and the Common Law*. Chicago: University of Chicago Press.

Skal, David J. (1993). *The Monster Show*. New York: Norton.

Skogan, W. (1975). "Measurement Problems in Official and Survey Crime Rates." *Journal of Criminal Justice* 3:17–32.

Slade, Michael ([1984] 1986). *Headhunter*. New York: Onyx.

———— ([1987] 1989). *Ghoul*. New York: Signet.

Slotkin, Richard (1992). *Gunfighter Nation*. New York: Atheneum.

Smith, Carlton (1993). *Fatal Charm*. New York: Onyx.

Smith, Carlton and Thomas Guillen (1990). *The Search for the Green River Killer*. New York: Onyx.

Smith, E. H. (1927). *Famous Poison Mysteries*. New York: Dial.

Smith, Michelle and Lawrence Pazder (1980). *Michelle Remembers*. New York: Congdon and Lattes.

Soothill, Keith and Sylvia Walby (1991). *Sex Crime in the News*. London: Routledge.

Sparks, R. (1992). *Television and the Drama of Crime: Moral Tales and the Place of Crime in Public Life*. Bristol, PA: Open University Press.

Spector, Malcolm and John Kitsuse (1987). *Constructing Social Problems*. Hawthorne, New York: Aldine de Gruyter.

Spencer, Judith (1989). *Suffer the Child*. New York: Pocket.

Spinrad, Norman (1969). *Bug Jack Barron*. New York: Avon.

Squitieri, Tom (1990). "Slayings of Prostitutes Linked." *USA Today* (March 14).

Stam, Robert (1989). *Subversive Pleasures*. Baltimore: Johns Hopkins University Press.

Starr, John, et al. (1984). "The Random Killers" *Newsweek* (November 26).

Stasio, Marilyn (1989). "The Homicidal Maniac: A Novelist's Best Friend." *New York Times Book Review* (October 15).

Stevens, Phillips (1992). "Universal Cultural Elements in the Satanic Demonology." *Journal of Psychology and Theology*.

Stevens, Shane ([1979] 1990). *By Reason of Insanity*. New York: Carroll and Graf.

Stingl, Jim (1992). "Autopsies Show Three of Dahmer's Victims Had Holes in Skulls." *Milwaukee Journal* (January 22).

Stratford, Lauren (1988). *Satan's Underground: The Extraordinary Story of One Woman's Escape*. Eugene, OR: Harvest House.

Straub, Peter ([1988] 1989). *Koko*. New York: Signet.

———— ([1990] 1991). *Mystery*. New York: New American Library/Dutton.

Straub, Peter (1993). *The Throat*. New York: Dutton.

Suggs, Donald (1992). "Did the Media Exploit the Lesbian Serial Killer Story?" *The Advocate* (March 10).

Sullivan, Terry, and Peter T. Maiken (1984). *Killer Clown*. New York: Pinnacle.

Summers, Anthony (1993). *Official and Confidential: The Secret Life of J. Edgar Hoover*. New York: G. P. Putnam's.

Suplee, Curt (1991). "Serial Killers: Frighteningly Close to Normal." *Washington Post* (August 5).

Surette, Ray (1992). *Media, Crime and Criminal Justice: Images and Realities*. Pacific Grove, CA: Brooks Cole/Wadsworth.

Sutherland, Edwin (1950). "The Diffusion of Sexual Psychopath Laws" *American Journal of Sociology* 56:142–48.

Tallant, Robert (1946). *Voodoo in New Orleans*. New York: Macmillan.

Taubin, Amy (1991). "Demme's Monde." *Village Voice* (February 19).

Terry, Don (1991a). "Milwaukee Grasping for Answers as Horror Mounts Over Killings." *New York Times* (July 29).

———— (1991b). "Serial Murder Case Exposes Deep Milwaukee Tensions." *New York Times* (August 2).

Terry, Maury (1987). *The Ultimate Evil*. New York: Dolphin Doubleday.

"Text of President's Speech on Drug Control Strategy" (1989). *New York Times* (September 6).

Tharp, Julie (1991). "The Transvestite as Monster." *Journal of Popular Film and Television* 19:106–13.

"Thirty-Five Murderers of Many People Could Be at Large, Says U.S." (1983). *New York Times* (October 26).

Thomas, Cal (1991). "Serial Murders Underscore Evil's Presence." Syndicated column, *Centre Daily Times* (State College, PA, August 6).

Thompson, E. P. (1991). *Customs in Common*. London: Merlin Press.

Toch, Hans and Kenneth Adams (1989). *The Disturbed Violent Offender*. New Haven, CT: Yale University Press.

Trinkaus, Erik and Pat Shipman (1992). *The Neandertals*. New York: Knopf.

"Troubled Past for Drifter in Serial Killing Claims" (1991). *New York Times* (August 17).

Turner, Patricia A. (1993). *I Heard It Through the Grapevine*. Berkeley: University of California Press.

U.S. Attorney General (1986). *U.S. Attorney General's Commission on Pornography: Final Report*. Washington, DC: U.S. Government Printing Office.

U.S. Congress, House Committee on Human Resources (1984). *Hearings on the Missing Children Assistance Act, April 9, 1984*. Washington, DC: U.S. Government Printing Office.

————, House Committee on Government Operations, Government Information, Justice and Agriculture Subcommittee. (1986). *The Federal Role in the Investigation of Serial Violent Crime. Hearings before a subcommittee of the Committee on Government Operations, House of Representatives, 99th Congress, second session, April 9 and May 21, 1986* Washington, DC: U.S. Government Printing Office.

U.S. Government (1969–1970). *Report of the National Commission on the Causes and Prevention of Violence*. 13 volumes. Washington DC: U.S. Government Printing Office.

U.S. Justice Department (1992). "Serial, Mass and Spree Murderers in the United States: Search of Major Wire Services and Publications January 1977–April 1992." Working list.

———— (1993). "Serial Murderers in the U.S." Working list.

U.S. Senate (1982). *Exploited and Missing Children: Hearings before the Subcommittee on Juvenile Justice of the Committee on the Judiciary, U.S. Senate, 97th Congress, 2nd Session, on S. 1701 . . . April 1, 1982.* Washington DC: U.S. Government Printing Office.

———— (1983). *Child Pornography: Hearings before the Subcommittee on Juvenile Justice of the Committee on the Judiciary, U.S. Senate, 97th Congress, 2nd Session, on S. 2856 . . . December 10, 1982.* Washington DC: U.S. Government Printing Office.

———— (1984). *Serial Murders: Hearings before the Subcommittee on Juvenile Justice of the Committee on the Judiciary, U.S. Senate, 98th Congress, 1st Session, on patterns of murders committed by one person in large numbers with no apparent rhyme, reason or motivation. July 12, 1983.* Washington DC: U.S. Government Printing Office.

———— (1985). *Effects of Pornography on Women and Children: Hearings before the Subcommittee on Juvenile Justice of the Committee on the Judiciary, U.S. Senate, 98th Congress, 2nd Session, on oversight on pornography, child abuse, child molestation and problems of conduct against women, Washington DC August 8, Sept. 12 and 25, and October 30, 1984, Pittsburgh, PA, October 18, 1984.* Washington DC: U.S. Government Printing Office.

———— (1993). *The Response to Rape: Detours on the Road to Equal Justice.* Prepared by the Majority Staff of the Senate Judiciary Committee, May.

Ungar, Sanford J. (1976). *FBI.* Boston: Little Brown.

Vachss, Alice (1993). *Sex Crimes.* New York: Random House.

Vachss, Andrew (1993). "Sex Predators Can't Be Saved." *New York Times* (January 5).

Van Arman, Derek ([1992] 1993). *Just Killing Time.* New York: Onyx.

Van Hoffman, Eric (1990). *A Venom in the Blood.* New York: Donald I. Fine.

Victor, Jeffrey (1993). *Satanic Panic.* Chicago: Open Court.

Viguerie, Richard (1981). *The New Right: We're Ready to Lead.* Falls Church, VA: Viguerie Co.

Vonnegut, Kurt (1975). "There's a Maniac Loose Out There." Pp. 65–76 in *Wampeters, Foma and Grandfalloons.* New York: Delta Press.

Walker, Robert W. (1992). *Killer Instinct.* New York: Diamond.

Walkowitz, Judith (1982). "Jack the Ripper and the Myth of Male Violence." *Feminist Studies* 8:543–74.

Wambaugh, Joseph (1989). *The Blooding.* New York: Bantam.

Warnke, Mike (1972). *The Satan Seller.* South Plainfield, NJ: Bridge Books.

Weaver, Michael (1993). *Impulse.* New York: Warner.

Weisman, Steven B (1990). "A New Era Comes to Korea, Followed by Crime." *New York Times* (December 18).

Wertham, Fredric (1947). *Dark Legend.* Garden City, NJ: Doubleday.

———— (1949). *The Show of Violence.* Garden City, NJ: Doubleday.

———— (1966). *A Sign for Cain: An Exploration of Human Violence.* New York: Macmillan.

West, Donald (1974). *Sacrifice Unto Me.* New York: Pyramid.

Wetlaufer, Suzy ([1992] 1993). *Judgment Call.* New York: Avon.

Wilcox, Robert K. (1977). *The Mysterious Deaths at Ann Arbor*. New York: Popular Library.

Williams, Emlyn (1967). *Beyond Belief*. London: Hamish Hamilton.

Wilson, Colin (1988). *Mammoth Book of True Crime*. New York: Carroll and Graf.

―――― (1992). *Ritual in the Dark*. New York: Ronin.

Wilson, Colin and Robin Odell (1987). *Jack the Ripper: Summing Up and Verdict*. London: Bantam Press.

Wilson, Colin and Patricia Pitman (1984). *Encyclopaedia of Murder*. London: Pan.

―――― (1983). *Encyclopaedia of Modern Murder*. New York: Perigee.

Wilson, Colin and Donald Seaman (1992). *The Serial Killers*. London: Virgin True Crime.

Wilson, Des (1974). "Slaughter on West 77th Street." *Observer*, London (November 10).

Wiltse, David ([1991] 1992). *Prayer for the Dead*. New York: Berkley.

Winn, Steven and David Merrill (1980). *Ted Bundy: The Killer Next Door*. New York: Bantam.

Wolf, Marvin J. and Katherine Mader (1986). *Fallen Angels*. New York: Ballantine.

Wooden, Kenneth (1976). *Weeping in the Playtime of Others*. New York: McGraw Hill.

―――― (1981). *The Children of Jonestown*. New York: McGraw Hill.

―――― (1988). "Light Must be Shed on Devil Worship." Letter to the editor, *New York Times* (November 23).

Woods, Stuart ([1981] 1987). *Chiefs*. New York: Avon.

Woodward, Bob (1987). *Veil*. New York: Simon and Schuster.

Worthington, Peter (1993). "The Journalist and the Killer." *Saturday Night* (Canada, July–August).

Wright, Lawrence (1993). "Reporter's Notebook: Remembering Satan." *New Yorker* (May 17):24.

Wright, S. P. (1945). *Chicago Murders*. New York: Duell, Sloan and Pearce.

Yarvis, Richard M. (1992). *Homicide: Causative Factors and Roots*. New York: Lexington Books.

Young, Robert J. (1992). "Deadly Persuasions: The Story of Philadelphia's Arsenic Murder Ring" M.A. dissertation in history, Pennsylvania State University, University Park.

"Youth Accused of Attempt to Murder Two Women" (1987). *Los Angeles Times* October 31.

Zarefsky, David (1986). *President Johnson's War on Poverty*. Tuscaloosa: University of Alabama Press.

Index

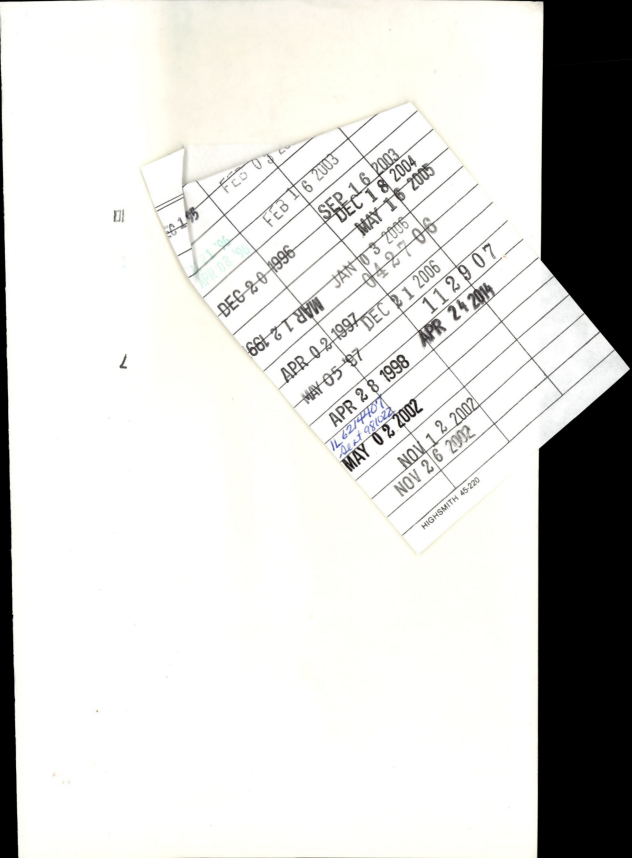